The Dying Child

The Dying Child

The Death and Personhood of Children in Ancient Israel

KRISTINE HENRIKSEN GARROWAY

OXFORD
UNIVERSITY PRESS

Oxford University Press is a department of the University of Oxford.
It furthers the University's objective of excellence in research, scholarship,
and education by publishing worldwide. Oxford is a registered trade mark of
Oxford University Press in the UK and in certain other countries.

Published in the United States of America by Oxford University Press
198 Madison Avenue, New York, NY 10016, United States of America.

© Oxford University Press 2025

All rights reserved. No part of this publication may be reproduced, stored in a retrieval system, transmitted, used for text and data mining, or used for training artificial intelligence, in any form or by any means, without the prior permission in writing of Oxford University Press, or as expressly permitted by law, by license or under terms agreed with the appropriate reprographics rights organization. Inquiries concerning reproduction outside the scope of the above should be sent to the Rights Department, Oxford University Press, at the address above.

You must not circulate this work in any other form
and you must impose this same condition on any acquirer

Library of Congress Cataloging-in-Publication Data
Names: Garroway, Kristine Henriksen, author.
Title: The dying child : the death and personhood of children in Ancient
Israel / Kristine Henriksen Garroway.
Description: New York, NY : Oxford University Press, [2025] |
Identifiers: LCCN 2024030416 (print) | LCCN 2024030417 (ebook) |
ISBN 9780197566688 (hardback) | ISBN 9780197566701 (epub) |
ISBN 9780197566695 (updf) | ISBN 9780197566718 (Digital-Online)
Subjects: LCSH: Children—Israel—Death.
Classification: LCC BV4907 .G44 2025 (print) | LCC BV4907 (ebook) |
DDC 933.0083—dc23/eng/20240907
LC record available at https://lccn.loc.gov/2024030416
LC ebook record available at https://lccn.loc.gov/2024030417

DOI: 10.1093/9780197566718.001.0001

Printed by Marquis Book Printing, Canada

Contents

List of Tables	vii
Preface	ix
List of Abbreviations	xi
Archaeological Periodization and Chronology	xiii

Introduction: Households, Children, Death, and Personhood	1

PART I.   THE BURIALS OF CHILDREN IN ANCIENT ISRAEL

1. Archaeological Overview of Child Burials in the Bronze and Iron Ages	25
2. Surveying Iron Age Infant and Child Burials on the Philistine Coast	43
3. Surveying Iron Age Infant and Child Burials in Phoenician-Influenced Areas	64
4. Surveying Infant and Child Burials in Iron I Israel and Iron II Judah and Israel	83

PART II.   INTERPRETING THE BURIALS OF CHILDREN IN ANCIENT ISRAEL

5. Memorializing Death	105
6. Children and Infants in Judahite Family Tombs	125
7. The Death of Children in the Hebrew Bible: Child Sacrifice, Personhood, and Judahite Ideals	148
8. The Personhood of Children Revealed in Death	167

Bibliography	177
Index	197

Tables

1.1	Number of Burial Sites with Child and Infant Burials Correlated with Burial Method and Time Period	26
1.2	Infant and Child Burials: Locations, Number of Individuals, and Time Periods	27
1.3	Overview of Grave Goods by Time Period: Age Not Specified	30
1.4	Overview of Grave Goods for Infants and Children by Time Period	31
1.5	Grave Goods: Ceramic and Personal Items Found with Children and Infants	32
2.1	Intramural Burials in Sites on the Philistine Plain	44
2.2	Intramural Infant and Child Burials in Ashkelon Grid 38	48
3.1	Skeletal Analysis of Remains from the Built Chamber Tomb T. C.1., Achzib	68
3.2	Cremated Child and Infant Burials at 'Atlit	71
3.3	Skeletal Analysis of the Cremated Remains at Tell el-Far'ah South	74
4.1	Rock-Cut Tombs in Judah with Benches/Repository Pits	86
4.2	Skeletal Remains from the Caves South of Ḥorbat Tittora by Age	88
4.3	Burials in the Samarian Hills	94
4.4	Intramural Burials of the Iron II Levels at Dothan	96
6.1	Ages of Individuals in the Bench Tombs at Tel 'Ira	134

Preface

The present study on children and death has been something percolating in the back of my mind for many years. I first broached the issue in *Children in the Ancient Near Eastern Household* (Eisenbrauns, 2014). There I focused specifically on the variation in the method of burials for children, asking why different methods were chosen. I pushed the topic further in Chapter 8 of *Growing Up in Ancient Israel* (SBL, 2018) in the discussion of child burials and reactions to burials in the archaeological data, where I asked questions such as why some children were buried under floors and others were not, why some children were included in family tombs and others were not, and whether parents grieved at the death of an infant or child. Short on time and space, I concluded: "Questions such as these demonstrate the need for further study of burial practices" (*Growing Up in Ancient Israel*, 262). Here then, is the product of that further study. I most likely do not have all the pieces of the puzzle, which means that the answers suggested in this study could change. More child burials are constantly being uncovered, as archaeologists are now paying more attention to the presence of children in the household, and bone preservation methods have improved. As additional information becomes available and more scholars take up the mantle of studying children, statements in this study might be strengthened, might need to be tweaked, or might be outright rejected. I am happy to have my conclusions tested and even proven wrong as long as the conversation on a very important component of the ancient Israelite household—children—keeps going. For in understanding how a society thought about children we can learn how they thought about their future. More importantly, as the Hebrew Bible remains an important text for three major world religions, understanding how the societies that comprised ancient Israel, reflected within the Hebrew Bible, treated their children remains a valuable endeavor.

A note of appreciation to those without whom this project would not have come to fruition. Many people, institutions, and libraries have been instrumental in helping the book come together. First, thanks go to my home institutions, the Hebrew Union College–Jewish Institute of Religion and the University of Southern California, and to Lucas Steinberg, who provided

X PREFACE

invaluable help locating sources. Much of the manuscript was completed during my sabbatical, supported by the Hebrew Union College– Jewish Institute of Religion. Fuller Theological Seminary Library was also instrumental in my research, providing access to its stacks. The project was edited by the able hands of Erika Zabinski.

Thanks are due to those colleagues who are always ready to offer a word of support or help me track down information. To Michal Bar-Asher Siegal, Angela Erisman, Laura Lieber, David Ilan, John W. Martens, Julie Faith Parker, and Shawn Flynn for your endless encouragement. To Christopher B. Hays, Jeremy Smoak, Matthew Suriano, Deirdre Fulton, and Rachel Kalisher, who share my love of burials and never tire of tossing around ideas with me about children and death in the ancient world. You are a treasure!

Most important, I offer my thanks to my family. To my parents, Sue and Denny, and my in-laws Neil and Cindy, who are a continual source of positive energy. To my three boys: Cyrus, Leo, and Abner, you continue to make my research come alive. And of course, to Josh, for all your love and support, represented by the sign you commissioned for my home office door saying: "Mom's working, get Dad."

Abbreviations

AABNER	*Advances in Ancient, Biblical, and Near Eastern Research*
AB	Anchor Bible
ABS	Archaeology and Biblical Studies
ANE	ancient Near East
ANEM	Ancient Near East Monographs/ Monografías sobre el Antiguo Cercano Oriente
AOAT	Alter Orient und Altes Testament
BAIAS	*Bulletin of the Anglo-Israel Archaeological Society*
BAR	*Biblical Archaeology Review*
BASOR	*Bulletin of the American Schools of Oriental Research*
BHS	Biblia Hebraica Stuttgartensia
BJS	Brown Judaic Studies
BR	*Biblical Research*
c.	century
ca.	circa
CAD	*Chicago Assyrian Dictionary*
CBQ	*Catholic Biblical Quarterly*
CHANE	Culture and History of the Ancient Near East
COS	*The Context of Scripture*, ed. William W. Hallo (Leiden: Brill, 1997–2002)
CRAI	Comptes rendus de l'Académie des inscriptions et belles-lettres
EANEC	Explorations in Ancient Near Eastern Civilizations
EB(A)	Early Bronze (Age)
EI	*Eretz Israel*
FAT	Forschungen zum Alten Testament
HAR	*Hebrew Annual Review*
HB	Hebrew Bible
HBM	Hebrew Bible Monographs
HSM	Harvard Semitic Series
HUCA	*Hebrew Union College Annual*
IA	Iron Age
IEJ	*Israel Exploration Journal*
JAA	*Journal of Anthropological Archaeology*
JANER	*Journal of Ancient Near Eastern Religions*
JANES	*Journal of the Ancient Near Eastern Society*

xii ABBREVIATIONS

JAOS	*Journal of the American Oriental Society*
JBL	*Journal of Biblical Literature*
JNES	*Journal of Near Eastern Studies*
JPF	Judean pillar figurines
JSOT	*Journal for the Study of the Old Testament*
LB(A)	Late Bronze (Age)
LHBOTS	Library of Hebrew Bible / Old Testament Studies
MB(A)	Middle Bronze (Age)
MNI	minimum number of individuals
NAR	*Norwegian Archaeological Review*
NEA	*Near Eastern Archaeology*
NJPS	New Jewish Publication Society
OBO	Orbis Biblicus et Orientalis
OIS	Oriental Institute Seminars
OTL	Old Testament Library
PEQ	*Palestinian Exploration Quarterly*
QDAP	*Quarterly of the Department of antiquities in Palestine*
RB	*Revue biblique*
SBLMS	Society of Biblical Literature Monograph Series
SEL	*Studi epigrafici e linguistici sul Vicino Oriente antico*
SHR	Studies in the History of Religions (supplements to *Numen*)
TA	*Tel Aviv*
VT	*Vetus Testamentum*
WA	*World Archaeology*
ZDPV	*Zeitschrift des deutschen Palästina-Vereins*

Archaeological Periodization and Chronology

Early Bronze Age	ca. 3700–2400 BCE
Intermediate Bronze Age	ca. 2400–1900 BCE
Middle Bronze Age	1900–1530 BCE
Late Bronze Age	1530–ca. 1200/1150 BCE
Iron Age IA	1200–ca. 1140/1130 BCE
Iron Age IB	1150/1130–ca. 980 BCE
Iron Age IIA	ca. 980–ca. 840/830 BCE
Iron Age IIB	ca. 840/840–732/701BCE
Iron Age IIIA	732/701–605/586 BCE
Iron Age IIIB	586–520 BCE
Persian Period	550–330 BCE
Hellenistic Period	330/323–63/31 BCE

Introduction

Households, Children, Death, and Personhood

The death of a child is tragic. While some might state this sentiment is rooted in a specific time and place—the contemporary Western world—I would argue that we have no idea whether this sentiment was true in ancient Israel. To make this argument requires understanding how the death of children was perceived there. Many studies have explored death by examining types of burial, burial rites, biblical notions of death and the afterlife, care for the dead, and cults of the dead, yet no single study has been devoted to children and death.[1] The present study starts the conversation, offering a social history of the death of children in the land of ancient Israel. It engages with previous studies that address adults, by both adding to and challenging prior conclusions.[2]

The study of childhood death is tightly entwined with the concerns of a field that is relatively new to the scholarship of ancient Israel: personhood.[3] Personhood is understood in terms of social recognition and marked by public rituals confirming and conveying personhood. Such rituals provide protection from physical harm. While personhood is usually discussed with respect to an individual during the person's life, personhood can also extend into death.[4] From an anthropological perspective, the idea that burial is a public form of ritual and that burial provides protection from physical harm argues strongly for including the dying individual in a discussion of personhood. The position that death is relational also supports the inclusion of personhood as a subject related to the dead as well as the living.[5] The lens of personhood is important because the lives of children are just starting to be uncovered in the archaeological record, and often scholars face the issue of how to link the material record with children. For example, archaeologists are reticent to say that items found in a domestic context, such as figurines, miniature vessels, or rattles, might be objects associated with children.[6] That children are present in a household is a given, but demonstrating their presence, much less their personhood, archaeologically is difficult. One way of

The Dying Child. Kristine Henriksen Garroway, Oxford University Press. © Oxford University Press 2025.
DOI: 10.1093/9780197566718.003.0001

2 INTRODUCTION

assessing whether children had personhood in life is through examining how their personhood is not erased but revealed in death.

As this brief overview suggests, the current work brings together disparate elements, providing a study concentrated on how the death of infants and children was perceived in the lands of Iron Age Israel, and how infants and children were incorporated into the household of death, through the so-called cult of the dead. While it is impossible to be definitive, it is possible to pose ideas that are plausible, even probable. Such a study adds not only to the understanding of children but also to the understanding of the cult of the dead *en large*. Additionally, it addresses infants and children first from the mortuary record, and secondarily from the biblical record. In doing so it moves beyond the limitations of what the biblical record can say about infants and children in ancient Israel vis-à-vis the dying process, the cult of the dead, and personhood.[7] Finally, in understanding the tomb as an extension of the household in the afterlife, the study provides more information on the personhood of infants and children and their place in the Iron Age household.

Household Archaeology of the Living

Understanding a child's place in the households of the living and the dead is predicated on an understanding of what comprised a household and how the household in ancient Israel has been understood.[8] Households can be defined in different ways, but for the purposes of this study, a household refers to the people, physical spaces and items, and activities comprising the smallest and most abundant social unit, or the social, material, and behavioral aspects.[9] The same tripartite structure applies to urban and agricultural households alike.[10] For households in the Southern Levant, some of these elements are more accessible to the archaeologist than others. The social component might be considered the most difficult to assess on a macro level as it requires inferring kinship groups and affinities.[11] On a micro level, we can understand the social element to be the people living in the household: the men, women, and, most important for this study, the children. For ancient Israel, the smallest social unit has been identified as the *bet 'av*—the nuclear family or an extended family group living in the same compound.[12]

The material aspects, the physical house and items, are easier to see from an archaeological perspective, as these are what the households of the past left behind. Drawing conclusions from the material record is an interpretive process, but one that, if done carefully, can provide information regarding the activities of the household.[13] The activities or behaviors engaged in can be further delineated as the production, distribution, transmission, and reproduction/socialization of a household.

This explanation of the behavioral aspect falls in line with processual archaeology; it views the household and the actors in it as behaving in a system. More recent studies of household archaeology in the Southern Levant have reached beyond the processual view of the household and taken up questions more germane to post-processual thinking, especially in the areas of embodied and gendered space.[14] As Bradley Parker and Catherine Foster have pointed out, household archaeology is not just one thing but a "diffuse subfield with no unified definitions, theoretical underpinnings, or methodological techniques."[15] The current project follows their lead and takes the diversity in the field as a positive, for "the skirting of canonization in household archaeology assures that household studies will always be on the cutting edge of archaeological research, constantly evolving to explore more refined and deeper questions about life in the ancient and historic past."[16] Indeed, the focus on children and their lives within the household system reflects the ever changing nature of how household archaeology is engaged.[17]

Children and Infants in the Household

When considering households, it cannot be denied that children and infants were an important component of the household. Not only were they contributors to the household economic system but they also embodied the continued future of the household.[18] In a patriarchal system, having an heir was tantamount to an afterlife. The Epic of Gilgamesh encapsulates this concept as the hero-king, bereft of his best friend Enkidu and fearful of his own mortality, journeys to discover eternal life. The moment he unlocks this secret, it is snatched away from him. Crushed, the king returns to his city, where he is greeted by his wife and newborn son. In seeing his son, Gilgamesh realizes that his life continues through the next generation. To this end, children would have been socialized in a manner consistent with the goals of recreating the next generation. For ancient Israelites this meant instilling in them the values and beliefs that made them Israelites.[19] Studies on the enculturation of children are usually concerned with how

4 INTRODUCTION

the younger generation actively learns and what the transfer of culture looks like in a society.[20] The household—the people, physical space, and behaviors therein—is essential to understanding children, for "the domestic arena is the place where socialization begins."[21] In this approach, it is crucial that children be understood as actors, people in their own right who observe, imitate, and transmit the things they are learning and will in turn reproduce future households.

Archaeologists often look to material culture used by, created for, or created by children to provide evidence not only of the presence of children but of the ways in which they were socialized into the household. Previous attempts have often found archaeologists stymied because without labels such as "child's toy" it can be difficult to determine what children interacted with.[22] Some studies have creatively approached this issue and have found success in identifying children in ancient households. Investigations of lithics and knapping, miniature objects, fingerprints left on ceramics, and spatial analysis of households has begun to place children within the ancient household.[23] As these studies demonstrate, understanding children in the living household requires creative approaches. Taking seriously the call for creative approaches, the investigation in this present study offers another creative method. It contends that to understand the place of a child in the household of the living we can look to how children are perceived in the household of death.

How to Identify Children?

A child's importance in the household notwithstanding, placing children in any ancient household can be difficult. Broadly speaking, sources for locating children in this study include archaeological realia found in domestic and mortuary contexts, as well as the texts of the Hebrew Bible and surrounding lands. Texts are not written by children; neither are they concerned with the everyday life of a child. The difficulties do not end there, as the terminology for children found in the ancient texts can make it hard to determine the age of the child. Relational terms such as son or daughter apply to infants, older children, teenagers, and adults alike. Only in knowing the context can one begin to make guesses regarding the age of a referred to in relational terms.[24] Terms that utilize social ages are more useful for identifying children in the textual record. In the Hebrew Bible social ages are indicated by terms such as *yeled* or *bətûlâ*. Texts from Mesopotamia also rely on social ages, with categories such as "suckling," "weaned," "small child," "infant," "one pulled from the mother's womb," and "infant in the birthing waters," to name a few. Social ages can be helpful because they situate the child in the family structure of the household. Julie Faith Parker's overview of twenty-eight terms used to describe children in the Hebrew Bible demonstrates a preference for social age over chronological age.[25] Ancient Near Eastern records also favored social stages or relative ages.[26] Joanna Sofaer Deverenski has cautioned, however, against using social ages. She notes that aging is a fluid process. Individuals do not all mark a growth stage at the same chronological moment. She warns that generalized social categories might lead one to overlook changes to the aging process.[27] Indeed, Shawn Flynn has demonstrated the mental gymnastics needed at times in deciding to what social age a term might refer.[28] While the warning is a valid one, it is difficult to avoid social ages when studying children in the past.

The archaeological record would seem to provide a more reliable, if not more visible, indicator of the presence of children in the household as well as the age of a child. Here too there are obstacles. Early excavations were not always attuned to younger individuals. "A lack of familiarity with immature remains has led, on more than one occasion, to their identification as 'non-human.'"[29] Without archaeologists properly trained in juvenile osteology the record for children at some sites is incomplete.[30] Improper terminology and definitions also led to the assumption that children simply could not be seen in the skeletal record. Reviewing why children were generally thought of as invisible, Patrick Beauchesne and Sabrina Agarwal provide the following list: children's bones preserve poorly, children's bones were overlooked, children received differential burials (away from adults), and children were marginalized because of their association with women.[31] Many of the reasons listed here stem from a much older issue, namely that the early, foundational studies of funerary archaeology focused on adults.[32] Even when children were identified successfully, archaeologists and osteologists continually wavered in their terminology. Terms like "subadult" and "nonadult" were used to describe any individual who did not fit the criteria of adult. These terms have come under scrutiny as they can imply a binary, ageist view of young individuals that starts with adult as the normative category. Everyone else, then, is otherized.[33]

Children remained invisible for a long time simply because scholars were not looking for them. The tide has begun to change, and the past few years

6 INTRODUCTION

have seen a rise in full-length studies dedicated specifically to the archaeology and bioarchaeology of children.[34] These studies add important information to our understanding of children in the archaeological record, yet, as
they themselves note, the studies do not use shared terminology for children.
Children are listed in reports as neonate, infant, child, young child, older
child, juvenile, adolescent, pubescent, and so forth. The ages corresponding
to these terms varies from one study to the next.[35] Part of the problem can be
attributed to the fact that biological age, chronological age, and social age do
not match up for any one young individual or across a group of individuals.[36]
Most ancient texts use social ages, while bioarchaeologists rely upon the biological age determined by skeletal age and dentition.[37] In addition, while
the skeletal age of an individual is listed in two-year increments (when possible), skeletal ages might not align with chronological age if the individual
has experienced severe sickness, famine, or other environmental stressors
that would affect growth.[38]

Despite, or perhaps because of, the difficulties mentioned here, it is important to define how this study employs terminology for children. The
study uses a combination of social ages and skeletal ages. It is very difficult to know exact chronological ages.[39] Since the data for this study concern archaeological remains, terminology and ages will be given as they
are listed in the physical anthropology reports. In general, the term "child"
will be used as a broad category to describe individuals from the time of
birth through age fourteen, by which time most individuals would have
entered adolescence. Such individuals would be ready for marriage, or at
least ready to take on more responsibilities in the household akin to those
of adults. The study further divides the category "child" into infant (through
two years of age), young child (three to six years of age), and older child
(seven to thirteen years of age).[40] As will be seen, the term "infant" and the
age range attached to it will be of importance when it comes to interpreting
differentiated burials.[41]

Mortuary Archaeology and the Household of the Dead

The study of dying children involves a double entanglement. On the one
hand, as dying individuals children are not actors but acted upon. Devoid of
life and the ability to act, their bodies are arranged, cared for, protected, and
deposited without their directives. Living adults bury the dying child.[42]

Burials would reflect *not* the realities of the lives of the people buried in them, but images of their lives and of their role in society in the minds of those arranging the burial and participating in the ritual. These images (or in other words: the ideal world) may coincide with the real world—but then again, they might not.[43]

In this case, we can understand the household of the living as the ones responsible for creating objects (the burial, grave goods, ritual items) for a child. On the other hand, the dying body of the child is still an actor. This statement goes toward personhood, which will be discussed more below. As members of their households, Israelite children were buried according to the family's cultural traditions. I will suggest that the manner of their burial is further dictated by their place within the household. Just as adults transition from the household of the living to the household of the dead, so too do children.

The opening overview of household archaeology and some of its underpinning theories is helpful for thinking about the household in death. For example, scholars suggest cemeteries or family tombs reflect an ideology wherein the household of the living is continued in the household of the dead.[44] The cemetery at Bab edh-Dhra' provides one example of how society organized itself in households of life and death.[45] Meredith Chesson's analysis explains the social connection there between the households of life and death. The living bury their dead and maintain ties with the dead through rituals, while the dead themselves are gathered in household kin groups that reflect the way their society was organized in life. Chesson hypothesizes that what we see in the EB II-III mudbrick charnel houses are House Societies.[46] Houses were a corporate entity, which reflect groups comprising both blood relatives and fictive kin. Those upper-class, socially elite charnel houses are correlated with the elite kin groups of Bab edh-Dhra' and the Lesser Houses with the socially lower-status kin groups. The post-urban EB IV saw a shift away from the charnel houses and House Societies and a return to the use of shaft tombs.[47] In this way, "Expressions of mourning and identity in mortuary contexts are shaped by the structuring forces within a community."[48]

Rachel Hallote's study of Middle Bronze Age II tombs is another example of how societal intent and perspectives can be seen in the mortuary complex, which in turn mirrored the ideologies of the living society.[49] "Tombs of the MBA Southern Levant can be accepted as the mortuary equivalent of dwellings."[50] Hallote concludes that each tomb served as a house for the dead,

8 INTRODUCTION

and each burial served to highlight the status a person had in life. Her study is important because it demonstrates that we can see households continued into death both inside of and outside of a cemetery complex. Importantly, both of these studies indicate how the physical burial space itself aligns with the physical component of a household.

These examples also demonstrate that burials were invested with meaning and that the household of the living could extend beyond the grave. Death is, in this respect, relational.[51] The living had a choice in how they wished to present their dead, and the way in which they did so provides us with an insight into the social structures, ideologies, and beliefs they had. Previous studies, like the ones just referenced, have thought about burials as they represented society either as a whole or as a society full of adults. For example, Hallote refers to infant jar burials under house floors and notes their prevalence in the Middle Bronze mortuary record. However, when she analyzes societal beliefs about the dead, she seemingly dismisses them from the burial record. Her conclusions state that burial under house floors is related to ancestor worship. The dots are left unconnected. Are the infant jar burials indicators of infants being worshiped as ancestors, or does her conclusion only apply to adults buried under the floors? Conclusions such as hers are not uncommon.[52] A more robust investigation of the household in death needs to integrate children into the analysis.

The studies above all fall into the category of mortuary archaeology, whose focus is to understand burials as culturally and socially significant.[53] Other mortuary archaeologists focus on the ritual aspect of the burial as the primary organizing factor of the burial.[54] A delicate balance between the two approaches is needed; death tears at the social fabric, and burials are a means of mending this tear.[55] These two approaches are popular and their use is evident in the scholarship reviewed below. Another, equally important but less addressed aspect of burials also exists—emotion. Anthropological studies have shown that burial and mortuary rituals are not devoid of emotion.[56] Locating emotions in a mortuary context is difficult, especially in an archaeological setting. While not a traditional part of mortuary archaeology, emotion is still an important aspect to consider. Those who do address emotion in burials are quick to point out that emotion can be culturally bound and that in any given culture or society age, gender, status, and kinship groups can play an important role in what emotion is expressed.[57] When we think about child burials, placement, social relationships, religion, rituals, and emotions must all be considered.

History of Studies Addressing Death and Dying in the Ancient Near East / Hebrew Bible

Dying is transitional.[58] It is a process by which the body transitions from a living being to a corpse, through decomposition, to bones, and then to the final form it will have in the afterlife.[59] Dying is also a social process as the body is transformed from one form to the next. By way of nomenclature, the term "dying body" is used in recognition that the body is in transition.

Studies of death and dying in ancient Israel address the dying body with the assumption that it is an adult body and address the ideal transition process as one wherein adults are gathered to their ancestors. Implicit in this understanding is the notion discussed above that the (family) tomb is the expression or continuation of the household in the afterlife. Theories that address dying and mortuary rituals or treatment of the dead, often called the cult of the ancestors, treat dying members of the household in a uniform manner—as adults. As stated, my goal in this study is to push the envelope further, to broaden the discussion of the dying body from adults to children. Such work cannot be done without both acknowledging and reviewing the work on adults that has paved the way.[60]

The study of death and dying is related to religion, inasmuch as religion functions as the means by which the living process the transition of their dead.[61] Just as contemporary religions have rites and practices that help their followers grapple with the hereafter, so too did those in the ancient world. "The communication at mortuary events focuses on reweaving and simultaneously renegotiating the social fabric of the community damaged by death."[62] The question "What happens next?" has captured the imaginations of people for thousands of years. The biblical text offers not a single picture but a multiplicity of images attesting to the afterlife, many of which are heterodox. This phenomenon has been called the "cult of the dead." Echoes of practices stemming from Egypt, Mesopotamia, the Neo-Hittite state, Ugarit, and the indigenous Canaanite groups are revealed in ancient Near Eastern (ANE) texts, uncovered in the archaeological record, and are sprinkled through the biblical text, presenting a veritable cornucopia of ideas on what the cult of the dead looked like.[63]

As the crossroads between major international powers, Israel was populated by many peoples. Whereas scholarship on Philistine, Phoenician, and other surrounding cultures acknowledges such a cult existed, scholarship has been divided with regards to whether such a cult existed in ancient

10 INTRODUCTION

Israel. Minimalist views have not found favor in the scholarly community; the pendulum definitely swings to the side of scholarship that sees death cult vocabulary in the texts of the Hebrew Bible and ANE, as well as the mortuary remains of the Levant, for what it is: evidence that cults of the dead were practiced. Scholars who reject any kind of cult of the dead push back against the idea that the biblical text retains any reflections of an indigenous Syria-Palestinian tradition. Here I follow Christopher B. Hays, who says that it is possible to excuse individual references to ancestor worship (or a cult of the dead), but you cannot ignore all the references together as an entire corpus.[64]

What the biblical text describes, then, is not a single "cult of the dead," but is better understood as cults of the dead, specifically dead men.[65] Those who argue on behalf of cults of the dead use texts from the Levant, Mesopotamia, and Egypt, along with archaeological evidence.[66] The Ugaritic evidence has been particularly influential. Based on it, William F. Albright acknowledged a widespread cult of the ancestors that was related to a cult of heroes, which in turn drew upon Hebrew and Canaanite practices.[67] Others, such as Klaas Spronk, Theodore Lewis, and Marvin Pope, also found links between the Ugaritic references to necromancy, Rephaim, and the *mrzḥ* (biblical מרזח) and the practices alluded to in the Hebrew Bible.[68] Mark Smith suggests that biblical practices related to the dead are intricately linked to and reveal their Canaanite heritage,[69] while Chanan Brichto saw the social organization of the ancient Israelites—cult, kin, and land—as connected to what happens in the afterlife, an idea echoed in both Francesca Stavrakopoulou's and Matthew Suriano's work.[70] Taking into consideration the past studies, Hays concludes that Israelite society engaged in the worship of chthonic gods, care for dead, and necromancy, and that the elite knew the mythologies of their neighbors and tried them out, especially when Yahweh was not responsive.[71] He elaborates further that ancestor cults included mortuary practices similar to neighboring regions: the *marzēaḥ*, Rephaim, necromancy, *avot/ʒbot* statues, kispu-like rituals, and feeding the dead.[72] Kerry Sonia's work also considers the wider ANE context to situate a discussion on what she calls the cult of the dead kin in the Hebrew Bible. She demonstrates that the care given to the dead is done by family and is situated within the realm of family religion.[73] Sonia's addition of the word "kin" to the phrase "cult of the dead" is important, for it highlights the relational aspect of death. While anthropology and archaeology make appearances, most of these studies, save Suriano's, have approached the cult of the dead (adults) and evidence for it in ancient Israel

INTRODUCTION 11

primarily through texts. The current study adds to this picture by supplying additional data to address a different section of the population—children—and privileging another medium of inquiry, archaeological realia.

Personhood in the Households of the Living and Dead

Personhood, broadly defined, is the state of being a person. What constitutes a person is culturally and socially constructed. "Persons are constituted, de-constituted, maintained and altered in social practices through life and after death. This process can be described as the ongoing attainment of personhood."[74] Personhood as constructed in ancient societies is different from the way it is understood in contemporary Western cultures. In the West, personhood is synonymous with individuality and indivisibility; personhood is fixed, and personal identity is more important than relational identities.[75] Personhood in the West is confined to a physical body, meaning that one's personhood is one's own. However, there are other ways to understand personhood. Kin-based societies, such as those found in the ANE, stress the collective over the individual; we see this in the societal construction of the *bet 'av*.[76] Such societies stress relational aspects of personhood. Personhood in these societies is dividual, "a state of being in which the person is recognized as composite and multiply-authored. People are composed of social relations to others to the degree that they owe parts of themselves to others."[77] Dividual concepts of personhood further understand the individual to comprise many parts.[78] We see this kind of personhood in ancient Egypt, where a person has, among other things a *ka* (vital essence), *ba* (personality), *khet* (physical body), and *ren* (name). Within dividual personhood, one can experience a partible personhood. This type of personhood involves the transfer of part of one's own personhood to another to whom it is owed.[79] Here the ideas of Mauss and his theories about societies in which reciprocal gift-giving was demanded is a useful example.[80] In giving a gift, individuals imbue the gift with some of their own personhood (Mauss called it *hau*) through the permeable materiality of the object.[81] The receiver receives the gift and in doing so receives some of the personhood of the giver. The counter-gift reverses this process, and the relational aspect important in these cultures is highlighted as in the end the two individuals are more closely bound together as they impart and share personhood.

12   INTRODUCTION

Taking into consideration that personhood can extend into death and that burials represent individuals in their idealized form, the mortuary record can provide insight into the degree of personhood bestowed on infants and children.[82] This study suggests that personhood grew with the child and that the degree of personhood given an individual could be reflected in the burial record. Adults represent the fullness of personhood, and the burial rites and rituals accorded them represent the possibility of obtaining the ideal, the ancestor. The lives of infants and children, cut short of this ideal by untimely death, are memorialized in different manners in accordance with age and the way their society understood the child to fit into the household. If the mortuary record indeed reflects the beliefs of the living about the dead, then these conclusions also have larger implications for how infants and children were understood within the household broadly.[83]

Progression of the Book

The study addresses two broad issues. It is concerned narrowly with the place of children in the Judahite cult of the dead kin and more broadly with issues of personhood that might be revealed in burial practices. Yet these aims cannot be accomplished without also understanding how children were treated in the mortuary record of surrounding regions and times. Thus, a comparative approach is necessary. So, too, one cannot simply begin to discuss the data because no study has yet collected information on child burials in one place. Therefore, this study is divided into two parts. Part I presents the data for child burials in various regions of the land of Israel.[84] It begins with regions outside of Judah, ending with an overview of children in Judahite burials. Recognizing that it is impossible to be comprehensive and that excavations continue to turn up new evidence, this study presents a start. Conclusions on child burials and their place in the household of death will likely need to be updated and expanded as more information becomes available and more scholars engage in their study. After the data are presented in Part I, Part II shifts to examine larger themes. It continues to investigate the theme of personhood seen cross-culturally through the use of memorials and place-making, before turning to focus specifically on the region of Judah and a child's place within the cult of the Judahite dead kin.

Chapter 1 presents an overview of child burials, which highlights that most Early Bronze Age through Iron Age societies had a propensity to bury infants, and at times young children, differently than the adults in their community. The chapter provides a broad overview of when and how children and infants were buried and with what they were buried. Most often the youngest are buried inside the site, under house floors, inside store jars. Intermural jar burials are found throughout the Southern Levant from the Neolithic to Persian Periods, with a spike in the practice showing up during the Middle Bronze Age. The presence of intermural burials appears as a challenge to the commonly held idea that death and the dying were excluded from the house. Such burials also bring into question when and if the dying body of an infant brought lasting impurity upon the house. In establishing what mortuary practices occurred in prior periods, we can then ask if the mortuary practices carried out in the Iron Age represent a continuity of past practices or something new. The chapter both frames the analysis of personhood by highlighting when, where, and how children and infants were buried and begins the discussion of how children fit into beliefs about the afterlife.

Chapters 2, 3, and 4 examine the different burial practices for infants and children in the various regions of ancient Israel. On the one hand, these chapters emphasize that Judah did not exist in a vacuum; cities such as Jerusalem and Lachish were international melting pots. On the other hand, examining whether infants and children are buried in the same manner throughout ancient Israel helps us assess whether a more general understanding of infants or children and their personhood, one that is not culturally bound, existed. In these lands, the infant and child burial methods of earlier periods, such as infant jar burials, continue well into Iron Age I and II. Since little is known about cults or beliefs about the dead (adults) outside of Judah proper, the burial of infants and children can offer insights into how one member of the household, the dying child, was perceived in these lands.

Chapter 2 addresses infant and child burials in the Philistine Plain. The continued use of intramural infant burials is noted as a hallmark of Iron Age Philistine burials in the Pentapolis cities. Yet even though this style is preferred, there are differences in the way they are carried out between sites. The discussion therefore also adds to the broader understanding of the diverse nature of Philistine sites. Burials on the Phoenician coast are examined in Chapter 3. The introduction of cremation into the burial repertoire has been well established as a Phoenician trait. However, there are variances between the way that cremation was used in the Phoenician homeland and in its areas of influence within the lands of ancient Israel. It appears that cremation was

14   INTRODUCTION

not used for infants or children in Phoenicia proper; however, the same is not true for Phoenician-influenced sites on the coast of Israel. Moreover, cremation is not the only burial option for infants and children. Rather, the variety that characterizes Phoenician burials in general also extends to children buried on the southern Phoenician coast. While infants and children were often buried individually, they were never far from the burials of their community. The infant and child burials in Philistine and Phoenician-influenced sites demonstrate different ways in which the personhood of these young individuals was understood in their societies.

Chapter 4 continues the geographically centered discussion of infant and child burials, looking first to the missing burials in the Iron I highlands before moving to a discussion of Iron II burials. It provides an overview of the secondary burials and bench/niche tombs that have become the hallmark of the mortuary record for Iron Age Judah. These tombs are often called "family tombs," based on the presence of a bone repository pit. However, these pits are usually found empty, and even when they do contain bones, the skeletal breakdown is not always taken into consideration. Chapter 4 examines those extant skeletal remains to discover whether the moniker "family tomb" is accurate. The chapter also includes a discussion of jar burials in Israel, noting that areas within Judah did not employ jar burials with the same frequency as the surrounding lands. Emphasized throughout is the way in which the personhood of infants and children is preserved within the mortuary record.

Part II opens with a discussion of how infants and children were memorialized in death. Chapter 5 explores structural memorials (burials or tombs) and written memorials (funerary inscriptions). By memorializing an individual through burial or words, the community or family engages in a public ritual. Rituals and protection, in turn, are two of the ways that societies acknowledge an individual's personhood. This chapter addresses why some infants and children were afforded burials and how their personhood was memorialized. Written memorials include an inscribed jar burial from Ashkelon, the Khirbet Beit Lei inscriptions, and the Ketef Hinnom amulets. In looking at structural memorials, the chapter returns to a discussion of jar burials marked with stone circles, pavement, fire pits, and other architectural features, analyzing them through the lens of place- marking and place- making. The chapter closes with a discussion of the tomb as a structural memorial that served as a symbolic return to the womb. A materiality approach to bench tombs and jar burials presents the possibility of rebirth as represented by the clay, shape, and location of the jar burials, while

INTRODUCTION 15

dismissing the possibility of rebirth in stone bench tombs. Though each of the different memorials should be understood in its own cultural location, the various memorials point to an overarching belief that threads its way through each memorial: living adults actively worked to bring dying children into a collective generational space through the process of commemoration and place-making.

Chapter 6 moves to address infants and children specifically within the Judahite bench tomb, investigating the tripartite transitional nature of dying from corpse, to liminal being, to the final form in the afterlife. Focusing on the corpse of the dying child, the chapter addresses ethnic marking through burial, arguing for the perceived necessity to mark children as Judahite in death. During the transition to the liminal state, the ethnic marking is in flux; the liminal stage is the time in the tomb when an individual has no fixed state of being. As common to liminal phases, this is the time when a dying individual needs the most care and protection. The deposition of grave goods, placement of goods and bones within the repository, and the nourishing of the dead are discussed through the lens of partible personhood. The chapter closes by assessing how infants and children fit into the Judahite cult of the dead kin and their place in the household of the dead.

Using the lenses of religious anthropology and the anthropology of gift-giving, Chapter 7 turns to biblical texts of violence, specifically child sacrifice, to address one of the strongest arguments against assigning a measure of personhood to a child. Pushing back against such a view, the chapter asserts that a child did have personhood, despite arguments to the contrary. Children would have been sacrificed because of their special status and perceived personhood that went along with that status. The chapter then investigates why, if child sacrifice was the ultimate example of devotion to the divine and undertaken in order to gain fertility, the rhetoric surrounding child sacrifice was negative. It suggests that the answer to this question might be found in the archaeological record of Phoenicia and other non-Judahite sites. It concludes that, in a world where the Exile loomed large, the texts on child sacrifice can be understood as a polemic against non-Judahite burials, pushing forward the Judahite agenda regarding the cult of the dead kin (as laid out in Chapter 6). Jar burials and child sacrifices then become metaphors for assessing the Other, the non-Judahite.

Chapter 8 draws the study to a close with a reassessment of a child's personhood revealed in death. In comparing and contrasting the different regions, it concludes that unlike other regions that may have placed an emphasis on

16 INTRODUCTION

adults in their community, or thought about people as individuals, Iron II Judahite burials placed an emphasis on the entire family, including infants and children. In this way, I argue, the terminology for and conception of the Judahite afterlife needs to change. What appears in the archaeological record of Judah should not be called a cult of the ancestors but is truly a cult of the dead kin.

Notes

1. See below for a review of scholarship related to adults. Some soundings into the death of children and their place in religion have been done, but a comprehensive study of how the death of children was perceived in ancient Israel and their place in the afterlife and the cult of the dead is missing and needed. See B. A. Nakhai, "When Considering Infants and Jar Burials in the Middle Bronze Age Southern Levant," in *Tell It in Gath: Studies in the History and Archaeology of Israel. Essays in Honor of A. M. Maier on the Occasion of His Sixtieth Birthday*, Ägypten und Altes Testament 90, ed. I. Shai, J. R. Chadwick, L. Hitchcock, A. Dagan, C. McKinney, and J. Uziel (Münster: Zaphon, 2018), 100–128; S. Flynn, *Children in Ancient Israel: The Hebrew Bible and Mesopotamia in Comparative Perspective* (Oxford: Oxford University Press, 2018); K. H. Garroway, *Children in the Ancient Near Eastern Household*, EANEC 3 (Winona Lake, IN: Eisenbrauns, 2014), esp. 198–244; K. H. Garroway, "Children and Religion in the Archaeological Record of Ancient Israel," *JNEAR* 17 (2017): 116–39; K. H. Garroway, *Growing Up in Ancient Israel: Children in Material Culture and Biblical Texts* (Atlanta: SBL, 2018), esp. 223–65.
2. For example, in assessing the death of adults, prior studies struggle with the tension between what is assumed based on texts and what can be seen archaeologically. For example, they assume that aspects of the cult of the dead, like other religious practices, may have been carried out in the house. From an archaeological perspective, studies argue that the data are not there, for all we have are the dedicated extramural burial grounds. Children offer an important set of data in this respect, since they are not always buried extramurally but can be found within the house.
3. To date, T. M. Lemos's monograph is the only full-length treatment of personhood in ancient Israel: *Violence and Personhood in Ancient Israel and Comparative Contexts* (Oxford: Oxford University Press, 2017). Her work focuses on personhood as it relates to violence and the erasure of personhood, concentrating primarily on personhood as related to the living (adult) as presented by biblical texts. Her study addresses children in a single chapter but as living members of society whose personhood can be erased. Infants, she argues, have no personhood. The current study counterbalances this perception by addressing personhood from an archaeological perspective.
4. M. Cradic, "Transformations in Death: The Archaeology of Funerary Practices and Personhood in the Bronze Age Levant" (PhD dissertation, University of California, Berkeley, 2017).
5. On death as relational see M. Suriano, *A History of Death in the Hebrew Bible* (Oxford: Oxford University Press, 2018).
6. Garroway, *Growing Up*, 203, 203 n. 22.
7. Lemos, *Violence and Personhood*, 132–70.
8. Early days of excavation found archaeologists of the Southern Levant invested in the discovery of monumental buildings and the uncovering of ancient city-plans. In the 1980s and 1990s, research questions narrowed to focus on group identity and ethnicity. A. Yasur-Landau, J. Ebling, and L. Mazow, "Introduction: The Past and Present of Household," in *Household Archaeology in Ancient Israel and Beyond*, ed. A. Yasur-Landau, J. Ebling, and L. Mazow (Leiden: Brill, 2011), 2. Arising out of these questions came a shift in focus to the domestic sphere. The movement started slowly, with studies focused first on domestic architecture and demography. See the review of scholarship in J. Hardin, "Understanding Houses, Household, and the Levantine Archaeological Record," in Yasur-Landau, Ebling, and Mazow, *Household Archaeology*, 12–13. Lawrence Stager's 1985 study is widely regarded as breaking new ground and setting the

stage for household archaeology in the Southern Levant, as it utilized an integrative methodology to analyze space, demography, architecture, text, and material remains of Iron Age Israel. L. Stager, "The Archaeology of the Family in Ancient Israel," *BASOR* 260 (1985): 1–35. Since then, excavations have taken seriously to engaging in household archaeology in order to understand the relationship between a site and the people living within the site. Hardin notes that "to understand fully the ancient sites one must not look only to the larger monumental structure, but to where people lived" ("Understanding Houses," 9).

9. R. Wilk and W. Rathje, "Household Archaeology," *American Behavioral Scientist* 25.6 (1982): 618. On other ways to define household, see the review in C. Foster and B. Parker, "Introduction: Household Archaeology in the Near East and Beyond," in *New Perspectives in Household Archaeology*, ed. B. Parker and C. Foster (Winona Lake, IN: Eisenbrauns, 2012), 1.

10. This is important to note since most extant burials are linked to a city, yet the majority of people are hypothesized to have lived in an agricultural setting. D. A. Knight, *Law Power and Justice in Ancient Israel* (Louisville, KY: Westminster John Knox, 2011), 70–79; S. Bender, *The Social Structure of Ancient Israel: The Institution of the Family* (beit 'ab) *from Settlement to the End of the Monarchy* (Jerusalem: Simor, 1996); Stager, "Archaeology of the Family"; J. D. Schloen, *The House of the Father as Fact and Symbol: Patrimonialism in Ugarit and the Ancient Near East*, SAHL 2 (Winona Lake, IN: Eisenbrauns, 2001); C. Meyers, *Rediscovering Eve: Ancient Israelite Women in Context* (Oxford: Oxford University Press, 2013), 112.

11. Hardin, "Understanding Houses," 13.

12. The house of the mother (*bet 'em*), while not as common as the *bet 'av*, appears to have also functioned in ancient Israel. C. Chapman, *The House of the Mother: The Social Roles of Maternal Kin in Biblical Hebrew Narrative and Poetry* (New Haven, CT: Yale University Press, 2016).

13. On the movement from excavations to inferences regarding the archaeological community, see Wilk and Rathje, "Household Archaeology," 617–39, esp. 618–19.

14. Foster and Parker, "Introduction," 2; C. Meyers, "Engendering Syro-Palestinian Archaeology: Reasons and Resources," *NEA* 66 (2003): 185–97. See too the essays in the volumes by Yasur-Landau, Ebling, and Mazow, *Household Archaeology*; Parker and Foster, *New Perspectives*, and C. Shafer-Elliott, *The 5 Minute Archaeologist in the Southern Levant* (Sheffield: Equinox Publishing, 2016), as well as, inter alia, T. Frank, *Household Food Storage in Ancient Israel and Judah* (Oxford: Archaeopress, 2018); J. Hardin, *Lahav II: Households and the Use of Domestic Space at Iron II Tell Halif: An Archaeology of Destruction*, Reports of the Lahav Research Project at Tell Halif, Israel, ed. J. Seger (Winona Lake, IN: Eisenbrauns, 2012); C. Meyers, *Households and Holiness: The Religious Culture of Israelite Women* (Minneapolis: Augsburg Fortress, 2005); Meyers, *Rediscovering Eve*; Garroway, *Growing Up*.

15. Foster and Parker, "Introduction," 8.

16. Foster and Parker, "Introduction," 8.

17. Garroway, *Children*; Garroway, *Growing Up*; R. Avissar Lewis, *Children of Antiquity: A View of Archaeology and Childhood in the Land of Israel during the Biblical Period* (Haifa: Haifa University Press, 2020) (Hebrew); J. Uziel and R. Avissar Lewis, "The Tel Nagila Middle Bronze Age Homes: Studying Household Activities and Identifying Children in the Archaeological Record," *PEQ* 145 (2013): 284–92.

18. On children as economic assets in the household see L. Koepf-Taylor, *Give Me Children or I Shall Die* (Minneapolis: Fortress, 2013); N. Steinberg, *The World of the Child in the Hebrew Bible*, HBM 51 (Sheffield: Sheffield Phoenix, 2013); Garroway, *Growing Up*.

19. Garroway, *Growing Up*, 137–71; Garroway, "Children and Religion," 116–39.

20. G. Lillehammer, "A Child Is Born: The Child's World in an Archaeological Perspective," *NAR* 22 (1989): 89–105; J. S. Deverenski, "Engendering Children, Engendering Archaeology," in *Invisible People and Processes: Writing Gender and Childhood into European Archaeology*, ed. J. Moore and E. Scott (London: Leicester University Press, 1997), 192–202; P. Bourdieu, *The Logic of Practice*, trans. R. Nice (Stanford: Stanford University Press, 1990); J. Arnett, "Broad and Narrow Socialization: Family in the Context of a Cultural Theory," *Journal of Marriage and Family* 57 (1995): 617–28.

21. Garroway, "Children and Religion," 120.

22. R. Kletter, *Judean Pillar Figurines and the Archaeology of Ashera*, BAR International Series 636 (Oxford: Tempus Reparatum, 1996), 73; Lillehammer, "A Child Is Born," 89–91. See also the discussion of these problematized objects in Garroway, *Growing Up*, 202–19.

23. N. Finlay, "Kid Knapping: The Missing Children in Lithic Analysis," in Moore and Scott, *Invisible People and Processes*, 203–12; L. Grimm, "Apprentice Flintknapping: Relating Material

18   INTRODUCTION

Culture and Social Practice in the Upper Paleolithic," in *Children and Material Culture*, ed. J. Sofaer Derevenski (New York: Routledge, 2000), 53–71; Uziel and Lewis, "Tel Nagila," 284–92; M. Králik, P. Urbanová, and M. Hložek, "Finger, Hand and Foot Imprints: The Evidence of Children on Archaeological Artefacts," in *Children, Identity and the Past*, ed. L. H. Dommasnes and Melanie Wrigglesworth (Newcastle: Cambridge Scholars, 2021), 1–15; B. Roveland, "Footprints in the Clay: Upper Palaeolithic Children in Ritual and Secular Context," in Derevenski, *Children and Material Culture*, 26–38.

24. For example, the rebellious son laws of Deuteronomy 21:19–21 and the children to whom the commandment to honor one's father and mother are directed are likely adults who are tasked with taking care of their parents in their old age.

25. J. F. Parker, *Valuable and Vulnerable: Children in the Hebrew Bible, Especially the Elisha Cycle*, BJS 355 (Providence, RI: Brown Judaic Studies, 2013), 41–74.

26. R. Harris, *Gender and Aging in Mesopotamia: The Gilgamesh Epic and Other Ancient Literature* (Norman: University of Oklahoma Press, 2000), 3–7; I. Gelb, "The Ancient Mesopotamian Ration System," *JNES* 24 (1965): 238–41; J. Tenney, *Life at the Bottom of Babylonian Society: Servile Laborers at Nippur in the 14th and 13th Centuries B.C.*, CHANE 51 (Leiden: Brill, 2011); Garroway, *Children*, 18–19.

27. J. Sofaer, "Towards a Social Bioarchaeology of Age," in *Social Bioarchaeology*, ed. S. Agarwal and B. Blencross (New York: Wiley-Blackwell, 2011), 285–311.

28. Flynn, *Children in Ancient Israel*, 9–13.

29. L. Scheuer and S. Black, eds., *Developmental Juvenile Osteology* (San Diego, CA: Academic Press, 2000), 1.

30. Speaking on skeletal remains as a whole, Knüsel and Robb make the following observation: "Many skeletal assemblages remain uninvestigated, often because they are perceived as too small or too fragmented to repay study." C. Knüsel and J. Robb, "Funerary Taphonomy: An Overview of Goals and Methods," *Journal of Archaeological Reports* 10 (2016): 656.

31. P. Beauchesne and S. Agarwal, "Excavating Childhood from the Skeletal Record," in *Children and Childhood in Bioarchaeology* (Gainesville: University Press of Florida, 2018), 4.

32. A. A. Saxe, "Social Dimensions of Mortuary Practice" (PhD dissertation, University of Michigan, 1970); L. Binford, "Mortuary Practices: Their Study and Their Potential," in *Approaches to the Social Dimension of Mortuary Practices*, Memoirs for the Society for American Archaeology 25, ed. J. A. Brown (New York: Society for American Archaeology, 1971), 6–29; J. M. O'Shea, *Mortuary Variability: An Archaeological Investigation*, Studies in Archaeology Series (Orlando, FL: Academic Press, 1984); I. Hodder, "Post-processual Archaeology," *Advances in Archaeology Method and Theory* 8 (1985): 1–26.

33. Garroway, *Children*, 17; S. Sheridan, "Coming of Age at St. Stephen's: Bioarchaeology of Children at a Byzantine Jerusalem Monastery (Fifth to Seventh Centuries CE)," in *Children in the Bible and the Ancient World: Comparative and Historical Methods in Reading Ancient Children*, ed. S. W. Flynn (London: Routledge, 2019), 152; M. Lewis, *The Bioarchaeology of Children: Perspectives from Biological and Forensic Anthropology* (Cambridge: Cambridge University Press, 2007).

34. Inter alia, Lewis, *The Bioarchaeology of Children*; M. Lewis, *Paleopathology of Children* (London: Academic Press, 2018); B. Baker, T. Dupras, and M. Tocheri, *Osteology of Infants and Children* (College Station: Texas A&M University Press, 2005); Beauchesne and Agarwal, *Children and Childhood*; E. Murphy and M. LeRoy, eds., *Children, Death and Burial: Archaeological Discourses* (Oxford: Oxbow, 2017); K. Bacvarov, ed., *Babies Reborn: Infant/ Child Burials in Pre- and Protohistory*, BAR International Series 1832 (Oxford: Archaeopress, 2008); E. Scott, *The Archaeology of Infancy and Infant Death*, BAR International Series 819 (Oxford: Archaeopress, 1999); M. Lally and A. Moore (eds), *(Re) thinking the Little Ancestor: New Perspectives on the Archaeology of Infancy and Childhood*, BAR International Series 2271 (Oxford: Archaeopress, 2011); S. Crawford, D. Hadley, and G. Shepherd, eds., *The Oxford Handbook of the Archaeology of Childhood* (Oxford: Oxford University Press, 2018).

35. See the comparison listed in chart form in Murphy and LeRoy, *Children, Death and Burial*, 10. See also Garroway, *Children*, 16–17; J. Baxter, *Archaeology of Childhood: Children, Gender and Material Culture* (Walnut Creek, CA: AltaMira Press, 2005), 97; Lewis, *The Bioarchaeology of Children*, 5.

36. J. Buckley, "Techniques for Identifying Age and Sex of Children at Death," in Crawford, Hadley, and Shepherd, *Oxford Handbook*, 55–70; Garroway, *Growing Up*, 7–8.

INTRODUCTION   19

37. Skeletal ages are based on the ability to read centers of ossification. Especially useful in this respect are long bones. Teeth, often the only thing preserved in a child's remains, start developing in utero and the pattern of growth is fairly well studied. Dental ages are often preferred because they are not affected by things like nutrition, endocrine events (growth spurts), and other environmental factors affecting the skeleton (Scheuer and Black, *Developmental Juvenile Osteology*, 5–13).
38. Scheuer and Black, *Developmental Juvenile Osteology*; Buckley, "Techniques for Identifying Age," 55–70. Scheuer and Black press the point that juvenile skeletons are biased. On the one hand, they represent individuals who are ill or deficient (i.e., they were ill and did not grow up). On the other hand, they do not correspond to the number of juveniles one would expect in the burial populations (Scheuer and Black, *Developmental Juvenile Osteology*, 14).
39. Graves do not have headstones with convenient born-on and died-on dates.
40. Garroway, *Growing Up*, 8; K. H. Garroway, "Children in the Ancient World: A Methodology," in *A Handbook to Children and Childhood in the Biblical World*, ed. J. F. Parker and S. Betsworth (London: T & T Clark, 2019), 74 and Table 4.1.
41. Most of the differential burials that are seen in the archaeological record of ancient Israel belong to infants, i.e., individuals up to two years of age.
42. S. Lucy, "Children in Early Medieval Cemeteries," *Archaeological Review from Cambridge* 13 (1994): 24–25; R. Hallote, "Mortuary Archaeology in the Middle Bronze Age Southern Levant," *JMA* 8.1 (1995): 95; M. Chesson, "Libraries of the Dead: Early Bronze Age Charnel Houses and Social Identity at Urban Bab edh-Dhra', Jordan," *JAA* 18 (1999): 140; E. Murphy and M. LeRoy, "Archaeological Children, Death and Burial," in Murphy and LeRoy, *Children, Death and Burial*, 1.
43. H. Härke, "Data Types in Burial Analysis," in *Prehistoric Graves as a Source of Information: Symposium at Kastlösa, Öland, May 21–23, 1992*, ed. B. Stjernquist (Stockholm: Kungl. Vitterhets Historie och Antikvites Akademien, 1994), 32.
44. These theories will be explored more in the following chapters.
45. Chesson, "Libraries of the Dead," 140. See also S. Kan, *Symbolic Immortality: The Tlingit Potlatch of the Nineteenth Century* (Washington, DC: Smithsonian Institution Press, 1989); P. Metcalf and R. Huntington, eds., *Celebrations of Death: The Anthropology of Mortuary Ritual* (Cambridge: Cambridge University Press, 1991).
46. Chesson's description of House Societies is reminiscent of the contemporary fraternity and sorority houses on college campuses. The bonds formed between the housemates is fictive, yet they refer to each other as "brothers" or "sisters." This fictive bond continues to exist between generations of sorority sisters / fraternity brothers. Similar to Chesson's House Societies, contemporary fraternity and sororities are understood to have different ranks on campus, as well as different group identities.
47. Chesson, "Libraries of the Dead," 160.
48. Chesson, "Libraries of the Dead," 140.
49. Hallote, "Mortuary Archaeology," 93–122.
50. Hallote, "Mortuary Archaeology," 100.
51. Suriano addresses the relational aspect of death in depth. See discussion below.
52. Hallote, "Mortuary Archaeology," 102–5.
53. R. Hertz, *Death and the Right Hand*, trans. R. Needham and C. Needham (Glencoe, IL: Free Press, 1960); A. van Gennep, *The Rites of Passage* (Chicago: University of Chicago Press, 1960); Binford, "Mortuary Practices"; Saxe, "Social Dimensions."
54. M. P. Pearson, "Mortuary Practices, Society and Ideology: An Ethnoarchaeological Study," in *Symbolic and Structural Archaeology*, ed. I. Hodder (Cambridge: Cambridge University Press, 1982), 99–113; I. Hodder, *Symbols in Action: Ethnoarchaeological Studies of Material Culture* (Cambridge: Cambridge University Press, 1982).
55. Chesson, "Libraries of the Dead," 142. For scholarship addressing both approaches see L. G. Goldstein, "One-Dimensional Archaeology and Multi-dimensional People: Spatial Organization and Mortuary Analysis," in *The Archaeology of Death*, ed. R. Chapman, G. Kinnes, and K. Randsborg (Cambridge: Cambridge University Press, 1981), 53–69; I. Hodder, "Social Structure and Cemeteries: A Critical Appraisal," in *Anglo-Saxon Cemeteries, 1979: The Fourth Anglo-Saxon Symposium at Oxford*, BAR British Series 82, ed. P. Rahtz, T. Dickinson, and L. Watts (Oxford: British Archaeological Reports, 1980), 160–69; J. Brown, "On Mortuary Analysis—with Special Reference to the Saxe-Binford Research Program," in *Regional Approaches to Mortuary Analysis*, Interdisciplinary Contributions to Archaeology, ed. L. A. Beck (Boston: Springer, 1995), 3–26.

20 INTRODUCTION

56. Kan, *Symbolic Immortality*, 17.
57. Kan, *Symbolic Immortality*, 18–22; A. A. Radcliffe-Brown, *The Andaman Islanders: A Study in Social Anthropology* (Cambridge: Cambridge University Press, 1922); Hertz, *Death and the Right Hand*; Binford, "Mortuary Practices"; C. Lévi-Strauss, *The Way of the Masks* (London: Jonathan Cape, 1983).
58. This concept is not unique to me or this work. See C. Bell, *Ritual Theory, Ritual Practice* (New York: Oxford University Press, 1992); V. Turner, *Ritual Process: Structure and Anti-structure* (New York: de Gruyter, 1995). Matthew Suriano (*History of Death*) uses it extensively in his work on the Judahite tomb.
59. R. Hertz, *A Contribution to the Study of the Collective Representation of Death*, Reprinted (Glencoe, IL: Free Press, 1960); orig. pub. *L'Année Sociologique* (Paris: Presses Universitaires de France, 1907). 9781119151746.excerpt.pdf (wiley.com)
60. The most recent work is that of Matthew Suriano (*History of Death*) with his thought-provoking study of the dying body and the Judahite tomb. It was in reading his work that I began to see the many areas where the treatment of children might be different and that the study of the dying child could offer a new contribution to the discussion of death in ancient Israel.
61. On the category of religion as a modern construct, see J. Z. Smith, *Imagining Religion* (Chicago: University of Chicago Press, 1982), xi. The comparative approach to Israel's religion and its rituals is well established.
62. Chesson, "Libraries of the Dead," 142.
63. For references to Canaanite traditions, see the discussion below. On Egyptian connections, see T. Lewis's review of *Israel's Beneficent Dead* in *JAOS* 119.3 (1999): 512–14, and C. B. Hays, *A Covenant with Death: Death in the Iron Age II and Its Rhetorical Uses in Proto-Isaiah* (Grand Rapids, MI: Eerdmans, 2011). For Mesopotamia, see inter alia J. Scurlock, "Ghosts in the Ancient Near East: Weak or Powerful?," *HUCA* 68 (1977): 77–96; J. Scurlock, *Magico-Medical Means of Treating Ghost-Induced Illnesses in Ancient Mesopotamia*, Ancient Magic and Divination 3 (Leiden: Brill, 2002); K. van der Toorn, "Funerary Rituals and Beatific Afterlife in Ugaritic Texts and the Bible," *BO* 48 (1991): 40–66; K. van der Toorn, *Family Religion in Babylonia, Syria, and Israel: Continuity and Change in the Forms of Religious Life* (Leiden: Brill, 1996).
64. Hays points to Lewis, who notes that, to argue this, one must hold fast to a minimalist understanding of the biblical text and see the Hebrew Bible as a literary creation of the Deuteronomist, creating religion out of whole cloth (Hays, *A Covenant with Death*, 144).
65. Just as Judaism today has a prescribed means of burying and memorializing the dead—burial in a plain wood coffin, without any means of preserving the body, and burial to happen within three days of the death—yet not every person who identifies as Jewish follows this tradition. Some choose to prolong the time between death and burial or choose other kinds of coffins or even cremation.
66. G. von Rad, *Old Testament Theology*, vol. 1, *The Theology of Israel's Historical Traditions*, trans. D. M. G. Stalker (Louisville, KY: Westminster John Knox, 2001) (German orig., 1957); H. Brichto, "Kin, Cult, Land and Afterlife—a Biblical Complex," *HUCA* 44 (1973): 1–54; W. F. Albright, *Yahweh and the Gods of Canaan* (Winona Lake, IN: Eisenbrauns, 1968); K. Spronk, *Beatific Afterlife in Ancient Israel and in the Ancient Near East*, Alter Orient und Altes Testament 219 (Neukirchen-Vluyn: Neukirchener Verlag, 1986); T. Lewis, *Cults of the Dead in Ancient Israel and Ugarit*, HSM 39 (Atlanta: Scholars Press, 1989); M. Pope, "Notes on the Rephaim Texts from Ugarit," in *Essays on the Ancient Near East in Memory of Jacob Joel Finkelstein*, Memoirs of the Connecticut Academy of Arts and Sciences 19, ed. M. de Jong Ellis (Hamden, CT: Archon Books, 1977), 163–82; M. Pope, "The Cult of the Dead at Ugarit," in *Ugarit in Retrospect: Fifty Years of Ugarit and Ugaritic*, ed. G. D. Young (Winona Lake, IN: Eisenbrauns, 1981), 159–79; M. Smith and E. Bloch-Smith, "Death and Afterlife in Ugarit and Israel," *JAOS* 108 (1988): 277–84; Hays, *A Covenant with Death*; K. Sonia, *Caring for the Dead in Ancient Israel*, ABS 27 (Atlanta: SBL, 2020). For a more in-depth history of scholarship on the matter, see Hays, *A Covenant with Death*, 135–47.
67. Albright, *Yahweh*, 204.
68. The place of necromancy and self-laceration has been debated, with Lewis, Spronk, Bloch-Smith, and Smith categorizing them as part of the cult of the dead, while Schmidt does not. Lewis, *Cults of the Dead*; Spronk, *Beatific Afterlife*, 257; Smith and Bloch-Smith, "Death and Afterlife," 277–84; B. B. Schmidt, *Israel's Beneficent Dead: Ancestor Cult and Necromancy in Ancient Israelite Religion and Tradition* (Winona Lake, IN: Eisenbrauns, 1996).

INTRODUCTION   21

69. M. Smith, *The Early History of God: Yahweh and the Other Deities in Ancient Israel*, 2nd ed. (Grand Rapids, MI: Eerdmans, 2002).
70. F. Stavrakopoulou, *Land of Our Fathers: The Roles of Ancestor Veneration in Biblical Land Claims*, LHBOTS 473 (London: T & T Clark, 2010); Suriano, *History of Death*. The relationship between land and the afterlife, incidentally, follows the description of land transmission and the investment in land when it is a scarce resource (Wilk and Rathje, "Household Archaeology," 627).
71. Hays, *A Covenant with Death*, 134.
72. Hays, *A Covenant with Death*, 162–72.
73. Sonia, *Caring for the Dead*, esp. 129–64.
74. C. Fowler, *The Archaeology of Personhood: Anthropological Approach* (London: Routledge, 2004), 4.
75. Fowler, *The Archaeology of Personhood*, 4, 9– 10; S. Gillespie, "Personhood, Agency, and Mortuary Ritual: A Case Study from the Ancient Maya," *Journal of Anthropological Archaeology* 20 (2001): 73–78.
76. N. Steinberg, *Kinship and Marriage in Genesis: A Household Economics Perspective* (Minneapolis: Fortress, 1993), 18–19; Fowler, *The Archaeology of Personhood*, 48–52.
77. Fowler, *The Archaeology of Personhood*, 5.
78. In Western society the individual might be understood to have a soul, but it is confined within the body.
79. Fowler, *The Archaeology of Personhood*, 5.
80. M. Mauss, *The Gift: Forms and Functions of Exchange in Archaic Societies* (New York: Norton, 1967).
81. On permeability and materiality of objects, see L. Quick, *Dress, Adornment, and the Body in the Hebrew Bible* (Oxford: Oxford University Press, 2021).
82. For applications of personhood studies and death within archaeological contexts see J. Cerezo-Roman, "Unpacking Personhood and Funerary Customs in the Hohokam Area of Southern Arizona," *American Antiquity* 80 (2015): 353– 75; Gillespie, "Personhood, Agency"; E.- J. Graham, "Becoming Persons, Becoming Ancestors: Personhood, Memory and the Corpse in Roman Rituals of Social Remembrance," *Archaeological Dialogues* 16 (2009): 51–74. On the investigation of personhood in an archaeological context, Cerezo-Román demonstrates the necessity of taking into consideration the relationship between the individual and material culture ("Unpacking Personhood," 354).
83. While some recent studies have started to address the issue of children in the household, most concentrate on the biblical data, and none have addressed the nexus of a child's or infant's personhood and the household.
84. I use the term "land of Israel" or "Israel" throughout the study to refer to the geographic region that reaches from the Upper Galilee to the Negev, and the Mediterranean coast to the Jordan Rift Valley.

PART I
THE BURIALS OF CHILDREN
IN ANCIENT ISRAEL

1

Archaeological Overview of Child Burials in the Bronze and Iron Ages

This chapter provides a broad overview of infant and child burials from the Bronze and Iron Ages. In establishing what mortuary practices occurred in prior periods, we can then ask if the mortuary practices carried out in the Iron Age represent a continuity of past practices or show something new. The chapter interacts with the discussion of personhood by highlighting when, where, and how children and infants were buried and in doing so introduces the conversation about a cult of the dying infant and child.

Differentiated Burials of the Dying Child

Infants and children were buried in different ways. The most popular burial methods include interment in caves, cists, coffins, jars, pits, and tombs. The terms here refer to generic styles. One might further divide these generic methods into specific types, such as bench, chamber, or shaft tomb or store jar and pithos jar. Because this chapter is an overview, and broad patterns will be discussed, I am using the key generic terms recorded by the excavators rather than differentiating between each kind of burial.[1] As the data sample below exemplify, many types of burials were employed in a single period.

Table 1.1 shows the results of a study cataloging almost one hundred infant and child burials sites at over sixty locations.[2] The results find that, despite the ebb and flow of use, jar burials are consistently the most common type of burial for infants and young children. Reasons for the high numbers of extant remains in jar burials might be due to a very practical reason—as opposed to a simple pit burial, jars kept the dying body protected from later disturbances. Yet this explanation only addresses why excavators found large numbers of jar burials; it does not explain why a society would choose to

The Dying Child. Kristine Henriksen Garroway, Oxford University Press. © Oxford University Press 2025.
DOI: 10.1093/9780197566718.003.0002

26 THE BURIALS OF CHILDREN IN ANCIENT ISRAEL

Table 1.1 Number of Burial Sites with Child and Infant Burials Correlated with Burial Method and Time Period

	EB I	EB II	EB III	EB IV–MB I	MB II	LB I	LB II	IA I	IA II	Total number of sites
Jar burial	4	0	0	0	17	2	5	6	5	39
Cave	1	2	0	1	2	2	2	4	1	15
Tomb	0	1	0	4	7	2	2	2	2	20
Pit	2	0	0	1	6	2	2	3	4	20
Total burials	7	3	0	6	32	8	11	15	12	94

Note: The sites and their bibliography can be found in K. H. Garroway, *Children in the Ancient Near Eastern Household*, EANEC 3 (Winona Lake, IN: Eisenbrauns, 2014), 281–316 and K. H. Garroway, *Growing Up in Ancient Israel: Children in Material Culture and Biblical Texts* (Atlanta: SBL, 2018), 257–60.

bury infants and young children in this manner. From a practical standpoint, a society might use a jar burial because it requires a relatively low amount of energy expenditure. Other types of burials, such as caves, tombs, and cists, require multiple steps in creating a location or preparing it for later reuse. Digging a trench and lining it with bricks, hewing benches and repository pits, clearing away previously deposited items and deceased individuals, or reopening the location are all time-consuming and labor-intensive activities. A small individual may not have been considered worthy of such energy output. The dimensions of a store jar, on the other hand, provide a ready-made coffin for a small individual.

In analyzing the various burials, it is important to note not only the burial methods but also who is buried in the graves. Some graves include only a single individual (the child/infant), while others include multiple burials.[3] Tombs and caves generally include multiple individuals and are frequently interpreted as kin-based burials. When infants and children are found in these burials, they are found alongside adults. Pit and cist burials include fewer individuals. Often they are single interments, but infants and children have also been found buried alongside one or two adults. Jar burials, on the other hand, overwhelmingly include only one infant or young child. Again, jar burials stand out as burials specifically meant for infants and young children.

ARCHAEOLOGICAL OVERVIEW OF CHILD BURIALS 27

Table 1.2 Infant and Child Burials: Locations, Number of Individuals, and Time Periods

Location	Individuals	EBI–III	EB IV / MB I	MB II	LBI–II	IA I	IA II
Intramural	Single	41	–	89	8	28[a]	6
	Multiple	1	–	5	–	–	2
Extramural	Single	–	–	26	4	5	27[b]
	Multiple	4	12	18	6	34[c]	8

Note: An earlier form of this table can be found in Table 4, in Garroway, *Children*, 222.

[a] Of these twenty-eight intramural burials, twenty-six belong to sites on the Philistine coast.

[b] Of these twenty-seven burials, eighteen were found in the Ashkelon cemetery.

[c] Of these thirty-four, thirty children and infants were found within the burial cave associated with Tel es-Safi/Gath, discussed in Chapter 2. The cave is dated to the Iron I–II period.

Another factor to consider is the relationship of infant and child burials to the wider community. Table 1.2 highlights how relative age affects not only the method of burial but the placement of that burial. Extramural burials are located outside of a site. At times these may be cemeteries adjacent to a site, such as those found at Jericho and Achzib, while at other times they may be a family tomb or cave located near a site, such as the burial caves near Nazareth or near Tel es-Safi/Gath.[4] Intermural burials can be described as burials that are located within a settlement. In most cases, those individuals found within a site are not adults but infants or children buried within simple pit burials or jar burials.[5] These burials have been found on the slopes of a site, near doorways or gate areas, and within domestic confines.[6] The use of intermural burials for infants and children reaches its zenith in the Middle Bronze II, where 17% of houses are estimated to have infant jar burials under their floors.[7]

Studies of household religion posit that religious practices took place in the domestic sphere.[8] Scholars also suggest that the cult of the dead had "a lasting appeal in certain forms of popular religion,"[9] yet a tangible link between religious practices and the cult of the dead has been missing. "Texts bear little direct witness to popular religion and a dearth of excavated common graves means that archaeology is largely mute on the topic as well."[10] Here is another place where an adult-centric view of death has overlooked a fertile piece of evidence, for as the data above show, children are often buried within the domicile. Because burials are marked with rituals, the intramural burials of infants and children should be considered as having a place both

28 THE BURIALS OF CHILDREN IN ANCIENT ISRAEL

within household religion and within the cult of the dead kin. Furthermore, considering the emphasis that household religion placed on children and fecundity, it would be irresponsible to exclude the death of children from the broader view of household religion. In thinking about the rituals that might have surrounded these intramural burials, Émile Durkheim's definition of a death cult (or cult of the dead) can be helpful: death cults included "repeated standardized practices oriented toward the dead" that were generally done at specific "ritual locations associated with the dead."[11] By this definition, rituals need not only be done at a tomb or in a public place of worship but can take place in the domicile or any other place associated with the dead.[12]

Lewis Binford argued that the totality of an individual's social persona determined the level of community participation in the person's burial and the degree to which the ritual attached to the death disrupted daily life.[13] Given that intramural jar burials are often found within residential buildings, it seems likely that, at a minimum, the routine of the immediate household would be disrupted with death-related rituals. What the exact rituals looked like is difficult to say. Both funerary rites and mortuary rites vary in how long they last, how many phases are involved, and the emotions that surround them.[14] At the very least, practices that are repeated and standardized imply that a group of people has agreed upon certain actions. Because the act of interring young individuals within jars has been found throughout sites and across many time periods, it qualifies as a repeated and standardized practice. Moreover, the grave goods found with jar burials, explored more below, also appear standardized. While the exact meaning behind the burials and the goods deposited might vary between societies, their standardization argues in favor of a generalized shared understanding underlying the practice. To this end, scholars have offered the possibility of the jar burial as a return to the womb and, more specifically, the domicile as a womb located within the natal house.[15] The differentiated burials might also indicate an ephemeral social personhood in which the individual has not yet been afforded full personhood.

Graves and Grave Goods

The cave tomb, prevalent in the Early and Middle Bronze Ages, evolved into a different style of hewn tomb in the Late Bronze II and Iron Ages.[16] These tombs had an elongated entrance, sometimes with steps leading down, which led to a central space. The central space had niches or benches. Side chambers with additional niches and benches on which to lay out the dead might branch off from the central space. Such tombs also included a repository pit used to collect the bones and grave goods associated with the individual. In later periods, the architecture of the tombs changed yet again. The benches gave way to catacomb-esque tombs in the Hellenistic, Roman, and Byzantine periods. Deposition of grave goods also changed. In earlier periods, goods were initially associated with the primary burial and then swept into a collective.[17] During the Second Temple Period onward, grave goods remained with the primary burial. The change in both the architecture of tombs and the associated grave good deposition demonstrates a shift away from the family collective (Bronze Ages) to a focus on the individual (Second Temple Period).[18] Motivations for this change have been linked to an evolution in the belief about the afterlife and the relationship between the living and the dead.

The shift from collective toward the individual might not seem to apply to infant and child burials, especially because they are often left out of family tombs in the earlier periods. Furthermore, when children and infants are found, they are most often within *individual* intramural burials. If the burial pattern of the youngest individuals does not follow that of adults, does this also mean that beliefs about the afterlife were different for infants and children? Or more to the point, would the argument made concerning the evolution of the adult burials suggest that individuals had no afterlife until they were of an age such that they were buried in a manner similar to other members of their society? Two answers present themselves, both of which argue that regardless of the method of burial, infants and young children did have a place in the afterlife. First, intramural jar burials are important because they are *intramural*. While the infants were buried in a manner different from that of other members of their family, they were nonetheless buried in a location that, like a family tomb, associated them with the family collective. In this regard, while they were buried individually, they were not disassociated from the family. Rather than severing links to the family, one might argue, keeping infants within the house actually formed a stronger link between the deceased infant and the living members of the household. The second answer has to do with the grave goods afforded to infants and children.

Grave goods can be divided into three broad categories: personal, status, and essential goods.[19] Essential goods are classified as items needed for

30 THE BURIALS OF CHILDREN IN ANCIENT ISRAEL

Table 1.3 Overview of Grave Goods by Time Period: Age Not Specified

Time Period	Ceramic Goods
Early Bronze Age (and continuing through the rest of the Bronze Ages)	Bowls, lamps, juglets, jars and jugs, beads, earrings, rings, daggers, and mace heads
Iron Age I	Bowls, chalices, pilgrim flasks, pyxides, jars, jugs, juglets, storage jars, and lamps
Iron Age II	Bowls, chalices, pilgrim flasks, pyxides, jars, jugs, juglets, storage jars, lamps, table amphorae, plates, storage jars, dipper juglets, cooking pots, and wine sets
Persian Period	One or two juglets and a few bronze objects (quantity of essential goods greatly decreased)

feasting and provisions in the afterlife, such as ceramics related to food preparation, drinking, and eating.[20] Personal grave goods are those items closely related to one's persona (jewelry, combs, makeup boxes, favorite possessions, toys, game pieces, etc.), while status-related items indicate one's place within society (imported goods, luxury goods, tools, weapons, seals, etc.).[21] Most Canaanite burials included a core group of items identified as a funeral kit. These were items given to an individual to help in the afterlife. In Canaanite Ashkelon, where this idea was first identified, the kit consisted of packaging for commodities, food-service vessels, tableware, scarabs, and toggle pins.[22] Jill Baker conducted a broad overview of the ceramic and non-ceramic items within the funeral kit at its genesis and decline.[23] Table 1.3 is based on her observations.

The results of the items linked to adults in family or group tombs can be compared with the items found buried with infants and children. Table 1.4 is the result of an earlier study conducted on over 440 infant and child burials.[24]

Table 1.4 shows the variety of items that might be found associated with a child or infant's burial. On the whole, the assemblage matches the grave goods afforded to adults. However, most of the child and infant burials examined found young individuals were buried with nothing.[25] When infants were buried with items, the number was generally one to three items. Jar burials contained the most standardized set of grave goods. The majority of jar burials included, besides the store jar itself, a juglet and a bowl covering the lid of the jar. The most important item here is the juglet. While juglets might be present in adult burials, they were not routinely included in every burial, and this presents an interesting opening for a thought

Table 1.4 Overview of Grave Goods for Infants and Children by Time Period

Time Period	Items Found in Burials
Early Bronze Age I–III	Bowls, juglets, jars, store jar, kernoi, cups, beads, bone/shell, plant/animal, metal, loom weight/whorl
Early Bronze Age IV	"Vessels," lamps, juglet, jars, toggle pin, ring/bracelet, knife/dagger
Middle Bronze Age II	"Vessels," lamps, bowls, juglets, jars, store jars, cups, cooking pot, toggle pin, beads, bone/shell, plant/animal, metal, loom weight/whorl, scarab, faience/alabaster, knife/dagger
Late Bronze Age I–II	"Vessels," lamps, bowls, juglets, jars, imports, cups, toggle pin, beads, bone/shell, plant/animal, metal, scarab, knife/dagger
Iron Ages	"Vessels," lamps, bowls, juglets, jars, store jars, cooking pots, toggle pin, beads, bone/shell, plant/animal, metal, loom weight/whorl, scarab, knife/dagger

experiment. Most commonly, ceramic items were thought to be placed with the deceased to serve their needs in the afterlife.[26] Yet recent studies have questioned whether the ceramic items deposited with adults were meant for the deceased in the afterlife or whether they were used by the living as a part of the funerary feast by the living and subsequently left in the burial. Along this logic, ceramic items were thought to be left behind in the tomb because they were contaminated through their association with death.[27] The routine presence of juglets in infant jar burials, however, suggests a different picture, one that supports the earlier idea that the dead needed sustenance in the afterlife. First, juglets alone would not be enough to provide food and drink for a funerary feast unless the feast given for the infant took a very different shape than the feast envisioned for adults. Second, deposition within the house or within settlements suggests that infant burials did not contaminate these areas. Therefore, I would suggest that the juglets were deposited with the infants not because they were deemed impure after the funerary banquet but rather because the infants needed them in the afterlife.[28] The most reasonable explanation for the use of juglets specifically, as opposed to miniature bowls, cups, plates, or other ceramic ware, has to do with their function. Because infants drank breast milk, the juglet may symbolize a container for milk, like a bottle. The fact that juglets were found near the infants' heads also supports this idea. It would seem, then, that juglets were designated as a miniature funeral kit for infants, especially during the Bronze Age.[29]

32 THE BURIALS OF CHILDREN IN ANCIENT ISRAEL

Table 1.5 Grave Goods: Ceramic and Personal Items Found with Children and Infants

	MB II	LB I–II	IA I–II		MB II	LB I–II	IA I–II
"Vessels"	9	3	5	Toggle pin	5	2	3
Lamp	5	1	1	Rings / bracelet	0	3	17
				beads	9	6	8
Bowl	21	6	3	Bone/shell	1	1	2
Juglet	52	5	1	Plant/animal	6	1	1
Jar	13	2	4	Metal	1	2	4
Store Jar	2	0	2	Loom weight/ whorl	2	0	1
Imports	0	6	0	Scarab	9	7	2
Cups	1	0	1	Faience/ alabaster	1	0	0
Cooking Pot	1	0	1	Knife/dagger	4	1	2

Table 1.5 offers a breakdown of the number of items found in the 440 infant and child burials examined.[30] Regarding ceramics, the Middle Bronze II period shows a much higher number of ceramic items found in child and infant burials. Ceramics decreased in the Late Bronze I/II and into the Iron Ages. This is seen most clearly in the deposition of bows, juglets, and jars. A different trend is seen in personal adornments. The number of beads remains relatively the same across the periods. Scarabs and toggle pins are more numerous in the Middle Bronze II than Iron Age, but the sample size here is relatively small. It is with rings and bracelets that one finds the most appreciable difference. Within the sample size, no jewelry was found on or near infant and child Middle Bronze II burials. In the Iron Age, however, seventeen skeletons were found with either a ring or bracelet. Through this overview of grave goods, it is tempting to see the same shift in infant and child burials as was found in adult burials, that is away from the family collective and toward individualization.[31]

Missing Burials

The mortality rate of infants was high in the ancient world. Upwards of 50% of infants were estimated to have died within the first year of life.[32] Most of these deaths occurred in the first week of life and were thought to result from a low birth weight.[33] Correlating burials and population estimates, archaeologists project that another 50% of individuals died between one and fifteen years of age. Some deaths were accidental, but the majority of skeletal remains suggest death was related to pathological factors. Disease, epidemics, malnutrition, and infection rank highest among these. Death could also be intentionally caused through war, cannibalism, and sacrifice. While the archaeological record attests to infant and child death caused by war, it does not readily present evidence linked to sacrifice.[34] Nonetheless, it should not immediately be discarded as a possibility since it was known in the ancient world.[35] Given the high death rates, one would expect the archaeological record to be rife with infant and child burials. However, as hinted at above, the extant number of immature skeletal remains does not correlate with the projected number of deaths given the mortality rate in ancient Israel.[36]

The reason for their absence can be attributed to several different factors. As referenced in the introduction, until recently archaeologists were not looking for children in the burial record. Thus, earlier reports may have overlooked children because they were concerned with different theoretical issues that did not involve children. Skeletal remains of children were simply bypassed or not recorded in a uniform manner.[37] Small bones could be easily overlooked for other reasons as well. For example, children's bones were sometimes confused with animal bones.[38] Because infant bones are small and fragile, they also break more easily and get lost in the recording process.[39] In addition, because of their size, infant and child bones can get swept aside. This can happen both in cases when tombs were opened and reused in antiquity, and when they are opened and excavated. As a result, small bones that were pushed aside are sometimes grouped with unstratified skeletal material. Adding insult to injury, because it is difficult to assign bones like this to a particular stratum, unstratified skeletal material often gets neglected in favor of more well-preserved, primary burials.[40]

Despite these difficulties, the lack of burials does not mean that infants and children were not cared for in death, their burials are just missing in the archaeological record. This is an important point. In as much as scholars assume non-elites were buried in simple pits, so too we can assume that a majority of children were also non-elites and buried in a similar manner.[41] Without the protection of a built tomb, cave, or jar, bones could go missing and seemingly vanish from the burial record. This means that the infants and children were not necessarily excluded from the mortuary community,

34 THE BURIALS OF CHILDREN IN ANCIENT ISRAEL

rather that our access to their burials has been lost to time. The most important conclusions to be drawn from infant and child remains, then, come from contexts where it is clear that we should expect infants and children to be present. For example, if there is a family tomb or cemetery setting in which multiple burials are found, one should ask whether children and infants are also present. If not, then one might ask why. Similarly, when infants are found in intramural jar burials, one can ask whether the number of jar burials corresponds with the projected number of infants at a site for any given time. If the answer is no, here too one needs to ask why some infants were afforded a special burial and others were not. Cases where infants and children are obviously lacking in the mortuary record, and not just overlooked or lost to time, present areas that need to be analyzed.

Personhood and Child Burials

The archaeological record presents a complex picture regarding children's burials. It leaves us with a tension. Why did societies that buried children bury some in marked graves but not others? Why did some infants and children receive grave goods but not others? What does this say about the personhood of children in the Southern Levant?

The most notable pattern within burial styles across time periods is the fact that infants are buried, for the most part, differently than other members of their community. A differentiated burial can mean either a different style of burial or a burial separated from other members of society. Based on the available data, the differentiated burial of infants and children are most often jar burials. However, there is also the absent data that needs to be accounted for. It was suggested that these missing infants and young children were either not given a burial or buried in a simple, unmarked pit away from other settlement burial sites. One wonders, then about the personhood afforded to the youngest members of these societies. If social recognition is a defining element of personhood, then what do differentiated burials say about personhood?

An analysis of these burials must be approached again with the caveat that all burials are carried out by living members of a society who project their own ideals onto the dead.[42]

Though inferences from the dead will never be perfect reflections of the social structure or ideologies of the living, we should nonetheless be able to extract some insights about how a group perceived itself through the images left to us through mortuary remains.... [A]rchaeological remains... should be able to serve for ideological statements about societal identity.[43]

Moreover, it is important to remember that the social identity or personhood of a child seen in the mortuary context is created by *adults*, who project their own ideals onto the deceased child. Children did not leave a will with directions on how they wish to be buried. Granted, it is speculative to suggest that anyone other than elite members of a society would leave such a will, but the point is that the agency of children over their own burials is lacking. Personhood, or an individual's social identity, is, like death, relational. A person is "an individual human being who is recognized by his or her society as having value, not as a commodity but as a participant in social relations."[44] Value is marked by a society in a number of ways, one of which is inclusion in public ritual. Rituals surrounding death can range from simple to complex.[45] Anthropologists have noted that the relationship between a person's age and achieved status affects the kind of burial given, which again stresses the relationship between the living and the dead and the fact that their relationship plays a role in the public ritual of burial.[46]

The act of constructing a grave can be understood as a facet of public funerary ritual, for the constructed grave was meant to afford some kind of protection for the dying body and whatever form the individual took in the afterlife. T. M. Lemos persuasively argues that one of the markers of personhood is protection, "particularly protection from physical harm."[47] The very act of creating a tomb, vessel, or other built construction in which to place a deceased individual argues in favor of living individuals understanding the personhood of the dead to continue in some form past biological death. So too, the act of marking a grave with a physical construction also supports a continued personhood after biological death. Markers might include the tomb itself, a jar, pillar, *maṣṣebot*, headstone, and so on. A marked grave, moreover, serves as a location to which a living individual can return either to carry out elements related to the cult of the dead or to remember the deceased.[48] Thus, a marked grave can be identified as a location of public ritual.[49] Given this understanding of personhood, the following questions naturally arise: Why did some infants and young children receive marked burials, such as a jar or constructed grave, while others did not? What made these young individuals so special that they are commemorated in the burial record? Questions such as these are difficult to answer with certainty but are important to ask.

36 THE BURIALS OF CHILDREN IN ANCIENT ISRAEL

Megiddo Strata XII–IX: A Case Study

Thinking broadly, one possible answer to the questions posed above might lie with social status. The Middle Bronze Age II–Late Bronze Age I intramural tombs (Str. XII–IX) from Megiddo provide an interesting case study with respect to social status. During this period at Megiddo, fifteen intermural masonry-constructed tombs were used.[50] In addition to the masonry-constructed tombs, intramural jar burials, stone-lined pits, and simple pit burials were also uncovered. Over two hundred individuals were found within the site, including infants, children, and adults.[51] As an example, burials associated with the courtyard building 12/K/15 included twenty-four individuals buried in simple pits and jars.[52] Tomb 100, the built tomb associated with building 12/K/15, included the remainder of the population for that area.[53] The grave good assemblage for all types of burials across Area K was the same—relatively rich.

While the excavators stated that differentiated burials were par for the course at Megiddo,[54] this would seem to pertain to differentiated burials that were used for adults and children alike. The catch lies with the jar burials. These have been found across the site, including in areas not associated with intramural family burials. They are also a form of differentiated burial, but this burial is used primarily for very young children.[55] One way to account for differentiated burials for children and infants would be to think about their family's place within the society. It could be that the families who were buried in the masonry-built tombs held a different status within the larger Megiddo community. If, as has been argued, the inhabitants of Tomb 100 acquired a special status in death that was maintained for up to 150 years,[56] then we might understand that family group to be a different ranked status in the community. Perhaps these were the families who were considered the line of communal ancestors, or perhaps these households were the socially elite lineages. Infants and children connected with these family burials might be considered ancestors *in potentia*. Burials within jars located outside of the family burials would therefore need to symbolize some other status within a family. For example, Beth Alpert Nakhai suggests that health may have been a qualifying factor. She posits that those too fragile to have undergone initiation rituals into society were excluded from family burials and instead placed in intermural jar burials.[57] This is certainly one possible explanation for jar burials.

Social memory is also a powerful way to consider the issue of personhood related to intramural burials. From an architectural perspective, "The burials became part of the architecture and biography of the building in which they were embedded. . . . Each burial created a specific locus of embedded social memory of the household that was intimately tied to the lives and deaths of its members."[58] The excavators note that the one distinguishing element of the Megiddo Middle Bronze II burials was the body disposal method; within the masonry tombs the bodies were found in disturbed, secondary burials, while in the simple pits and jar burials the bodies were in a primary burial position. Furthermore, excavators noted that the secondary burial in the masonry tombs indicated an intentional interaction between the living and the dead, so that social memory was continued and (re)created every time people used the masonry tombs for subsequent burials.[59] "Manipulation of the corpse after burial through various means, such as repositioning, decoration, furnishing with grave goods, and even destruction, involved interaction with the dead, even after the body became unrecognizable due to decomposition."[60] Since infants and children were also found in Tomb 100, this would mean that by extension social memory could have been afforded to even some of the youngest members of a household, which would further support the stance that infants and children had a type of personhood that extended into death.

Concluding Thoughts: Infant and Child Burials

Many times, burial grounds are found outside a city; indeed, they often define the borders of a settlement.[61] Structuralist studies suggest boundary marking as the driving impetus for this practice. The boundaries in question were many: dead/living, village/tomb, order/chaos, pure/impure.[62] One might expect that if infants and children had some amount of personhood, they would also be routinely found in burials outside of the city in order to maintain said boundaries. At times this is true: infants and children are found buried outside the settlements. Yet the practice of intramural jar burials appears in all periods, making them boundary-crossers, in a way.[63] In this framework, differentiated burials, such as jar burials, raise questions about whether the individuals buried within the jars were recognized by society as people. Did the living bury the youngest of their society differently because they were not considered persons?

Regardless of a family's status, the infant or young child interred in a jar appears to have had some degree of personhood: (1) they were afforded

38 THE BURIALS OF CHILDREN IN ANCIENT ISRAEL

a burial that was marked with a physical object (the jar), (2) the burial protected the dying body from harm, and (3) they were interred in the ground, implying that an associated ritual took place. Anthropological studies of personhood note that individuals can accrue personhood.[64] It seems possible, then, to see a link between marked burial and personhood. I have argued elsewhere that the type of burial individuals receive is related to their perceived membership in society.[65] The older one becomes, the greater the chances one is buried in a manner similar to other members of the society. All individuals are born with the recognition that they have the potential to become full members of society. Personhood and status are different conceptual categories, but closely related: "Shifts in personhood always result in shifts in status, but not all status changes affect an individual's personhood."[66] Infants and young children buried in jars did not have the same status as other members of the household, but this does not mean de facto that they were not afforded any personhood whatsoever. Instead, it is proposed that the youngest members of society are best understood as persons *in potentia*. Because of their liminal and developing personhood, at times these individuals were buried with other members of their family and society, and at other times they were buried differently, away from other family members.

As we move into the following chapters, there are a few important points to take away from this overview of infant and child burials in the Bronze through Iron Ages in the Southern Levant. First is the recognition that infants and children were intentionally buried. While this statement might sound obvious, it demonstrates that because they held some degree of personhood, the youngest individuals in a society were not automatically discarded in death but cared for via burial and grave goods. The second point is that there was a general Canaanite burial pattern, which will become important when thinking about how infants and children were understood in later Judahite Israel. This burial pattern saw infants in the Bronze Ages buried within jars, which were in turn buried within the settlement site, often under house floors. These jar burials generally included a "baby burial kit" consisting of the store jar itself and a juglet, with the possibility of a bowl also being included as a cover to the jar. By and large, during the Bronze Ages children—yet seldom infants—were found buried along with other adult members of their society either in caves/tombs or cemeteries. During the Iron Age, the burial pattern shifts, and regionalized differences become even more prominent. Elements of the Bronze Age Canaanite burial practices remain for much of the region and are adapted and integrated as new groups come on the scene. This will be seen clearly with the arrival of the Sea Peoples groups on the coastal plain. The rise of the bench tomb's popularity in Judah becomes another way we will see a shifting burial trend as infants become incorporated into the family tombs. For their part, jar burials decrease in popularity, although they do make appearances, especially in regions outside of Judah.

Notes

1. When discussing the Iron Age in subsequent chapters, variations in burial methods will be discussed in depth. To do so here would take the study too far afield.
2. There may be multiple burial sites at a single location. For example, Azor has three Iron II cemeteries. This counts as one location with three burial sites. Other locations, such as Gezer and Megiddo, have child burials in multiple time periods, each of which would count as a different burial site at a single location.
3. See Garroway, *Children*, 283–88. Tables 6–12 provide information on the method of burial, time period, and whether adults were present along with the children.
4. See, Garroway, *Children*, 299, 305–6; Y. Alexandre, "Burial Caves from the Intermediate Bronze, Middle Bronze and Iron Ages at Nazareth," '*Atiqot* 93 (2018): 1–44.
5. The extensive use of intramural burials for adults, children, and families during the Middle Bronze II period at Megiddo are the exception rather than the norm.
6. See, for example, Mevorakh, Dothan, and Tell el-Far'ah North. Garroway, *Children*, Appendix C, 299–316.
7. R. Hallote, *Death, Burial, and Afterlife in the Biblical World* (Chicago: Ivan Dee, 2001), 37.
8. Inter alia, R. Albertz and R. Schmitt, *Family and Household Religion in Ancient Israel and the Levant* (Winona Lake, IN: Eisenbrauns, 2012); R. Albertz, B. A. Nakhai, S. Olyan, and R. Schmitt, eds., *Family and Household Religion: Toward a Synthesis of Old Testament Studies, Archaeology, Epigraphy, and Cultural Studies* (Winona Lake, IN: Eisenbrauns, 2014); C. Meyers, *Rediscovering Eve: Ancient Israelite Women in Context* (Oxford: Oxford University Press), 2013.
9. T. Lewis, *Cults of the Dead in Ancient Israel and Ugarit*, HMS 39 (Atlanta: Scholars Press, 1989), 174.
10. C. B. Hays, *A Covenant with Death: Death in the Iron Age II and Its Rhetorical Uses in Proto-Isaiah* (Grand Rapids, MI: Eerdmans, 2011), 143.
11. É. Durkheim, *The Elementary Forms of Religious Life*, trans. C. Cosman (Oxford: Oxford University Press, 2001), 64.
12. Consider the *oferenda* with its various traditional elements that is set up in houses for Día de los Muertos. The *oferenda* transforms a quotidian space on a yearly basis into a ritual space using a standardized set of ritual elements.
13. Garroway, *Children*, 243; L. Binford, "Mortuary Practices: Their Study and Their Potential," *Memoirs for the Society for American Archaeology* 25 (1971): 19–22. While I do think that the social persona of the deceased individual should be considered when thinking about burials, caution should be taken in adopting a strict structuralist approach with respect to mortuary rites. See the following and sources therein: J. Brown, "On Mortuary Analysis—with Special Reference to the Saxe-Binford Research Program," in *Regional Approaches to Mortuary Analysis*, ed. L. Anderson Beck (New York: Plenum Press, 1995), 3–26; B. A. Holz, "A Recent Application of the Saxe-Binford Hypothesis in Establishing Social Persona" (MA thesis, University of Nevada at Las Vegas, 1996); I. Hodder, "Social Structure and Cemeteries: A Critical Appraisal," in *Anglo-Saxon Cemeteries, 1979: The Fourth Anglo-Saxon Symposium at Oxford*, BAR 82, ed. P. A. Rahtz, T. M. Dickinson, and L. Watts (Oxford: BAR Publishing, 1980), 161–69.

40 THE BURIALS OF CHILDREN IN ANCIENT ISRAEL

14. L. Nilsson Stutz and S. Tarlow, "Beautiful Things and Bones of Desire: Emerging Issues in the Archaeology of Death and Burials," in *The Oxford Handbook of the Archaeology of Death and Burial*, ed. S. Tarlow and L. Nilsson Stutz (Oxford: Oxford University Press, 2013), 5.

15. See Chapter 5 and also Garroway, *Children*, 240–43; B. A. Nakhai, "When Considering Infants and Jar Burials in the Middle Bronze Age Southern Levant," in *Tell It in Gath: Studies in the History and Archaeology of Israel. Essays in Honor of Aren Maeir on the Occasion of His Sixtieth Birthday*, Ägypten und Altes Testament 90, ed. I. Shai, J. Chadwick, L. Hitchcock, A. Dagan, C. McKinny, and J. Uziel (Münster: Zaphon, 2018), 101.

16. J. Baker, *The Funeral Kit: Mortuary Practices in the Archaeological Record* (Walnut Creek, CA: Left Coast Press, 2012), 113–17; E. Bloch-Smith, *Judahite Burial Practices and Beliefs about the Dead*, JSOT Supp. 123, JSOT/ASOR Monograph Series 7 (Sheffield: JSOT Press, 1992).

17. Matthew Suriano argues that once the items became disassociated with the primary burial, they ceased to serve their original purpose. M. Suriano, *A History of Death in the Hebrew Bible* (Oxford: Oxford University Press, 2018), 48–49.

18. Baker, *The Funeral Kit*, 109– 26; S. Burke, *God, Self, and Death: The Shape of Religious Transformation in the Second Temple Period* (Leiden: Brill, 2003).

19. Binford, "Mortuary Practices," 6–29; M. Parker Pearson, *The Archaeology of Death and Burial* (College Station: Texas A&M University Press, 2000); P. Wason, *The Archaeology of Rank*, New Studies in Archaeology (Cambridge: AltaMira Press, 2004).

20. J. H. L. Ginsberg, "Death in West Semitic Texts: Ugaritic and Nabatea," in *The Archaeology of Death in the Ancient Near East*, Oxbow Monographs 51, ed. S. Campbell and A. Green (Oxford: Oxbow Press, 1995), 189–90; Pearson, *Archaeology of Death*; W. T. Pitard, "Tombs and Offerings: Archaeological Data and Comparative Methodology in the Study of Death in Israel," in *Sacred Time, Sacred Place: Archaeology and the Religion of Israel*, ed. B. M. Gittlen (Winona Lake, IN: Eisenbrauns, 2002), 149–50.

21. Baker, *The Funeral Kit*, 27; Garroway, *Children*, 228.

22. Baker, *The Funeral Kit*, 58.

23. Baker, *The Funeral Kit*, 114–18.

24. For a fuller treatment of these objects and their find locations, see Garroway, *Children*, 228–44, Appendix A, and Appendix B.

25. Garroway, *Children*, Appendix A.

26. B. Crass, "Gender and Mortuary Analysis: What Can Grave Goods Really Tell Us?," in *Gender and the Archaeology of Death*, ed. B. Arnold and N. L. Wicker (Walnut Creek, CA: AltaMira, 2001), 105– 18; F. Ekengren, "Contextualizing Grave Goods: Theoretical Perspectives and Methodological Implications," in Tarlow and Stutz, *Oxford Handbook*, 173–92.

27. M. Suriano, "What Did Feeding the Dead Mean? Two Case Studies from Iron Age Tombs at Beth-Shemesh," *AABNER* 1.3 (2021): 117–42; J. Milgrom, "The Rationale for Biblical Impurity," *JANES* 22.1 (1993): 107– 11; D. P. Wright, *The Disposal of Impurity: Elimination Rites in the Bible and in Hittite and Mesopotamian Literature* (Atlanta: Scholars Press, 1987), 115– 28; Y. Feder, "Contagion and Cognition: Bodily Experience and the Conceptualization of Pollution (*ṭumʾah*) in the Hebrew Bible," *JNES* 72 (2013): 161.

28. It is also possible that juglets were understood as a status item associated with the infant.

29. For more on juglets, funerary kits, and jar burials, see Garroway, *Children*, 235.

30. After Garroway, *Children*, 296, Table 32, and Table 33. The Early Bronze I–III and Early Bronze IV / Middle Bronze I are not included in the Table because the sampling of infant and child burials was too small for comparison.

31. A greater sample size and more in-depth study needs to be done to verify this conclusion with certainty.

32. P. Smith and G. Avishai, "The Use of Dental Criteria for Estimating Postnatal Survival in Skeletal Remains of Infants," *Journal of Archaeological Science* 32 (2005): 86; P. Smith and M. Faerman, "Has Society Changed Its Attitude to Infants and Children? Evidence from Archaeological Sites in the Southern Levant," in *Nasciturus, infans, puerulus vobis mater terra: La muerte en la infancia*, ed. F. G. Jener, S. Muriel, and C. Olària (Castelló, Spain: Disputació de Castelló, Servei D'investigacions Arquelògiques Prehistòriques, 2008), 211. Well into the 1990s some developing countries still recorded similarly high mortality rates. D. C. Ewbank and J. N. Gribble, *Effects of Health Programs on Child Mortality in Sub-Saharan Africa* (Washington, DC: National Academy Press, 1993).

33. The World Health Organization has determined five and a half pounds to be the cutoff for low birth weight. http://apps.who.int/iris/bitstream/10665/43184/1/9280638327.pdf (accessed April 27, 2017).

ARCHAEOLOGICAL OVERVIEW OF CHILD BURIALS 41

34. The mass graves found inter alia at the following sites are attributed to casualties of war: Ashdod (Iron Age) (M. Dothan, *Ashdod II–III: The Second and Third Seasons of Excavations 1963, 1965: Soundings in 1967* [Jerusalem: Department of Antiquities, 1971]; Lachish (Iron II) (D. Ridson, "A Study of the Cranial and Other Human Remains from Palestine Excavated at Tell Duwier Lachish by the Wellcome-Marsont Archaeological Research Expedition," *Biometrika* 31 [1939]: 99–166); and the Halzi Gate at Nineveh (Iron II) (D. Pickworth, "Excavations at Nineveh: The Halzi Gate," *Iraq* 67.1 [2005]: 295–316).

35. On sacrifice in ancient Israel and the Punic world, see the comprehensive discussion by H. Dewrell, *Child Sacrifice in Ancient Israel*, EANAC 5 (Winona Lake, IN: Eisenbrauns, 2017).

36. P. Smith, "Approach to the Paleodemographic Analysis of Human Skeletal Remains from Archaeological Sites," in *Biblical Archaeology Today, 1990: Proceedings of the Second International Congress on Biblical Archaeology*, ed. A. Biran and J. Aviram (Jerusalem: Israel Exploration Society and Israel Academy of Sciences and Humanities, 1993), 2–13 ; M. Martin, M. Cradic, and R. Kalisher, "Area K: Intramural Pit and Jar Burials (Level K-10)," in *Megiddo VI: The 2010–2014 Seasons*, vol. 1, Emery and Claire Yass Publications in Archaeology, ed. I. Finkelstein and M. Martin (Winona Lake, IN: Eisenbrauns, 2022), 239–41.

37. Garroway, *Children*, 9; M. Lewis, "The Osteology of Infancy and Childhood: Misconceptions and Potential," in *(Re)thinking the Little Ancestor: New Perspectives on the Archaeology of Infancy and Childhood*, ed. M. Lally and A. Moore, BAR International Series 2271 (Oxford: BAR Publishing, 2011), 3–4.

38. N. Wicker, "Selective Female Infanticide as Partial Explanation for the Dearth of Women in Viking Age Scandinavia," in *Violence and Society in the Early Medieval West*, ed. G. Halstall (Woodbridge: Boydell Press, 1998), 205–21.

39. H. Guy, C. Masset, and C. Baud, "Infant Taphonomy," *International Journal of Osteoarchaeology* 7 (1997): 221–29.

40. J. Buckberry, *Where Have All the Children Gone? The Preservation of Infant and Children's Remains in the Archaeological Record*, paper presented at the "Archaeology of Infancy and Childhood" conference, May 6–8, 2005; Lewis, "Osteology of Infancy," 4.

41. Hallote, *Death, Burial and Afterlife*, 31.

42. Pearson, *Archaeology of Death*, 201–4; H. Härke, "Data Types in Burial Analysis," in *Prehistoric Graves as a Source of Information: Symposium at Kastlösa, Öland, May 21–23, 1992*, ed. B. Stjernquist (Stockholm: Kungl. Vitterhets Historie och Antikvites Akademien, 1994), 32.

43. R. Hallote, "Real and Ideal Identities in Middle Bronze Age Tombs," *NEA* 65 (2002): 105.

44. T. M. Lemos, *Violence and Personhood in Ancient Israel and Comparative Contexts* (Oxford: Oxford University Press, 2017), 11.

45. See also K. H. Garroway, "The Anthropology of Death in Ancient Israel," in *The T & T Clark Handbook of Anthropology and the Hebrew Bible*, ed. Emanuel Pfoh (London: Bloomsbury, 2023), 455–68; K. Sonia, *Caring for the Dead in Ancient Israel*, ABS 27 (Atlanta: SBL, 2020); Tarlow and Stutz, *Oxford Handbook*.

46. Binford, "Mortuary Practices," 6–29; P. Ucko, "Ethnography and Archaeological Interpretation of Funerary Remains," *WA* 1 (1969): 262–68; T. Shay, "Differentiated Treatment of Deviancy at Death as Revealed in Anthropological and Archaeological Populations," *JAA* 4.3 (1989): 225–43.

47. Lemos, *Violence and Personhood*, 11. Lemos is concerned with living individuals and so makes this argument for the living. Since personhood also applies in death, it would make sense that the living society would protect the personhood of the deceased in a manner fitting to each individual.

48. Sonia, *Caring for the Dead*.

49. Chapter 5 explores this question in depth for the Iron Age. On this point see too the summary of Maurice Bloch, Victor Turner, Robert Herz, and Catherine Bell by Ekengren, "Contextualizing Grave Goods," 173–94.

50. M. Cradic, "Residential Burial and Social Memory in the Middle Bronze Age Levant," *NEA* 81.3 (2018): Table 2, 193. Intramural burials of wealthy stratified societies near residential sites have been found at other Middle Bronze sites as well. For an overview see Nakhai, "Considering Infants," 107–8.

51. Cradic, "Residential Burial," 193–94; M. Faerman and P. Smith, "Human Skeletal Remains from Chamber-Tomb 100," in Finkelstein and Martin, *Megiddo VI*, 402–17.

52. M. Faerman, "Human Skeletal Remains of the Intermural Pit and Jar Burials from Area K," in Finkelstein and Martin, *Megiddo VI*, 418–42.

53. Cradic, "Residential Burial," 197–98.

42 THE BURIALS OF CHILDREN IN ANCIENT ISRAEL

54. Cradic, "Residential Burial," 198–99.
55. The majority of infants received a differential burial; these were found in various places intramurally throughout the site. Faerman and Smith, "Human Skeletal Remains," 406.
56. Cradic, "Residential Burial," 199. The MNI of individuals in this tomb totaled twenty-three: ten adults, two infants, six children, three juveniles, and two adolescents. Faerman and Smith, "Human Skeletal Remains," 404.
57. Nakhai, "Considering Infants," 108.
58. I. Hodder and C. Cressford, "Daily Practice and Social Memory at Çatalhöyük," *American Antiquity* 69 (2004): 17–40; N. Laneri, "A Family Affair: The Use of Intramural Funerary Chambers in Mesopotamia during the Late Third an Early Second Millennia B.C.E.," in *Residential Burial: A Multiregional Exploration*, Archaeological Papers of the American Anthropological Association 20, ed. R. L. Adams and S. M. King (Walden, MA: Wiley Periodicals, 2011), 121–35; Martin, Cradic, and Kalisher, "Area K," 254.
59. Cradic, "Residential Burial," 199.
60. Cradic, "Residential Burial," 199.
61. Burials outside of cities becomes a hallmark in the Iron Age. For example, Iron Age Jerusalem is surrounded with burials.
62. Suriano, *History of Death*, 45; M. Douglas, *Purity and Danger: An Analysis of Concepts of Pollution and Taboo* (Harmondsworth: Penguin, 1970), 35–41.
63. Of course, calling them boundary-crossers highlights the fact that ritual is complex and does not always operate according to set rules. It may be that the complexity of individual societies utilizing jar burials affects the way that they bury their infants. Or one may consider that some families may have decided, for whatever reason, to employ jar burials for some of their younglings but not others. Such possibilities emphasize that ritual is not a "one size fits all" and further call to mind issues that a strict structuralist approach can overlook.
64. B. Conklin and L. Morgan, "Babies, Bodies, and Production of Personhood in North America and Native Amazonian Society," *Ethos* 24 (1996): 667.
65. Garroway, *Children*, 243–44.
66. Lemos, *Violence and Personhood*, 13.

2

Surveying Iron Age Infant and Child Burials on the Philistine Coast

Chapter 2 brings the conversation to focus on the Iron Age. Before moving to a reassessment of Judahite burials and the so-called family tombs, this chapter begins by examining the different burial practices for infants and children in the lands surrounding Judah. On the one hand, an overview of the surrounding lands is important, for Judah did not exist in a vacuum; cities such as Jerusalem and Lachish were international melting pots. On the other hand, examining whether infants and children are buried in the same manner throughout the Southern Levant helps assess whether a more general understanding of infants and children and their personhood, one that is not culturally bound, existed. The data in Chapters 2 through 4 is arranged geographically and taken from a survey of sites that list Iron Age occupation or are identified as Iron Age burial grounds. The chapters will investigate whether burial trends from previous periods are continued or cease or new trends are introduced, as well as what the burials might say about the perceived personhood of infants and children vis-à-vis other members of their society.

Burials in Philistia

The sites examined here in Chapter 2 (see Table 2.1) fall into the area generally known as the Philistine Plain during the Iron Age. Of the five Philistine Pentapolis cities, four have been excavated: Ashdod, Ashkelon, Tel Miqne (Ekron), and Tel es-Safi (Gath).[1] As Joe Uziel and Aren Maeir note, "The paradigm of a unified Philistine origins and of a simplistic Philistine conquest of the southern Coastal Plain cannot be accepted anymore."[2] Gone are the days of understanding Philistine mono- or bichrome ware as a hallmark of a new singular culture that equates pots with people. The inhumations found at the different Pentapolis sites attest to a mixture of different burial

The Dying Child. Kristine Henriksen Garroway, Oxford University Press. © Oxford University Press 2025.
DOI: 10.1093/9780197566718.003.0003

44   THE BURIALS OF CHILDREN IN ANCIENT ISRAEL

Table 2.1 Intramural Burials in Sites on the Philistine Plain

Sites	Period	Interment[a]
Abu-Hawam	Iron I	Jar burial[b]
Ashkelon	Iron I	Intramural burials in the city
	Iron II	Cemetery with pit burials outside the city
Ashdod	Iron II	Mass pit burials and family burial[c]
Azor	Iron I	Jar burials in cemetery, including two cremations[d]
el-Khirbe	Iron II	Possible jar burial[e]
es-Safi/Gath	Iron I–II	Burial cave
		Intramural burials
Miqne-Ekron	Iron I	Intramural burials of infants
Timnah (Tel Batash)	Iron II	Infant under the house floor
Yavne-Yam	Iron II	No individuals aged 0–12 years found in the cemetery

Note: Many of these burials are discussed later on in the current chapter. For those that are not, the bibliography can be found in the notes to this table.

[a] When given in the excavation report, the number of burials is listed.

[b] Dothan reports that jar burials, covered with bowls, were found at Abu-Hawam. These burials are unpublished. M. Dothan, "The Excavations at 'Afula," *'Atiqot* 1 (1955): 40.

[c] The family burial included one female, one male, one younger child four to five years of age and one older child twelve to fourteen years of age. Dothan, *Ashdod II–III*, 212–14. The other burials are discussed later in the current chapter.

[d] The cremations included older children who were identified as more than ten years old and between twelve and sixteen years old (Ben-Shlomo, "The Cemetery of Azor," 38).

[e] The excavators report a jar covered with a bowl and a small juglet nearby. J. Ory, "Other Discoveries: 1 July 1938 to 30 June 1940," *QDAP* 10 (1944): 205. While not listed as a burial, this is the hallmark pattern for a jar burial. It is possible that the excavators did not investigate the contents of the jar.

practices. Whereas many Bronze Age and Iron Age sites employ a single type of burial method, during the Iron Ages the sites of the Philistine Pentapolis do not share a singular burial method. This appears to be true for other cities on the coastal plain as well. Rather than understanding the Philistine sites as monolithic, as demonstrating a single Philistine culture that is reflected in the burial patterns, the exploration of burials at these sites has been hailed as providing new insight into Philistine culture. Burials in particular show a mixture of Aegean, Cypriot, and Levantine grave goods, suggesting perhaps that the peoples burying their dead were not isolationists but members of a cosmopolitan society.[3] Reports on the cemeteries and intramural burials within the Philistine sites are careful to note the relative ages of the deceased; however, the emphasis in the reports generally concentrates on the multiplicity of burial methods rather than any relevance that age might have for the burials. The discussion here re-examines the information for the four Pentapolis sites as well as an additional three sites on the Philistine Plain with possible Philistine connections, analyzing how children are buried and what this can tell us about their perceived personhood.

Pentapolis Sites

Ashdod

Ashdod was the first of the Pentapolis sites to be excavated.[4] Situated on the coast, it is roughly twenty kilometers north of Ashkelon and thirty-two kilometers south of Tel Aviv. The excavations show the site was inhabited continually from the Middle Bronze II through the Hellenistic period.[5]

Ashdod presents a unique case among the Pentapolis cities. First, the intramural burials are all Iron II (eighth c. BCE), as opposed to Iron I. Second, the majority of the individuals that were found were in mass, intramural reburials, which are relatively unheard of during this time.[6] Because the mass burials are so exceptional, they deserve special attention. The discussion of the Ashdod mass burials in the final report is vague and adult-centric, referencing skulls, injury caused by weapons, and the ceramic finds. Yet if one pieces together the discussion of Area D, the physical anthropology report, and the ceramic finds, a different story appears, one that is rather surprising when it comes to the relative age of the individuals and the grave goods that accompany them.[7]

The data: the pit in locus 1006 contained forty-five individuals. None of these were infants and only four were children (0.8%).[8] Locus 1121 contained twenty-one individuals, twenty of whom were listed as adults. The only child was between two and fifteen years of age. The large pit in locus 1113 appeared to be a secondary burial or reburial of 2,434 individuals.[9] Twenty-two percent were children; fifteen infants and 523 children were identified. Locus 1114 presents yet another picture. This burial, like that of locus 1113, was in an open courtyard. Here 57% of the 376 individuals found were infants and children: eighty-five infants (up to one year old), twenty-four young children (two to six years old), seventeen older children (seven to fourteen years old), and eighty-nine children of indeterminate age

46 THE BURIALS OF CHILDREN IN ANCIENT ISRAEL

(somewhere between two and fifteen years old). This is remarkable considering the much lower percentages of children in other loci. Faunal remains were mixed into this pit as well as a number of bowls, jugs, and juglets. No other mass graves contained faunal remains.[10]

Observations: the relationship between the faunal remains and the burial of infants and children is intriguing. Were the faunal remains included as offerings to accompany the young? Was this one way the living of Ashdod cared for the deceased children and/or specifically for infants?[11] Furthermore, why did infants and children comprise over half the burials in locus 1114, but not in 1113 or 1121, and why were infants and children completely absent from locus 1006? While the mass burials at Ashdod leave many questions unanswered, they do give us an idea of the Stratum 3a inhabitants' burial customs.[12] Notably, the mass casualty inflicted on the 3b inhabitants did not necessitate burial outside of the city; instead, the mass burials in the potters' quarter were commemorated when sealed off with a plaster floor.[13] The casualty affected infants, children, and adults. It appears that issues of ritual impurity and or discomfort with keeping those killed by a massive destruction close to the living were not concerns.[14]

Ashkelon

Ashkelon was the only Pentapolis city located directly on the coast. As such it served as a port city and provided important inroads from the sea. Like the other Pentapolis cities, it too enjoyed a lengthy period of settlement. By way of contextualizing the Iron Age burials at the site, it is important to note that Ashkelon was under Egyptian hegemony prior to the arrival of the Sea Peoples. Grid 38 contains the Iron Age intramural burials; it also happens to provide an excellent stratigraphic overview of the Iron Age city.[15] The city moved from an Egyptian fortress city (1400–1175 BCE) to a city inhabited by both Egyptians and Sea Peoples in the early Iron Age (1175–1150 BCE). Sometime around 1100 BCE the Egyptians withdrew their presence from the city. It is during this time that the intermural infant burials become prominent in Grid 38.

The data: The Iron Age I spans four phases in Grid 38: Phases 20–17, with Phase 17 being the transition between Iron I and Iron II. The earliest infant burial appears in Phase 20A (1175–1150 BCE), during the initial appearance of the Philistines.[16] The analysis of the bones was not included in the osteological report, but the burial was listed in the overview as a pit burial of an infant less than two months old.[17] The burial was found south of the threshold in Room 191. The room also contained lots of other small pits, some of which were filled with animal bones. Phase 19 is dated to 1150–1100 BCE and Phase 18 to 1100–1050 BCE. During the time of the Egyptian withdrawal, Grid 38 contains nine intramural infant burials (Phases 19A and 19B). Each of the infants was very young, ranging from premature, to neonate, to newborn, up to two months old.[18] Table 2.2 represents the results of the data gleaned from the osteological report and the stratigraphic overview of the grid.

In the final seasons at Ashkelon a cemetery was uncovered adjacent to the city.[19] It is the first, and so far only, cemetery to be found at one of the Pentapolis sites. Based on pottery, the cemetery is dated to the Iron Age IIA.[20] It is described as densely populated with an estimated MNI of twelve hundred individuals if fully excavated. Three types of burials were discovered: simple pit graves, built cist tombs, and cremations. Of the pit burials, the majority were placed in an orientation following the line of the sea, in an east-west orientation with the head toward the sea.[21] The uniformity here contrasts with the seeming disregard for burial orientation seen within the site proper, suggesting a change in the way the Iron I and Iron II inhabitants treated the burials. The second kind of tombs were built chamber tombs.[22] No indication was given as to whether infants or children were a part of these tombs. Skeletal analysis of the final burial type, cremations, was also not included in the preliminary report. Six cremations jars were found, two of which were in situ. These jars included the charred remains of individuals and a juglet, all of which were sealed off with a bowl. The jars themselves were sunk into the ground.[23] Considering the assemblage as a unit, these cremations appear similar, albeit not the same, to the way that jar burials of infants were deposited in previous time periods. Yet without the final report it is difficult to say much more.

Observations: the intramural and extramural burials of infants and children show a different approach to the treatment of this age group. It is possible that the treatment changed over time as ideas about personhood and ritual purity changed. Then again, it may be that different social strata of the population chose to bury outside the cemetery.

Table 2.2 Intramural Infant and Child Burials in Ashkelon Grid 38

Burial	Square	Phase	Age	Location	Other Field Notes
Pit 223	64	20A	Infant	Room 191 near doorway along wall	Infant on back, head to door. Many weaving implements and fish scales in the room.
Not numbered	74	19	≤6 mo.	Room 1023[a]	Within a house. Facing west. No grave goods.
B. 191	74	19A	0–1 mo.	Room 957 north wall, near/under bench 942	Head facing west. Burial ringed with stones and possibly covered with mud brick.
B. 192	74	19A	1–2 mo. (m)[b]	Room 957 south wall	Head facing east.
B. 193	73	19A	Premature	Room 577 Northeast corner of room	On back, head facing west. May have been flexed and propped in a sitting position.
Pit 386	75	19A	≤2 mo. (f)	Room 392 South of threshold	Lots of pits, some with animal bones.
B. 881	74	18B	0–1 mo.	Room 892 Jar burial, west side of the threshold	Multipurpose room with lots of installations. Lying on side, semi-flexed position. Store jar used as coffin.
Not numbered	84	18B	neonate	Room 892 By wall 901	*Burial not recognized in the field. Discovered in debris layer 828 by wall 901.
Pit 962	74	18B	newborn (f) 1–2 mo. (m)	Room 905 Pit burial in southeast corner with two infants	The room had multiple installations. The burial was in a new floor with shells laid flat on top of the floor.
B. 375	75	18B	≤2 mo.	Room 365 Near street entrance Jar burial	Jar was Egyptian and inscribed. Burial jar placed in a field-stone capped pit. The pit was lined with stones and sherds.

[a] This burial was recorded in the overview of Grid 38 from Ashkelon I (Stager, Schloen, and Master, *Ashkelon I*, 262). This burial was not referenced at all in *Ashkelon 7*, in either the overview of Grid 38 or in the osteological report. Ashkelon I did not give sub-phases to Grid 38 but listed it simply as Phase 19. In comparing the grid plans from both volumes, it appears that Room 1023 of Ashkelon I occupies a space similar to Room 1074 in Phase 19A listed in *Ashkelon 7* (Stager, Master, and Aja, *Ashkelon I*, 51).

[b] Sexing the infants was limited by the condition of the bones. DNA could be amplified for only four of the burials. M. Faerman et al., "Infants," in Stager, Master, and Aja, *Ashkelon 7*, 701–3; Feldman et al., "Ancient DNA Sheds Light on the Genetic Origins of Early Iron Age Philistines," *Science Advances* July 5.7 (2019): eaax0061, published July 3, 2019, https://doi.org/10.1126/sciadv.aax0061.

Tel es-Safi / Gath

Located about midway between Ashkelon and Jerusalem, the ongoing excavations at Tel es-Safi / Gath have provided much insight into the Philistine culture within the Southern Levant. However, a cemetery associated with the site has yet to be uncovered. Some infant burials within the site and a burial cave nearby are the only Iron Age burials that are associated with the site. Notably, the intramural infant burials are described in the introduction as two subsurface jar burials that date to the late Iron I period.[24] Such burials are similar in nature to the Iron I jar burials found in Ashkelon in Phases 19 and 18.[25] The other burials of note for this study come from the Iron I/II burial cave discovered to the southeast of Tell es-Safi.[26]

The data: the manmade cave served as a burial location for multiple generations (ca. twelfth c. BCE to eighth c. BCE).[27] Dental analysis found rare inherited conditions present in multiple individuals, leading to the conclusion that this was a family burial cave.[28] Statistical analysis for all seventy-seven individuals found adults (aged thirteen- plus years) comprised 57.15%; children (aged two to twelve years) 28.57%, and infants (two years or younger) 14.28%.

Observations: the preliminary and final reports of the burial cave both took time to emphasize the presence of infants, the high number of younglings, and the poor health of the individuals. In particular, the high number of infants discovered merited the following comment:

> The existence of infant bones in the cave is of interest, since, as noted above, the use of infant jar burials in the Iron Age I Philistia has been documented both at Tell es-Safi / Gath and at other Philistine sites.... [This] might indicate that infants were buried during this period in various manners in the Philistine culture.[29]

In comparing this burial population with that of contemporary Phoenician burials from Achzib, it was noted that the life expectancy was relatively low.[30] One theory posited that this particular burial cave might have been used by individuals who were either of a lower socioeconomic standing or that the health of the Philistine population at es-Safi/Gath was simply inferior.[31] The former theory does not seem supported by the richness of the grave goods. It could also be that this is a case of the local population mixing with

50 THE BURIALS OF CHILDREN IN ANCIENT ISRAEL

the Philistine population. As it stands, Gath's position on the border of the Shephelah and Judean Hills makes it an ideal frontier town where various populations could mix.

Tel Miqne / Ekron

Tel Miqne / Ekron sits inland, a few kilometers north of Gath, on the border of what is known as Philistia and Judah. Like es-Safi/Gath, it is a multiperiod, borderlands site, which in the early Iron Age "suggests the initial presence of two distinct but contemporary cultural systems: one related to the indigenous people; and one foreign."[32] The report on the 1995–1996 season at Ekron references thirteen intermural infant burials discovered during the Early Philistine period / Iron Age I.[33]

The data: Field IV was dubbed the elite zone since the architecture and material culture found in the area were indicative of a richer portion of the population than was found in other areas of the site. The infant burials found in Field IV come from three different strata.[34] In Stratum VI (ca. 1170–1100 BCE) an infant was found under the surface of the floor (Room 355E). The information on this burial is extremely limited. The other burials were found in Building 350, Stratum V (ca. 1100–1050 BCE). Stratum VC contained an infant jar burial under the threshold to the main entrance of the building. A small juglet was placed on the infant's hip. A second jar burial nearby was filled with ash and small bones. The relationship between these two jar burials is not known. Building 350 contained a second burial in Stratum VB, at the base of a staircase. This burial was not a typical jar burial in that the body was placed in a pit and covered with large sherds from a store jar.[35]

The burials in Field I NE were described as simple burials in domestic areas, below floor levels. Field I NE was an industrial area during Stratum VII (ca. 1200–1170 BCE).[36] Stratum VIIA contained three burials, each associated with a different phase. In Phase 9 B2 (Room 14) an infant was found placed near the south-facing wall. In Phase 9 B1–2 (Room 14) an infant was found in the fill inside of a fire installation. No indication was given that this infant was cremated. In Phase 9 B1 (Room 16) an infant was buried near the north-facing wall. This room also contained a bathtub.[37] During Strata VI there was a large building complex with a "cult" room, so identified due to the votive vessels and incised scapulae found there. It also had a large outdoor area with pebble hearths.[38] Stratum VIB Phase 8 C (Room 23b) contained

BURIALS ON THE PHILISTINE COAST   51

the full skeleton of an infant in the fill. Stratum VIB Phase 8 B (Room 13k) contained an infant in a thin layer of brick material.[39]

Observations: the excavation report finds these intramural burials strange since infants, children, and adults are usually buried outside of the city during the Iron Age. They suggest that such burial behavior was either typical of the Philistines or "perhaps represents furtive in-house burials of unwanted babies."[40] Yet the infant burial pattern here is similar to other Pentapolis sites. Therefore, the explanation that these burials are typical of Philistine burial practices or, at the very least, of residents of a city with a mixed indigenous and foreign population is a better explanation than secretive burials of unwanted babies.

Other Sites with Philistine Connections

Azor

Tel Azor is located on the Philistine coast about six kilometers southeast of Tel Aviv and Jaffa. The remains of the ancient city of Azor are under the modern towns of Azor and Holon and have therefore not been uncovered. However, a salvage excavation undertaken at the site found an Iron I–II cemetery with at least fifty Iron Age graves associated with the site.[41] The cemetery site has been located in Areas A, D, and E.

Area D Cemetery
Three Iron Age phases were found in the Area D cemetery: Phases V and IV date to the late Iron I (Philistine bichrome) and Phase III (Cypro-Phoenician and local "black" juglets) to Iron IIA.[42] The Iron II burials in Area D did not contain many children.[43] The Iron I burials, however, included nine jar burials. The age span and character of these jar burials breaks from previous patterns and will be discussed below. In addition to the jar burials, children were also found in pit burials and cremations.[44]

The data on cremation burials of Phase IV:[45] while cremation is found at other sites in the land of ancient Israel, the appearance of cremation burials in an Iron I cemetery is unusual. Two burial pits, D62 and D63, contained a total of three individuals, two of which were older children. The skeletal remains of D62 were identified as an individual ten-plus years of age. Notably, the report did not say "adult." Grave goods associated with the burial

52   THE BURIALS OF CHILDREN IN ANCIENT ISRAEL

included two Philistine bichrome kraters, a jug, a double flask, and a carinated red-slipped bowl. The skeletal remains in D63 were of an adult male forty to fifty years old and a juvenile twelve to sixteen years old, along with pig and bird bones. Above the burned remains in the jar were placed a bronze bowl and gold foil mouthpiece, along with pottery sherds and shells. The jars were placed within pits. In the case of D63, the top of the jar, covered by a basalt slab, protruded from the pit. The pit itself was lined with stone, both setting it apart and marking its location.

The Cemetery: Areas A and E
Additional salvage excavations, undertaken in Areas A and E, also uncovered more of the Iron I cemetery.[46] While smaller in size, these two areas also contained pit and brick-cased burials; however, no infants and very few children were identified. Additional jar burials were found in these areas. The jars were described as being made specifically for burials.[47] Four jar burials were listed, with a total of five bodies. Jar T4 contained two jars joined at the neck. A child was placed in each jar; one child was older than four years old and one older than one year old. Tomb T5 again comprised two connected jars, but this jar only had one child older than two years old. Tomb T7 was the badly damaged grave of a male older than thirty years. It too consisted of two jars.

Observations on the Azor Cemeteries
The Iron I jar burials of Phase IV stand out for a few reasons. First, the jar burials were placed in a cemetery context. Other Iron I jar burials from the Philistine coast are primarily intramural burials within domestic contexts. Second, jar burials are not reserved for infants or young children but are used for adolescents as well. Third, there are cases where a single store jar was not large enough for the individuals. Rather than using pithoi or a larger vessel, at least eight examples from Azor Area D include multiple store jars lined up and/or connected in order to make the "coffin" larger.[48] One exception merits reference. In Buchennino and Yanni's 2010 report, T4 was listed as a jar burial where two wide-mouth jars were connected by inserting the broken end of one into the top of the other. T4 included the burial of two individuals. One jar contained a child less than four years old and the second jar a child less than a year old.[49]

The jar burials found at Azor are not oriented in one single direction, and many times pottery, such as a bowl, lamp, or flask, is found next to the jars. The deposition of bodies with this assemblage is a bit more familiar, hearkening back to the assemblage found with jar burials in the Middle Bronze Age. However, whereas the quintessential Middle Bronze jar burial grave good was a juglet, juglets are completely absent in Iron I Azor jar burials.[50] In two cases jewelry was found with the burials.[51] The excavators note: "As most of the jars were relatively small (about 50 cm long) they would be problematic for a primary burial, especially of an adult."[52] In most cases this comment would be out of place. Since jar burials are most often associated with very young infants, the store jars in question would be a fine fit. Infants, especially in the Middle Bronze Age, were placed in a flexed, fetal position within the jar. However, at Azor, the comment raises another set of questions. Nine Iron I jar burials were found in the cemetery. Of these, one belonged to a child one year old, one to a child nine years old, and two to an individual fourteen or fifteen years old. The remaining five were of unknown ages. Unless those five belonged to infants, the pattern of usage for jar burials is very different from any other group of jar burials from the Bronze through Iron Ages.[53] Why were some older children and adolescents buried in jars when the possibility of a pit burial was available? Were they of a different ritual status, ethnicity, or social class? Further adding to the mystery is the single grave good found with burial D88. This jar burial was one of the individuals of unknown age. Whoever this was, the individual was given a Philistine bell-shaped krater with cups, a rather elaborate gift with Aegean funerary origins.[54]

Timnah (Batash)

Like Ekron and Gath, Timnah is located on the border between the Philistine Plain and the Judean hill country. The site is in the Sorek Valley, just east of es-Safi/Gath. The city was well developed in the Iron I and Iron II and displays evidence of an important trade and industrial center. Control of the site appears to go back and forth between the Philistines and Israelites during the Iron Age.[55] The site becomes important in the Iron II as a Judean border town. The two intramural human remains date to the Iron II period.[56] An adult male was found among the smashed *lmlk* store jars of Building 737. The other individual was a child around two years old, who was placed under a stone floor (eighth c.) on the inside of the city wall.[57] The floor was built over in the next stratum.

54   THE BURIALS OF CHILDREN IN ANCIENT ISRAEL

Yavne

Tel Yavne sits on the coastal plain of Israel. It was located at the junction of the Sorek Valley and the Way of the Sea, making it an important city in the Sharon Plain. Located further north than Ekron, but not as far inland, Yavne has Philistine connections.[58] The ancient city has not been excavated, but a salvage excavation took place immediately north of the tell. The excavations uncovered a cemetery with Middle Bronze, Late Bronze, Iron Age, Byzantine, and Ottoman remains. The Iron Age cemetery is identified as containing twenty-eight graves of the Philistine city.[59] While the cemetery is labeled "Philistine," the contents challenge this designation.[60] What is notable here is what is not there. No material remains definitively indicate that this was a Philistine burial ground. In fact, the burial patterns would seem to argue otherwise. Not only are grave goods almost absent, but infants and children are missing in the Iron II cemetery. This is a significant break from the other Philistine-associated sites with extramural burials. Where the children and infants were buried remains to be seen, as well as whether this is actually a Philistine city.

Discussion of Child Burials on the Philistine Coastal Plain

While there are other sites on the Philistine coastal plain that might add to the corpus of infant and child burials, the extant burials are not numerous. Considering the dearth of Iron I burials in the Central Highlands, coastal sites with Iron I as well as Iron II provide an important insight into the ways different populations cared for their dead children during the Iron Age.

Extramural Burials

In a geographical area that is relatively small and uniform, the cemeteries are anything but uniform. Pits, cists, jars, built tombs, and cremations are all found together at Azor, while at Ashkelon pits and cist tombs are preferred. Both sites date to the Iron I/IIA time period, and both sites include burials of children. Yavne is nestled between the two sites. The cemetery there dates much later, to the Iron II (eighth to seventh c. BCE). By this time, the excavated areas of the cemeteries at Ashkelon and Azor are no longer in use. Yavne, linked cautiously to the Philistines, shows a weak similarity with Ashkelon in that the pit burials at both sites are oriented toward the sea. Additionally, children were not found at Yavne. This could mean that children were intentionally buried outside of the cemetery. Children made up only 16% of the pit burials at Ashkelon, so it is possible that if Yavne was also a Philistine site, children have yet to be uncovered in the cemetery.

Regarding Azor and Ashkelon, without final reports on the cemeteries, it is only possible to offer some tentative observations. The children found at both sites are cared for. They are placed in graves and afforded burials in a manner similar to, but not always the same as, the other members in the cemetery. At Ashkelon, the major differences between adult and child burials in pits was the lack of a ceramic burial assemblage. Perhaps this indicates that children were not thought to require the same burial kits for the afterlife.[61] At Azor, however, ceramic wares accompany all the pit burials. This might indicate a different set of values placed on the children or a different concept of what was needed for an afterlife. The children at Ashkelon, like the women, were often buried with metal bracelets, anklets, and rings. This is reminiscent of Tel es-Sai'diyeh, where there was a link established between gender and age.[62] Contrasting this is the lack of jewelry found on children in the Azor cemetery.[63]

The final observation here is that a significant number of infants are missing at both cemetery sites. This is not incredibly surprising since infants are often noted as missing in the burial record. There is the reference to a one-year-old individual in pit burial D91A at Azor, but that is it. The remainder of children referenced in the preliminary reports for both sites are more than two years old. Considering that the excavations were recent and undertaken with care, it is unlikely that small bones would have been overlooked. Infants and the majority of children must have been buried elsewhere, outside of the cemetery.[64] David Ben-Shlomo's comment, that "more archaeological data is needed in the form of excavated cemeteries," seems quite apt.[65]

As an aside, it is interesting that the multiple burial styles used at Azor in the Iron I/IIA cemetery are similar to the later Iron II cemeteries found further up the coast at Achzib, yet this comparison is not readily made in the literature. Perhaps this is due to the different coastal locations or time periods, or maybe the assumption that Achzib was a Phoenician site and

56   THE BURIALS OF CHILDREN IN ANCIENT ISRAEL

Azor a Philistine-influenced site. Given the similarities between the two sites from different time periods, it would appear either that various groups remained open to different expressions in how they treated their dead or that fixed traditions were held, but what we are seeing in the cemetery is an expression of truly mixed populations borrowing from each other and burying their dead together in the same space.[66] This would be significant, for it would demonstrate the peaceful commingling of different people groups both in life and into the afterlife.

The only other extant extramural burial site is the Iron I/ IIA cave at Tell es- Safi/Gath. This cave also suggests the commingling of different people groups but demonstrates a burial pattern radically different from the cemeteries at Azor and Ashkelon as it is a family burial cave. The term "family" burial cave is accurate because the individuals were not only shown to be related via DNA analysis, but all ages, infants through adults, were found inside. As noted above, the number of infants found was so stunning that it merited a special remark. The grave goods deposited in the cave consist of a typical Iron Age ceramic assemblage, plus Egyptianized or Egyptian glyptics and amulets, red- slipped and hand- burnished wares, beads, and bronze bracelets.[67] To whom exactly the goods belonged was not clear. However, the diameter of the bangles/bracelets matches well with the diameter of the bones of the infants and young children found in the cave. In addition, infants and young children were found in proximity to these pieces of jewelry. Because the metals were highly valuable, this "highlights the importance of personal status from a young age."[68]

While the method of burial is different, family cave burial versus pit burials, we see a connection between the Tell es- Safi / Gath and Ashkelon depositions of children in the extramural burials. Both buried the children in a manner similar to the others in their community, suggesting a measure of personhood. In addition, we can think about how articles of personal adornment deposited with the children represented the personhood of both the giver and the receiver.[69] The items were not simply generic shells strung on thread, or amulets placed with the body, but metal bangles that took time, energy, and valuable materials to construct. As Chapter 6 will discuss, the materiality of the metals is also important. Shiny metal items would produce a luminescence that could protect the children in their journey to the afterlife.[70] Moreover, the bracelets were personalized so that they fit the little individuals, again showing the care and investment that was put into the children at these sites.

Intramural Burials

When considering ethnicity and people groups, one of the main issues that keeps appearing in the literature has to do with how previous studies identified burial practices as Philistine. For example, studies often note the faulty attribution of anthropoid coffins as Philistine, or the overly simplistic rationale that if a burial contained Philistine wares, it must be a Philistine burial.[71] These reports successfully problematize the earlier approaches to Philistine burials but fail to consider what the intermural burials might tell us about the people living in the sites who presumably buried their population outside of the site. The emphasis is always on adults and, in the case of Pentapolis, on finding cemeteries that might illuminate "Philistine" burial practices. If we want to talk about Philistine burial behaviors, then a comparison of the intermural burials at the Pentapolis cities is appropriate.

The intramural burials across the sites in this chapter include simple pit burials and jar burials. The mass burials at Ashdod are often pointed out as atypical and not representative of Philistine burial practices. While this may be true, it is worth noting that the mass burial pits were not understood as contaminating the site or imparting lasting impurity to the area as the inhabitants of the next stratum continued to use the area above the inhumations. The pit with the highest number of younglings also displayed an additional burial behavior, the deposition of faunal remains. It seems that this pit was treated differently, perhaps due to the high percentage of infants and children contained within. Most importantly, the infants and children who died in the mass casualty event are buried together with adults who died in the same event, not in a separate location, which seems to indicate a desire to classify or group individuals of different ages together. Whether this is for familial, ethnic, practical, ritual, or other reasons is difficult to say.

The remaining intermural burials are all infant burials found primarily during the Iron I.[72] The burials at Ashkelon, es-Safi/Gath, and Ekron are found near walls or thresholds in domestic areas. The rooms in which the burials appear range as follows: the cramped multiuse rooms at Ashkelon; the elite zone, industrial area, and southern part of the tell at Ekron; and near a storage installation at es-Safi. The burials are therefore not limited to a certain socioeconomic class, professional class, location on a tell, or particular type of building. Furthermore, the burials are sometimes in pits and other times in jars. Unlike previous intermural infant and child burials in the Bronze Age, the intermural burials found in the Pentapolis do not contain

58 THE BURIALS OF CHILDREN IN ANCIENT ISRAEL

the typical jar, juglet, and bowl burial kit. In a few cases these two practices are deconstructed when there is a body in a pit that is covered with parts of a jar. This practice occurs at es-Safi and Ekron and in the Ashkelon cemetery but not in Ashkelon proper.[73] The appearance of intermural burials in the Greek and Mycenean world before the arrival of the Philistines and the resurgence of the practice within the Pentapolis sites around the arrival of the Philistines is a point that needs more investigation.[74] With the knowledge that the Philistines did come from an Aegean background, perhaps they brought with them a burial practice that meshed well with a practice already known from earlier Canaanite periods (intermural burials) and one that remained in vogue until the Philistines became fully enculturated with the native Levantine population.[75]

Regardless of where the practice came from, its use within the sites demands an explanation. Intramural burials do not appear associated with the construction of the building, so we can rule out foundation deposits. Rather, it appears that these infants were intentionally buried for another reason. As with the Canaanite Bronze Age intermural burials, not every infant was afforded burial within the house; it was reserved for a select few. Figuring out who exactly those few were and why they were chosen is a task that is archaeologically impossible. For example, DNA analysis from Ashkelon rules out the possibility that intermural infant burial was based on sex.[76] Age seems to be a more likely limiting reagent for the intermural burials at the Pentapolis sites, as only very young infants were buried in jars and pits.

The "why" behind the burials is also difficult to ascertain. Such burials may represent a belief in rebirth or the desire to anchor the child to the house.[77] Melissa Cradic suggests: "Residential inhumations may have been strategic components of place-making, commemoration, and group membership in death."[78] Since intermural burial is limited to infants, the notion of group membership in death is a bit different from what one might see with, for example, an intermural family burial. However, there might be an attempt to make an association between the infant and the people in the domestic area.[79] Given the high percentage of infant mortality, I think it is possible that such burials may have acted as sympathetic magic, protecting the household from the very thing that it feared, infant death.

The point is sometimes made that intramural infant burials are more private, and the number of people involved in the burial more limited, than with an extramural burial. The implication is that infant burials are less important or meaningful than those in which the whole community participated. While it is true fewer people may have been involved in the burial preparation and burial rites for these infants, they arguably have *more* regular visitors to their "gravesites" than a burial placed in a cemetery. Whereas extramural burials might require a more visible procession every time individuals went to commemorate their dead, I would argue that an intermural burial would be "seen" and perhaps even remembered daily as the inhabitants of the dwelling moved about their activities. Therefore, commemorating individuals with intramural burials demonstrates a particular degree of personhood attributed to the individual, which in this case happens to be an infant.

Notes

1. See, inter alia, M. Dothan, *Ashdod II– III: The Second and Third Seasons Excavations 1963, 1965, Soundings in 1967* ('Atiqot [ES] 9– 10) (Jerusalem: Israel Exploration Society, 1971); M. Dothan and Y. Porath, *Ashdod IV: Excavation of Area M* ('Atiqot [ES] 15) (Jerusalem: Israel Exploration Society, 1982); M. Dothan and Y. Porath, *Ashdod V: Excavation of Area G* ('Atiqot 23) (Jerusalem: Israel Exploration Society, 1993); M. Dothan and D. Ben- Shlomo, *Ashdod VI: Excavations of Areas H and K (1968– 1969),* IAA Reports No. 24 (Jerusalem: IAA, 2005); L. E. Stager, "New Discoveries in the Excavations of Ashkelon in the Bronze and Iron Ages," *Qadmoniot* 131 (2006): 2– 19 (Hebrew); L. E. Stager, J. D. Schloen, and D. M. Master, eds., *Ashkelon I: Introduction and Overview (1985–2006),* Final Reports of the Leon Levy Expedition to Ashkelon 1 (Winona Lake, IN: Eisenbrauns, 2008); M. Faerman, P. Smith, E. Boaretto, J. Uziel, and A. M. Maeir "'. . . in Their Lives, and in Their Death . . .': A Preliminary Study of an Iron Age Burial Cave at Tell es̩-S̩āfī, Israel," *ZDPV* 127 (2011): 129– 48; A. Maeir, ed., *Tell es- Safi / Gath I: Report on the 1996–2005 Seasons,* Ägypten und Altes Testament 69 (Wiesbaden, in press); A. Maeir and A. Zukerman, "Appendix A: Methodology of Excavation, Recording, and Processing of the Finds," in Maeir, *Tell es- Safi / Gath I;* T. Dothan and S. Gitin, *Tel Miqne- Ekron: Eighth Excavation Season and Field School: June 10– July 27, 1990: Program* (Jerusalem: W.F. Albright Institute of Archaeological Research, 1990); T. Dothan and S. Gitin, *Tel Miqne (Ekron) Excavation Project: Spring, 1982; Field Report, Field I NE-Areas 2, 3, 4, 5, 6, 7* (Jerusalem: Tel Miqne (Ekron) Excavation Project Publications Office, 1982); M. W. Meehl, T. Dothan, and S. Gitin, *Tel Miqne- Ekron Excavations 1995–1996: Field INE East Slope: Iron Age I (Early Philistine Period)* (Jerusalem: W.F. Albright Institute of Archaeological Research and the Hebrew University, 2007).
2. J. Uziel and A. Maeir, "Philistine Burial Customs in Light of the Finds at Tell es̩-S̩âfī / Gath," *NEA* 81.1 (2018): 20.
3. K. Birney and B. R. Doak, "Funerary Iconography on an Infant Jar Burial from Ashkelon," *IEJ* 61.1 (2011): 32– 53; A. Buchennino and E. Yannai, "Iron Age I Tombs in the Azor Cemetery," *'Atiqot* 63 (2010): 17– 40 (in Hebrew, English summary 231– 32); D. Ben- Shlomo, "The Cemetery of Azor and Early Iron Age Burial Practices," *Levant* 40 (2008): 29–54.
4. The site was dug during the 1960s and the publications of the site took a hiatus, with the final report coming out in 2005.
5. D. Ben- Shlomo, "Introduction," in Dothan and Ben- Shlomo, *Ashdod VI,* 2. The Iron I strata overlay a Late Bronze Age II site with Egyptian connections. Strata XII– XI represent Iron I and contain pottery and architecture indicative of a Philistine settlement. Stratum X marks the transition to Iron II with a shift away from Philistine bichrome ware and a move to red-slipped pottery (Ben-Shlomo, "Introduction," 5). Within the well-attested Iron I levels in Area H, intermural burials do not seem to be in vogue. No jar burials or pit burials of infants or children were discovered in Iron I levels. A single intramural burial of an adult man was found in Stratum X (M. Dothan and D. Ben-Shlomo, "Stratigraphy and Building Remains," in *Ashdod*

60 THE BURIALS OF CHILDREN IN ANCIENT ISRAEL

VI: The Excavations of Areas H and K (1968–1969), IAA Reports No. 24, ed. M. Dothan and D. Ben-Shlomo (Jerusalem: Israel Antiquities Authority, 2005), 42). It is notable, in light of the Ashkelon and Ekron information, that the only sunken jar installations found in Areas H and K were found in relatively close to the inhumation in Square U-7 (Dothan and Ben-Shlomo, "Stratigraphy and Building Remains," 41–42).

6. In addition to the mass burials, there were a few other more typically styled intramural human burials, three of which contained children. N. Haas, "Anthropological Observation on the Skeletal Remains Found in Area D (1962–1963)," in Dothan, *Ashdod II–III*, 212–14. Locus 1060, which is unstratified, contained two adults and two children, likely in a primary burial. Only two ceramic wares, a cooking pot and krater, were recorded in the finds. For the ceramics see Dothan, *Ashdod II–III*, 128–29.

7. Haas, "Anthropological Observation," 212–14.

8. Data on sex-age distribution comes from Haas, "Anthropological Observation," 214.

9. The table of sex-age distribution of individuals included in Haas's chapter (page 214) appears to have a typo. It lists locus 1151 as the mass burial with 2,434 and locus 1113 with only seven individuals. Both the full physical anthropology report (page 213) and the discussion of the stratigraphy and Area D list locus 1113 as the mass burial referenced earlier in the book (p. 94, Pl. XXXV:3). Hass, "Anthropological Observation," 212–14.

10. All the mass burials contained pottery and some jewelry.

11. The answer may be as simple as energy expenditure; the animals in question could also have been killed in the mass destruction and for sake of convenience they were buried in the same pit; however, this does not seem likely as other refuse pits contained only faunal remains.

12. Regarding the strata listed in the reports: The individual areas use localized strata, such as found here. Strata 3b and 3a are local strata dating to the 8th c. BCE, whereas Strata VIII–VII are site wide general strata dating to the 8th c. BCE. See, for example, Ben-Shlomo, "Introduction," 9, Table 1.1.

13. On the association of clay, jars, and rebirth, see Chapter 5.

14. On ritual impurity and its relationship to burials see M. Suriano, "What Did Feeding the Dead Mean? Two Case Studies from Iron Age Tombs at Beth-Shemesh," *AABNER* 1.3 (2021): 117–42.

15. For an overview of the stratigraphy and phases in Grid 38 see Stager, Schloen, and Master, *Ashkelon I*, 215–17.

16. "The date of Philistine settlement continues to be the subject of controversy. At Ashkelon, a scarab of Ramesses III was found embedded in the floor buildup of Phase 20B (see chapter 13, cat. no. 15). This scarab forms a terminus post quem for the occupation of the new Iron I inhabitants, the Philistines, at Ashkelon." A. Aja and D. Master, "Conclusions: Uncovering Philistines," in *Ashkelon 7: The Iron Age I*, ed. L. Stager, D. Master, and A. Aja (Winona Lake, IN: Eisenbrauns, 2020), 856.

17. This burial was located in Square 64 and identified as Pit 233. A. Aja, "Grid 38," in Stager, Master, and Aja, *Ashkelon 7*, 42.

18. In Phase 19A four infants were found buried in unlined pits. Phase 18B included two pit burials and two jar burials.

19. As of preparation of the current book, the cemetery has yet to be fully published. A preliminary report can be found in D. Master and A. Aja, "The Philistine Cemetery of Ashkelon," *BASOR* 337 (2017): 135–59.

20. Master and Aja, "Philistine Cemetery of Ashkelon," 144.

21. On pit burials, see Master and Aja, "Philistine Cemetery of Ashkelon," 135–41.

22. For chambers and cremations see Master and Aja, "Philistine Cemetery of Ashkelon," 141–44.

23. Unlike the cremations at Azor, discussed later in this chapter, the Ashkelon examples did not have stones circling them.

24. Maeir, *Tell es-Safi / Gath I*, 22. Another study from es-Safi also references multiple "baby burials" at Gath located in Area A. Faerman et al., "In Their Lives," 30.

25. The remaining infant burials of es-Safi/Gath in Area A still await publication. Personal communication, Aren Maeir, January 2023.

26. A. Maeir and J. Uziel, *Tell es-Safi / Gath II: Excavations and Studies*, Ägypten und Altes Testament Bd. 105 (Münster: Zaphon, 2020), 221–77; Faerman et al., "In Their Lives," 129–48; Uziel and Maeir, "Philistine Burial Customs."

27. E. Boretto, "Radiocarbon Dates from Cave T1," in Maeir and Uziel, *Tell es-Safi / Gath II*, 235. On the appearance of benches as early as the Late Bronze Age and continuing into the Iron Age see R. Gonen, *Burial Patterns and Cultural Diversity in Late Bronze Age Canaan*, American

BURIALS ON THE PHILISTINE COAST   61

Schools of Oriental Research, Dissertation Series 7 (Winona Lake, IN: Eisenbrauns, 1992); Ben-Shlomo, "The Cemetery of Azor," 50; E. Bloch-Smith, *Judahite Burial Practices and Beliefs about the Dead*, JSOT Supp. 123, JSOT/ASOR Monograph Series 7 (Sheffield: JSOT Press, 1992), 41–52.

28. Faerman et al., "In Their Lives," 41.
29. Faerman et al., "In Their Lives," 38.
30. M. Faerman and P. Smith, "The Human Remains from Cave T1," in Maeir and Uziel, *Tell es-Safi / Gath II*, 231.
31. Faerman et al., "In Their Lives," 44.
32. L. Mazow, "Competing Material Culture: Philistine Settlement at Tel Miqne- Ekron in the Early Iron Age," in *Material Culture Matters: Essays on the Archaeology of the Southern Levant in Honor of Seymour Gitin*, ed. J. Spencer, R. Mullins, and A. Brody (Winona Lake, IN: Eisenbrauns, 2014), 135.
33. Meehl, Dothan, and Gitin, *Tel Miqne-Ekron Excavations*, 54–55. In Field I, at the summit of the northeast acropolis, three intramural burials were found. The elite zone of Field IV on the lower portion of the tell contained four burials, and Field III contained one burial. Five burials were found in Field I NE.
34. Information on these burials comes from Mazow, "Competing Material Culture," 450.
35. Note the sherd blankets at Ashkelon and also in some Phoenician sites.
36. On stratigraphy for the excavation areas, see Mazow, "Competing Material Culture," 52–55.
37. A similar bathtub was discovered in secondary use at Ashkelon in Grid 38 Phase 19 (Iron I) in Room 25 at the southeast corner. No infants were found in the Ashkelon room. Stager, Schloen, and Master, *Ashkelon I*, 266.
38. Mazow, "Competing Material Culture," 54–55.
39. Gitin, Meehl, and Dothan, *Tel Miqne-Ekron Excavations*, 55.
40. Gitin, Meehl, and Dothan, *Tel Miqne-Ekron Excavations*, 55.
41. M. Dothan, "Excavations at Azor, 1960," *IEJ* 11.4 (1961): 171–75; Ben-Shlomo, "The Cemetery of Azor," 29–54.
42. On pottery forms and phases see Ben-Shlomo, "The Cemetery of Azor," 31, Table 1.
43. The seven Iron IIA pits all belonged to adults. There were six built structures that included anywhere from one to seven individuals dated to Iron IIA. Of these, only one included children. Burial D79A was listed as bones belonging to MNI five adults and children. Grave goods included pottery, scarabs, beads, and jewelry. Ben-Shlomo, "The Cemetery of Azor," Table 2.
44. Ben-Shlomo, "The Cemetery of Azor," 31, Fig. 3. For a list of the skeletons and discussion of individual graves see Ben-Shlomo, "The Cemetery of Azor," 31–34 and Table 2.
45. M. Dothan reports on these as burials in "Group B." M. Dothan, "A Cremation Burial at Azor–A Danite City," *EI* 20 (1989): 173. Ben-Shlomo reassesses the cremations and includes photos of the burials in "The Cemetery of Azor," 38–40.
46. Buchennino and Yannai, "Iron Age I Tombs," 17–40. For the relationship of the different fields, see Plan 1 in Buchennino and Yannai.
47. Buchennino and Yannai, "Iron Age I Tombs," 20.
48. The so-called double-jar burials are not unique to Azor. Buchennino and Yannai also found one in Azor Area A and note they were also reported at Tel Zeror, Megiddo, Kefar Yehoshua, Tell es-Safi / Gath, and Tel Nami. K. Ohata, *Tel Zeror III: Report of the Excavation Third Season, 1966* (Tokyo: Society for Near Eastern Studies in Japan, 1970), LVIA; Buchennino and Yannai, "Iron Age I Tombs," 21.
49. Buchennino and Yannai, "Iron Age I Tombs," 21.
50. This is surprising given that juglets make up 88% of the Iron II grave goods in Azor Area D. Ben-Shlomo, "The Cemetery of Azor," 46.
51. Burial D87 was an individual fourteen-plus years of age, and burial D78 is of unknown age. Ben-Shlomo, "The Cemetery of Azor," 32.
52. Ben-Shlomo, "The Cemetery of Azor," 36.
53. Even if one were to count those five as infants, this makes six infants, one older child, and two adolescents.
54. Ben-Shlomo, "The Cemetery of Azor," 36 and Fig. 17:5.
55. A. Mazar, *Timnah (Tel Batash) I*, Qedem 37 (Jerusalem: Hebrew University of Jerusalem, 1997), 8–9.
56. B. Arensburg, "Human Skeletal Remains from Tel Batash," in *Timnah (Tel Batash) III*, Qedem 45, ed. A. Mazar and N. Panitz-Cohen (Jerusalem: Hebrew University of Jerusalem, 2006), 313.

62 THE BURIALS OF CHILDREN IN ANCIENT ISRAEL

57. Arensburg, "Human Skeletal Remains," 313; A. Mazar, "Areas A and D," in Mazar, *Timnah (Tel Batash) I*, 199.
58. The biblical text states that Uzziah captured the city back from the Philistines in the eighth c. BCE (2 Chronicles 26:3, 6). The tendentious nature of this connection is pointed out by Master and Aja, "Philistine Cemetery of Ashkelon," 154–55.
59. R. Kletter and Y. Nagar, "An Iron Age Cemetery and Other Remains at Yavne," *'Atiqot* 81 (2015): 1–33.
60. Two of the jars were Phoenician types found on coastal sites, the jugs were Ashdod Ware or Late Philistine Decorated Ware (Iron II), and the remaining ceramics were typical of the Iron Age II local wares. The pit burials do, however, show a consistent pattern of orienting the graves perpendicular to the sea, a trait often found in Iron II Phoenician burials. Master and Aja, "Philistine Cemetery of Ashkelon," 155.
61. On the concept of burial kits and their appearance at Ashkelon, see J. Baker, "The Funeral Kit: A Newly Defined Canaanite Mortuary Practice Based on the MB and LBA Tomb Complex at Ashkelon," *Levant* 38 (2006): 1–31.
62. J. Green, "Anklets and the Social Construction of Gender and Age in the Late Bronze and Early Iron Age Southern Levant," in *Archaeology and Women: Ancient and Modern Issues*, ed. S. Hamilton, R. D. Whitehouse, and K. Wright (Walnut Creek, CA: Left Coast Press, 2007), 283–311.
63. For an overview of the burials, age, sex, and grave goods in Azor Area D, see Ben-Shlomo, "The Cemetery of Azor," 30, Table 2.
64. The explanation given for "missing infants" is often one of the following: previous excavations were not looking for them; their small bones were crushed or fell apart with quick digging; their bodies were overlooked because they were in pits that did not contain grave goods. See K. H. Garroway, *Growing Up in Ancient Israel: Children in Material Culture and Biblical Texts*, AB 23 (Atlanta: SBL, 2018), 261 and nn. 164 and 165; K. H. Garroway, *Children in the Ancient Near Eastern Household*, EANEC 3 (Winona Lake, IN: Eisenbrauns, 2014), 19 n. 14.
65. Ben-Shlomo, "The Cemetery of Azor," 51.
66. Ben-Shlomo, "The Cemetery of Azor," 51.
67. Faerman et al., "In Their Lives," 36.
68. J. Verduci, "The Iron Age I/IIA Jewelry from Cave T1," in Maeir and Uziel, *Tell es-Safi / Gath II*, 267.
69. Here partible personhood, as discussed further in Chapter 6, is a useful frame. For partible personhood applied to adornments given to children, see K. H. Garroway, "The Case of Joseph's Coat: Giving Gifts to Children in the Hebrew Bible," *AVAR* 1.2 (2022): 185–211.
70. On the properties of metal as protective, see J. Smoak, "You Have Refined Us Like Silver Is Refined (Ps 66:10): Yahweh's Metallurgic Powers in Iron Age Judah," *AABNER* 1.3 (2021): 83–84.
71. Ben-Shlomo, "The Cemetery of Azor," 47–51; Master and Aja, "Philistine Cemetery of Ashkelon," 156.
72. The adult male from Timnah is excluded from the discussion because it appears to be an outlier.
73. With the Ashkelon cemetery attributed with some certainty to the Philistines, the appearance of the sherd-blanket burials there and within the Pentapolis cities is highly suggestive of a burial practice that might be linked specifically to the Philistines. On the link between the Ashkelon cemetery and the Philistines, see Master and Aja, "Philistine Cemetery of Ashkelon," 135–36; L. Stager, "Introduction," in Stager, Master, and Aja, *Ashkelon 7*, 3–14.
74. A. Aja, "Philistine Domestic Architecture in the Iron Age I" (PhD dissertation, Harvard University, 2009), 391; Maeir, *Tell es-Safi / Gath I*, 22; Birney and Doak, "Funerary Iconography," 36–36; N. Polychronakou-Sgouritsa, "Children Burials in Mycenean Greece," Αρχαιολογικόν Δελτίον, Μελέτες 42 (1987): 8–29; C. Sourvinou-Inwood, *Reading Greek Death: To the End of the Classical Period* (Oxford: Oxford University Press, 1983), 45; M. R. Popham, and J. H. Musgrave, "The Late Helladic UIC Intramural Burials at Lefkandi, Euboea," *Annual of the British School at Athens* 86 (1991): 273–96. On the connection between Egypt and intermural burials see Birney and Doak, "Funerary Iconography," 35. Birney and Doak note that the intermural burials in Egypt cease in the thirteenth to twelfth c. BCE, 4.
75. On the gradual enculturation of the Philistines with Levantine populations, see the various publications by A. Maeir on es-Safi/Gath.
76. Faerman et al., "Infants."
77. See Chapter 6.

78. M. Cradic, "Residential Burial and Social Memory in the Middle Bronze Age Levant," *NEA* 81.3 (2018): 199; A. Brody, "Late Bronze Age Intramural Tombs," in Stager, Schloen, and Master, *Ashkelon I*, 516, 529; A. Brody, "New Perspectives on Levantine Mortuary Ritual: A Cognitive Interpretive Approach to the Archaeology of Death," in *Historical Biblical Archaeology and the Future: The New Pragmatism*, ed. T. Levy (London: Equinox, 2010), 126.
79. This idea is further examined in Chapter 6.

3

Surveying Iron Age Infant and Child Burials in Phoenician-Influenced Areas

The previous chapter examined the Philistine coastal sites, looking at the so-called Pentapolis cities and some areas that are thought to have had Philistine inhabitants. As the picture developed in that chapter, it became clear that the cities were indeed cosmopolitan, with new groups mixing with the indigenous population. The data are unsurprising, as geopolitical borders ebbed and flowed, and along with them mortuary practices. We see this when older mortuary practices remain, new practices are added, and known practices are adapted. An examination of the burials in Phoenicia, again outside of the traditional borders of Iron Age Judah, continues to demonstrate that it is not always easy to assign ethnicity to a site or to a particular burial practice. Despite this, some burial trends, such as cremation, do appear to be used more frequently in Phoenicia and do appear indicative of a Phoenician burial style.[1]

The Phoenician presence in the Southern Levant arose during the Iron Age.[2] The core of the Phoenician homeland extended across modern-day Lebanon and beyond, with various cities holding regional power. Phoenician colonies have been identified throughout the Mediterranean, with the best-known one being Carthage. Reference to Carthage in a study dedicated to child burials of course raises the issue of the infant tophets.[3] All of the known infant tophets are located in the Phoenician colonies of North Africa, Sardinia, Sicily, et cetera. Since none have been found in the Phoenician homeland or in the land of Israel, they remain outside the scope of the present chapter. However, the burial practice that is found at the tophets, cremation, is notably found at sites within the scope of the present study. While not common in the Southern Levant, cremation has generally been associated with Phoenician burials when other Phoenician elements are present. Yet, as will be shown, cremation was not the only type of burial employed by those in Phoenician lands.[4]

The Dying Child. Kristine Henriksen Garroway, Oxford University Press. © Oxford University Press 2025.
DOI: 10.1093/9780197566718.003.0004

BURIALS IN PHOENICIAN-INFLUENCED AREAS   65

To understand the Phoenician burials, it is perhaps first proper to note that there is no one single "Phoenician" burial style.[5] Maria López-Bertran offers a generalized view of Phoenician burial practices, stating that burial and corpse treatment moved from incineration between the ninth and sixth c., to inhumation in the sixth c. through 350 BCE,[6] and then to a combination of inhumation and incineration from the end of the fourth c. on.[7] However, as the survey below demonstrates, the real hallmark of Phoenician burials appears to be the variety of styles. While one site may follow López-Bertran's pattern, another may mix jar burials, inhumations, and cremations within one time period.

Cremations associated with Phoenicians were carried out in the Levant between the tenth and sixth c. BCE.[8] Just as there are a variety of methods used for inhumation, there are also a variety of ways to carry out a cremation burial. Possible styles included cremation in a pit covered with sand and cremation on a pyre followed by a secondary burial in an (un)covered urn. The degree to which the body was cremated also varies between sites. It should be noted that the fires used for cremation burned at lower temperatures than they do today. One estimate for ancient cremations gives a temperature of 315–482 degrees Fahrenheit, while today incinerators at crematoriums reach temperatures of 1400–1800 degrees Fahrenheit.[9] The difference in temperature affects how much of the body can be completely consumed. Thus, when one reads that an ancient body was cremated and placed within an urn, one should not picture an urn with "grandma's ashes," as one might find today. Rather, ancient urns often contained burned bones along with the ash of the soft body tissues.[10] Based on the well-preserved remains from the cremation site at Tyre Al-Bass, María Aubet has reconstructed the basic funerary sequence as follows:[11]

1. A funerary pyre is made, and the corpse is placed on top with personal grave goods.
2. The pyre is lit.
3. Feasting by the living happens while the pyre burns. This could be a means of associating the living with the dead in a collective identity. The burned food remains are kept aside.
4. The pyre is extinguished and remains are sifted.
5. Remains are placed in urns with additional personal items, like amulets.
6. A burial pit is (re)opened.

66 THE BURIALS OF CHILDREN IN ANCIENT ISRAEL

7. The urn is deposited in the pit with any additional grave goods, such as a drinking vessel, and then covered.
8. Secondary funerary rituals occur. This might include aromatic purifying fires, a second ritual meal, and the smashing of ceramics associated with this meal.
9. A commemorative monument may be erected, such as a stela, in order to mark the location as a burial or locale for an ancestor cult.[12]

This sequence is helpful for visualizing the funerary process that may also be found at other locations where cremations occurred.

Sites within the Carmel Region Containing Phoenician-Style Burials

To the south of the Phoenician homeland, a few sites on the Carmel coast contain Phoenician-style burials: Achzib, ʿAtlit, and Tel Bira. These sites demonstrate a relationship to each other not only in burial style but also in material culture. It is thought that the Tyrian polity expanded south into these areas as well as into western Galilee in order to gain a foothold in productive agricultural lands.[13]

Achzib

The site lies twenty-five kilometers south of Tyre and fifteen kilometers north of Acre. Excavations have found evidence of inhabitance from Middle Bronze II to Roman times. During Iron IIA, the site experienced a period of resettlement, as is evidenced by a reassessment of the burials in the Eastern Cemetery.[14] The burial complex of Iron Age Achzib is complicated. Over the course of many excavations, four cemeteries have been discovered, each labeled according to their relationship to the site: north, south, east, and center (on the tell itself).[15]

The data: it is not my intention to do a full review of the cemeteries here, but rather to highlight some similarities to other Phoenician burial practices and to point out when we see children and when we do not in the four Achzib cemeteries.[16]

BURIALS IN PHOENICIAN-INFLUENCED AREAS   67

Details of the burials in the Central Cemetery are limited. Three cist tombs built of ashlar stones were dated to the tenth c. Eliat Mazar suggests that these tombs may be related to the built ashlar stone chamber family tombs in the Southern Cemetery. She goes on to posit that the cist tombs were used for immediate families, while the chamber tombs were for extended family burials.[17]

The Eastern Cemetery contained cist and shaft tombs all dated to the Iron Age II.[18] The cist tombs were made of rough stone, similar in construction to two of the cist tombs found in the Southern Cemetery. Unfortunately, while the ceramics and other small finds survived, the skeletal remains were in poor condition. While more skeletal remains would be helpful, the analysis of the cist tombs demonstrates that, at the very least, the elite members of Iron IIA Achzib buried their children with them. Whether infants were also included in these family tombs remains unknown.

The Eastern Cemetery also contained shaft tombs with closed ceilings. A detailed analysis of the skeletal remains in the shaft tombs is not available. The publication of the Ben-Dor excavations describes the situation as follows: "A serious information gap, among others, is the lack of data concerning burials, in particular with regard to the type of burial—inhumation or cremation—as well as the presence of skeletal material and the position, number, gender, and age of the deceased."[19] However, a few pieces of information can be gleaned from Moshe Prausnitz's brief encyclopedia entry. He describes one early (eleventh to eighth c.) shaft tomb as having "remains of two to three hundred bodies . . . piled almost to the ceiling."[20] The later (eighth to sixth c.) shaft tombs he describes as having benches, upon which bodies and grave offerings were laid. While we cannot know for certain, it may be that they were also family burials that included children.

The Southern Cemetery contained built tombs, shaft tombs, and pit graves, as well as a few jar burials of infants and some cremated jar burials of adults.[21] Two of the built chamber tombs (T. C.1 and T. C.2) were used from the tenth c. through the end of the Iron Age.[22] They both include a repository pit at the front end of the tomb, presumably used to hold the remains of earlier burials when more room was needed for new burials. Each tomb was a family tomb, including the remains of adults, children, and infants.[23] The tombs also had a ceiling made of sandstone slabs with a hole in the center. Mazar suggested that the ceiling holes in these tombs functioned as a "drinking shoot" for libations and other items to be given to the dead.[24]

68 THE BURIALS OF CHILDREN IN ANCIENT ISRAEL

Table 3.1 Skeletal Analysis of Remains from the Built Chamber Tomb
T. C.1., Achzib

Location	0–1 years / Infant	2–5 years	6–10 years	11–15 years / Juvenile	Adult	Total Number
Jar burial #43	0	1	0	0	2	3
Jar burial #44	0	0	0	1	1	2
Jar burial #45[a]	0	1	0	0	1	2
Extended bench burials	0	0	0	0	2	At least 2[b]
Northwest corner	0	0	0	1	2	3
Northeast corner	1	0	3	1	7	12
Southeast corner	0	2	0	1	8	11
Central	0	1	1	0	2	4
Locus 219	0	2	1	0	1	4
Repository pit	1	2	0	1	7	10
Outside burial	0	0	0	0	2	2
Total burials	2	9	5	5	35	56

Note: Data taken from the report in P. Smith, L. Horowitz, and J. Zias, "Human Remains from the Iron Age Cemeteries at Achziv, Part 1: The Built Tomb from the Southern Cemetery," *Rivista di Studi Fenici* 18.2 (1990): 137–54.

[a] This burial included the full skeleton of a two- to three-year-old child. There were also sheep/goat bones.

[b] The burials on benches were not well preserved. Smith, Horowitz, and Zias, "Human Remains," 141.

The shaft tombs of the Southern Cemetery were all grouped together in the northern quadrant. Various types of shaft tombs were discovered, showing a progression in their development (ninth c. through the end of the Iron Age).[25] Unfortunately, a full skeletal analysis of these tombs was not included in the final report.[26]

Mazar suggests that because cremations are not common in the Southern Cemetery, there is a link between the cremation burials and the tombs. Perhaps these cremated individuals were placed "next to family tombs and relatives."[27] While in a different location of the cemetery, the placement of the cremation burials outside of, but next to, shaft tombs is reminiscent of the infant jar burials placed outside of, but next to, the ashlar built tombs. One wonders what caused these particular individuals to be placed outside of, rather than within, the tombs if they are indeed family tombs. The final major tomb type in the Southern Cemetery is pit graves. But because there was only a single reference to one child found in a rectangular pit, is unclear how many children were found in pit burials.[28]

The Northern Cemetery contained a single ashlar constructed tomb (ca. tenth to sixth c.), which was a family tomb akin to those found in the Southern Cemetery.[29] The cemetery is best known as the cremation cemetery (tenth to seventh c.).[30] Burial urns with cremated remains were found peppered throughout the site. According to Mazar, all cremations found at Achzib were adults.[31] However, a more recent analysis identified a total of fifty cremated individuals, including three subadults, described as two juveniles and one child aged six to nine years old, found in urns that also contained adult cremations.[32] During the sixth c., after the crematorium stopped being used, the site was used primarily for infant jar burials and child inhumations.[33]

Observations: during Iron II, people at Achzib had many different options for burying their children. In most cases, the infants and children are afforded burials similar to the other members of their society. While a few traditional infant jar burials make an appearance, they are not found interred under house floors or in a domestic space such as they were during the Canaanite Bronze Age, or in early Iron Philistia. Instead, the jar burials are associated with family burials, signaling an intention to join, rather than separate in death, the youngest members of society with their families in the afterlife.[34] Yet the fact remains that these children were still separated out and given different burials, which speaks perhaps to their differentiated personhoods.

The presence of infants and children in the ashlar tombs with so-called drinking holes is especially interesting. If these were in fact libation shoots, they prompt a question regarding who was receiving the libations and other offerings. Was it only for the adults in the tomb or for all of the individuals? If the answer is "for all individuals," then certainly this says something about the personhood of the individuals buried within. In addition, the reuse of these family tombs over hundreds of years and the inclusion of repository pits also brings up the issue of collective memory. Tombs opened and reopened, bodies laid out and moved, all point to continual interaction with the deceased. Indeed, if one explains the mass secondary burials in the built tombs as relocated from the Northern Cemetery, then this movement speaks to a desire to keep the memory of the deceased alive. Contra Mazar's statement that "since entering the tomb one must have had to step over these

70 THE BURIALS OF CHILDREN IN ANCIENT ISRAEL

(repository pit) burials, their location probably indicates their relatively less importance," I would argue their placement demanded interaction with all the deceased.[35] One would at the very least see the remains of the dead every time a new burial was added. Most importantly, these remains included adults, juveniles, children, and infants alike.

'Atlit

The site of 'Atlit is twelve kilometers south of Haifa. The cemetery is located at the site of Pilgrim's Castle at the southeastern corner of the fort. Excavators found shaft tombs and cremations in the necropolis.

The data: the rock-hewn shaft graves first appear in the Iron II and are used through the Hellenistic periods, signaling a long stretch of reopening and reuse of the tombs.[36] These shaft tombs contained at least fourteen graves and over one hundred burials. Unfortunately, most of the skeletal remains were too decomposed for analysis. There are only two references to the burial of children.[37] While C. N. Johns identifies both children as female, this should be taken with a grain of salt, seeing that the identification was based on the jewelry found with the children.[38]

The 'Atlit necropolis also contained a cremation area, which merits a fuller discussion here. These cremation burials are dated to the eighth to sixth c. BCE. Unlike cremations at other sites, 'Atlit did not have a central hearth used for incineration. Instead, the burials were all primary burials wherein the deceased was laid in a pit on a small pyre of branches. The body was then burned and covered with sand before it was completely consumed. Pottery was present in eleven of the eighteen burials and was placed at the head, feet, or head and feet of the individuals. Johns notes that in some cases the vessels were whole, while in other cases it appears the vessel was deliberately smashed—perhaps "killed"—before the grave was covered.[39] While there are eighteen burial locations, there are twenty-four cremated individuals. It appears that in some areas the burials were placed too closely together to assign them a new burial number.[40] The head and body position of the cremated individuals shows no particular pattern. Bodies are flexed, extended, and facing all directions.

Observations: Elizabeth Bloch-Smith makes a startling observation: "Virtually all the excavated burials were of children burned on a wooden pyre and then covered with dirt."[41] According to Johns, five

BURIALS IN PHOENICIAN-INFLUENCED AREAS 71

Table 3.2 Cremated Child and Infant Burials at 'Atlit

Burial	Age	Grave Goods
Iii	Child	No grave goods
Iva	Child	Grave goods crushed
X	Child	Oenoche, saucers, miniature bottle Mortar and saucer at the legs Perhaps 3 silver earrings and 4 silver eyelets associated with the grave
xi a	Infant	Bronze earring
xi b	Child	2 bottles, a goblet, amphoriskos, and a bowl
xi c	Infant	?
xiii a	Infant	No grave goods
xv	Small child (infant?)	
xvia	Probably a child[a]	Bronze earring and bronze granule
xviii	Probably a child	Bronze ornament with the skull, glass beads, earring Sherds scattered around the burial

[a] The excavation report states the burial was flexed and its upper part measured 60 cm (Johns, "Excavation of Pilgrims' Castle" 149). Accounting for the full, extended height gives us 120 cm, or 3'11". Even if the population was shorter than average, this height is still not adult height. Other bodies listed as adults were 130–150 cm, or 4'3"–4'11".

individuals were adults, six were children, and four were infants. There were an additional eight individuals whose age was not listed. Whether or not the remaining eight were adults, the percentage of children and infants is still quite high. Table 3.2 describes the ten cremated infants and children and the grave goods associated with those burials. Johns has included a drawing of the excavated portion of the 'Atlit cemetery, and from his drawing it appears that six of the ten infant and child burials are clustered around a pit. While there is not enough data to determine whether infant and child burials were intentionally clustered, it does provide some food for thought. It should also be noted that all twenty-four cremations were found in an excavated area that was roughly ten meters by ten meters.

As a whole, the sample of cremations from the 'Atlit necropolis demonstrates that this society buried infants, children, and adults in a similar manner. Unlike the cremations at Tyre Al-Bass or Tel Bira, there was no attempt to separate burial methods by age.[42] The manner of cremation also appears to be similar for all ages, as do the allotted grave goods. Only one

72 THE BURIALS OF CHILDREN IN ANCIENT ISRAEL

cremated individual was found buried in an urn. It appears that primary cremation where the individual was laid out in a pit was the typical practice, unlike the cremation necropolises further north in the Phoenician homeland where individuals were placed in urns.

Additional Southern Levantine Sites with Phoenician-Style Burials

Other sites in the south of Israel also contain burials that appear linked to Phoenicians based on grave goods and the use of cremation.[43] These sites include Tell er-Reqeish, Tell el-ʿAjjul,[44] and Tell el-Farʿah South. Clustered close to each other but far away from even the southernmost fringes of Phoenician influence, these sites are thought to perhaps be Phoenician trade outposts.[45] Like the Phoenician homeland and those sites in its sphere of influence, these next sites also demonstrate mortuary variability.

Tell er-Reqeish

A salvage excavation took place in 1940 at the site of Tell er-Reqeish, located in what is now the Gaza Strip, one kilometer south of Deir el-Balah.[46] The site is a low, sandy mound located on the shore. The results of this dig were given a cursory publication. It appears that thirty Iron II cremation burials were discovered.[47] They are described as "being calcined [burned], of human adults and rather well-grown children" placed in at twenty-four urns.[48] Unfortunately, the bones were taken to the Palestinian (Rockefeller) Museum and subsequently lost before a physical anthropologist could analyze them and a final report be issued.[49] In 1974 a second emergency excavation was undertaken at the site. Five strata spanning the Iron II through Persian periods were discovered, along with evidence of a town and cemetery. The cemetery was five hundred meters south of the town area. Three types of burials were found there. Avraham Biran's report of this excavation includes twenty inhumations, an unspecified number of open cremated burials, and six cremated burials placed in urns. This brings the total number of urn cremations up to thirty.

Observations: while the ethnic identity of the Tell er- Reqeish Iron II inhabitants is not definitively known, the ceramic evidence, along with the variety of burial styles, does suggest a Phoenician presence or at the very least a Phoenician influence at the site.[50] If the inhabitants followed suit with other Phoenician sites, it also raises the possibility that children may have been cremated here too.

Tell el-Far'ah South

Tell el-Far'ah South sits twenty kilometers east of Gaza, in the northern Negev region. William Flinders Petrie published the site under the name Beth Pelet. He found multiple cemeteries at the site. With its mixture of burial styles, Cemetery 200 is most interesting. It included large family tombs with children and adults "crammed" together, along with some unique, lavishly adorned child burials dug directly into the marl.[51] Such burials, separate from family tombs, but within the same vicinity of the family tombs, suggest that these children were treated differently for a reason. What that purpose was remains unknown. However, it does stand to reason that the children were understood to have some measure of personhood to receive such burials.

The data: within Cemetery 200 there is a cluster of burials listed as cremation jars.[52] The cremation urns have been dated to the tenth to eighth c. BCE.[53] Unlike other cemeteries, the urns at Tell el-Far'ah South were not buried on top of, within, or leaning against the other tombs in the cemetery. The placement led Tufnell to conclude that those depositing the urns were aware of the location of the stone tombs.[54] While a full anthropological report on the cremations was not undertaken, Petrie did include a brief report by Dr. Karl Pearson on nine of the cremated remains. It is difficult to assess whether these were the only skeletal remains that were discovered in the urns, or whether other remains were too fragmentary or friable to provide useful data.

Observations: the impact of Pearson's report, as laid out in Table 3.3, has not been fully appreciated in the scholarly literature. Put bluntly, Pearson identified cremated remains of children. The age of the children, whether they were infants or younger or older children, is unknown. Yet the fact remains that he identified children in the urns. The children were buried along

74 THE BURIALS OF CHILDREN IN ANCIENT ISRAEL

Table 3.3 Skeletal Analysis of the Cremated Remains at Tell el-Far'ah South

Burial	Child	Adolescent	Adult/Sex/Age	Total
F. 215	1		0	1
F. 219	0		1 (f)?	1
F. 250	0		1? (f?)	1
F. 251	0		1? (f?) ca. 40	1
F. 253	0	1 (unknown) *15–20 years old	0	1
F. 255	0		1 (m?) 35+	1
F. 257	0		1 (m)?	1
F. 262	1		0	1
F. 264	1		0	1
	3 children	1 adolescent	5 adults	9 individuals

Note: Based on the data from Petrie, Beth-Pelet I, 13.

with adults in a sort of cremation section of the cemetery. The urns were mostly large store jars that were local imitations of Cypriot ware. Within the urns, one or two small ceramic "pots" were found. The jars were described as "never more than 30 inches below the surface; a flat dish (types 2 or 3) was often inverted over the mouth of the jar and sometimes there would be a pile of small stones on top."[55] The description of the cremation jars fits in some ways with what we find in other cremation cemeteries: the jars were found holding one individual, no burned grave goods accompanied the burials, and the cremations burials appear clustered together. The most marked differences were that the cremation burials at Tell el-Far'ah South included individuals of all ages, including children, and that the vessels contained "pots" rather than juglets or bowls.

Discussion of Child Burials in Phoenician-Influenced Areas

The deposition of infant and children within sites under Phoenician influence are as varied as the sites themselves. Of the nine different sites examined, at least five different methods of burial were discovered: built tombs, pit tombs, shaft tombs, cremations, and jar burials. Although infants and children were included in the burial record, it should be noted that the number of infants and children found at sites within the Phoenician sphere should again be higher considering the infant mortality rate.[56]

The data leave one with the unsatisfying conclusion that infants and children were sometimes afforded the same burial rights as other members of the family and community, while at other times they were not. The discrepancy in the burial record between the number of infants and children found, versus the number we would expect to be found, can be answered in a few ways. First, these communities might not always find it efficient or necessary to treat infants and young children to structured burials. Regarding the practice of cremation specifically, it might be that the public nature of the rite, and the expense associated with it, made it not viable to engage on a regular basis.[57] It could also be that the status of the deceased individuals within the Phoenician community dictated whether they were cremated. For example, the adult cremation cemeteries might only have been used for adult elite, adult firstborn, adult priest or priestess, and so on.[58] However, a different explanation must then be sought for sites like 'Atlit and Tell el-Far'ah South, where young and old alike were cremated and placed together in a cemetery context.

Thinking broadly about the mortuary record, the lack of Phoenician infant and child burials has led to conclusions such as the following: "It was expressed in the fact that in many past societies, infants and children were not considered members of the community, or even fully human, until they had reached a specific stage of biological development."[59] This theory is possible and likely correct.[60] However, the relationship between membership in a community and concepts of personhood are put into tension when we consider that at least some infants and children are found in Phoenician family burials and in cemetery contexts. To put it another way, those holding the previous conclusion argue that there is a direct correlation between personhood in life and personhood in death. It would follow logically, then, if infants and children were not afforded any type of personhood, they should be completely absent from contexts in which individuals afforded membership/personhood were buried. This is simply not the picture.

Again, within sites under Phoenician influence, as in other areas, it seems most probable that factors other than personhood— for example, social status, economic status, circumstance of death, or even the health of other family members—affected the type of burial afforded to infants and children

76 THE BURIALS OF CHILDREN IN ANCIENT ISRAEL

in a way that such factors might not have affected the burial of individuals more vested in the community. For example, it might not have been viable to open a family tomb or create a new built grave every time an infant or child died. It might be that family vaults were opened only when other members of the extended family had died at the same time, or if the deceased was a firstborn or held another special status. In times when the community was struggling economically or family members were ill or overcome by grief, it might have been the practice to do a simple field burial. Yet the fact remains that in the Phoenician homeland and those areas it touched, infants and children were not always excluded from extant burial grounds. Such a fact means we should not assume de facto that infants and children had no measure of personhood in Phoenician society.

Locating Personhood in Phoenician Child Burials

Personhood is evidenced in several different ways within the extant child burials in Phoenicia. Where previous scholarship has addressed personhood and burial rituals with respect to adults, some of the observations can be applied to child burials as well. Because of its link with Phoenician society, I will use cremation as an example. Cremation has been understood in a number of ways, each of which attests to the social transformation of the individual's (read adult's) personhood. Aubet's comments summarize the general ideas, namely, that fire acts as a purifying agent that transforms the body into a new identity and through which "acts of display and competition are minimized, so that social differences vanish."[61] The swift disintegration of an individual through incineration not only speeds up the process of bodily decay but also rapidly transforms the community's relationship to the body.[62] The absence or presence of grave goods with cremated remains has been understood to indicate how a society related to individual adults as their personhood transformed. Ceramic items, such as the common trio of a mushroom jug, trefoil jug, and bowl or juglet, often accompany the remains, attesting to a need for sustenance on the journey to the afterlife.[63] Yet, while most urn cremations were provided with a ceramic kit, they did not include personal grave goods. At Achzib, this led Mazar to conclude that there was no need to provide the adult individuals with identity markers in death.[64] Others interpret this trend differently, suggesting that personal grave goods were only needed in cases where the individual's body (and personhood) underwent a longer period of transformation.[65] This argument follows for the child burials at 'Atlit, where personal grave goods were placed on the funeral pyres burned along with the individuals. The skeletal remains at 'Atlit were noticeably not as burned as those in cremation urns, which suggests a shorter time spent in the incinerating fires, perhaps in turn necessitating the inclusion of personal grave goods to assist the dead child in its transformation.

In addition to cremations, we can observe further indications that infants and children were afforded varying ritual rites associated with personhood. Here the individual child burials within cemetery complexes are notable. First, let us consider the burials that are not in family tombs. While family tombs are important for considering a place a child may have had in the family at death, individual graves are instructive for conceptualizing how the individual child was treated. At each of the sites examined above, an effort has been made to distinguish between individual child and adult burials.

Consider the following sites within the southern sphere of Tyrian influence, where we see children and adults separate yet together. At the Southern Cemetery of Achzib, we find children in jar burials. Notably, the jar burials placed within the tomb also contained adults, while the jar burials placed outside the tomb contained the more traditional interment of single infants, familiar within earlier time periods. 'Atlit's cremation cemetery utilized pits for single incinerations where children and adults alike were given various personal and ceramic grave goods. In the shaft grave area, infants were found with earrings, anklets, and bracelets, as well as a pendant with a bell, and beads. Finally, at Tell el- Far'ah South we might consider the two unique children's burials, placed just outside the family tombs, that were afforded a rich set of grave goods. While the jewelry given to all these children may represent a social status related to age or economics, it is also possible that, as with the Philistine children, the shiny metal was meant to protect the individual children in death, as it did in life.[66] For example, the appearance of a bell pendant at 'Atlit suggests warding off evil, perhaps an intentional nod to the danger that was present as the body decomposed and transformed into its final state.[67]

If we move to the family tombs, evidence of perceived personhood in death is also seen. The fact that we find infant and child bones within repository pits or pushed to the side of a chamber and commingled with adult bones argues for including children in the family or community's social memory.[68] Here one can consider the repository pits placed at the front of Tombs C.1 and C.2 at Achzib. Anyone entering the tomb would have interacted with

78   THE BURIALS OF CHILDREN IN ANCIENT ISRAEL

the dead by stepping over the pit. While it is difficult to know the degree of personhood afforded to infants and children at these sites, at the very least, one might argue that these infants and children were incorporated into the family in death to the same degree they were in life.

However personhood was envisioned at these sites, it appears that the community was invested enough in their infants and children to provide some of them with means for continuing a relationship with them into the afterlife. As the examples of both family and individual burials demonstrate, infants and children were cared for in death. At times they were subsumed into the family conglomerate, while other times children and infants remained apart from the family. Yet even when they remained apart, they were never far from the burials of others in their community.

Notes

1. By way of a caveat, I note that while the terms "Phoenician" and "Canaanite" are used as ethnic identifiers in the scholarly literature, there were regional ethnic variations. Gunnar Lehmann, "The Levant," in *The Oxford Handbook of the Phoenician and Punic Mediterranean*, ed. C. López-Ruiz and B. Doak (Oxford: Oxford University Press, 2019), 465.

2. The origins of the Phoenicians are not clear. They did not leave historical records. Suggestions for their origins and eventual uprise include the fall of Ugarit at the end of the Late Bronze Age, where a Canaanite base of peoples mixed with a contingent of Sea Peoples. Ann Killebrew, "Canaanite Roots, Proto-Phoenicia, and the Early Phoenician Period 1300–1000 BCE," in López-Ruiz and Doak, *Phoenician and Punic Mediterranean*, 42; C. C. López-Ruiz, *Phoenicians and the Making of the Mediterranean* (Cambridge, MA: Harvard University Press, 2021).

3. I use the term "infant tophets" to distinguish them from the other adult cremation sites in Phoenicia, which are also sometimes called tophets in the literature. The literature on tophets is extensive: inter alia, P. Smith, G. Avishai, J. A. Greene, and L. E. Stager, "Age Estimations Attest to the Practice of Infant Sacrifice at the Carthage Tophet," *Antiquity* 87 (2013): 1191–99; P. Smith, G. Avishai, J. A. Greene, and L. E. Stager, "Aging Cremated Infants: The Problem of Sacrifice at the Tophet at Carthage," *Antiquity* 85 (2011): 859–74; P. Xella, "'Tophet': An Overall Interpretation," *SEL* 29–30 (2012–13): 259–81; L. Stager, "Carthage: A View from the Tophet," in *Phönizier im Westen: Die Beiträge des Internationalen Symposiums über "Die phönizische Expansion im westlichen Mittelmeerraum" in Köln vom 24 bis 27 April, 1979*, ed. H. G. Niemeyer (Mainz am Rhein: Zabern, 1982), 155–66; P. Xella, J. Quinn, V. Melchiorri, and P. van Dommeln, "Phoenician Bones of Contention," *Antiquity* 87 (2013): 1–9. Biblical scholars in particular have struggled to make sense of biblical texts that appear to describe a tophet and child sacrifice. H. Dewrell, *Child Sacrifice in Ancient Israel*, EANEC 5 (Winona Lake, IN: Eisenbrauns, 2017); P. G. Mosca, "Child Sacrifice in Canaanite and Israelite Religion: A Study in *Mulk* and מלך" (PhD dissertation, Harvard University, 1975); P. G. Mosca, "The Tofet: A Place of Infant Sacrifice?," *ESL* 29–30 (2012–13): 119–36.

4. Unlike the study of burials in biblical Israel, the study of Phoenician burials has not been systematized until relatively recent times. In 1995 Helen Sader bemoaned the state of burial studies, noting that more systematic study needed to be done. "Necropoles et tombes phénicinnes du Liban," *Cuadernos de Arqueología Mediterránea* 1 (1995): 15–30. Helen Dixon took up this challenge eighteen years later in her dissertation, presenting a systematized description of Phoenician mortuary practice. "Phoenician Mortuary Practice in the Iron Age I–III (ca. 1200–ca. 300 BCE) Levantine 'Homeland'" (PhD dissertation, University of Michigan, 2013). Other studies of individual burial grounds have since gathered more traction, and the topic continues to be an area ripe for research.

BURIALS IN PHOENICIAN-INFLUENCED AREAS 79

5. Dixon, "Phoenician Mortuary Practice," 568; M. Aubet, "Cremation and Social Memory in Iron Age Phoenicia," in *Ritual, Religion and Reason: Studies in the Ancient World in Honour of Paolo Xella*, Alter Orient und Altes Testament 404, ed. O. Loretz et al. (Münster: Ugarit-Verlag, 2013), 77–79. Lehmann points out that the Phoenicians themselves were not a single entity. Regional differences appear, but the one thing linking all Phoenicians together was their penchant for maritime trade interests. Lehmann, "The Levant," 465; S. Sherratt and A. Sherratt, "The Growth of the Mediterranean Economy in the Early First Millennium B.C.," *WA* 24.3 (1993): 361–78.

6. The above pattern should be taken with the caveat that many children in Punic lands were still cremated in the sixth c. through 350 BCE.

7. M. López- Bertran, "Funerary Ritual," in López- Ruiz and Doak, *Phoenician and Punic Mediterranean*, 293–309; Dixon, "Phoenician Mortuary Practice," 566–68.

8. Y. Alexandre and E. Stern, "Phoenician Cremation Burials at Tel Bira," *'Atiqot* 42 (2001): 183–95; E. Bloch- Smith, *Judahite Burial Practices and Beliefs about the Dead*, JSOT Supp. 123, JSOT/ ASOR Monograph Series 7 (Sheffield: JSOT Press, 1992), 178–79, 210–14, 244–45.

9. López-Bertran, "Funerary Ritual," 294.

10. For images of burned bones in urns, see the plates in M. Aubet, "The Phoenician Cemetery of Tyre," *NEA* 73: (2010): 144– 55 and T. Macridy, "A travers les nécropoles sidoninnes," *RB* 1 (1904): Pl. VI:14, VI:15.

11. Aubet, "Phoenician Cemetery of Tyre," 151–54.

12. Hundreds of inscribed memorial stelae (eighth to sixth c. BCE) were found in the cemetery. Dixon provides a comprehensive study of the ones that have been saved and analyzed. Dixon, "Phoenician Mortuary Practice," 56–67.

13. M. Edrey, E. Arie, H. May, and A. Yasur-Landau, "The Iron Age II Tombs of Area E, Tel Achziv," *IEJ* 68.2 (2018): 173 and sources within.

14. Edrey et al., "Iron Age II Tombs," 152.

15. Excavations in the Southern Cemetery: I. Ben-Dor (1941–44), M. W. Prausnitz (1958, 1960, 1980– 81), E. Mazar (1988). Excavations in the Eastern Cemetery: Ben- Dor (1941– 44) and Prausnitz (1963). Excavations in the Central Cemetery: Prausnitz (1963– 64). Excavations in the Northern Cemetery: Prausnitz (1980, 1982, 1984), Mazar (1992, 1994, 2002, 2004). Further excavations have been undertaken by the Hebrew Union College and Lyon University. At least one family cist tomb (dated to the ninth c. BCE) built of field stones has been found. Buried within were a male, female, and child between three and five years old. The grave was richly furnished with luxury items. The child was wearing a complete necklace. P. Bohstrom, "Whole Nuclear Family Found in Ancient Phoenician Tomb in Israel," *Haaretz*, December 24, 2019; TOI Staff, "Archaeologists Discover Phoenician Family Tomb in Ancient City of Achziv," *Times of Israel*, December 25, 2019.

16. For a review of the Achzib cemeteries, see most recently Dixon, "Phoenician Mortuary Practice," 484–88.

17. E. Mazar, "The Achziv Burials: A Test-Case for Phoenician-Punic Burial Customs" (PhD dissertation, Hebrew University, 1996), 11.

18. These tombs were previously dated to Iron IB, but have since been redated to Iron IIA. Edrey et al., "Iron Age II Tombs," 150–81.

19. M. Dayagi- Mendels, *The Akhziv Cemeteries: The Ben- Dor Excavations, 1941– 1944* (Jerusalem: Israel Antiquities Authority, 2002), 2.

20. M. Prausnitz, "Achvib," in *New Encyclopedia of Archaeological Excavations in the Holy Land*, vol. 1, ed. E. Stern (Jerusalem: Israel Exploration Society & Carta; New York: Simon & Schuster, 1993), 34.

21. E. Mazar, *The Phoenicians in Achziv: The Southern Cemetery. Jerome L. Joss Expedition, Final Report of the Excavations, 1988– 1990*, Cuadernos de Arquelogía Mediterránea 7 (Barcelona: Laboratorio de Arqueología, Universidad Pompeu Fabra de Barcelona: Carrera Edicio, 2001).

22. Mazar, "The Achziv Burials," 5; Mazar, *The Phoenicians in Achziv*, 49.

23. The skeletal analysis for Tomb C.1 can be found in Table 3.1.

24. For more on drinking holes, see the discussion in Mazar, *The Phoenicians in Achziv*, 75– 76. There Mazar notes that ashlar constructed tombs with drinking holes are also found in 14th– 13th c. Ugarit, as well as on Cyprus at the 14th–13th c. site of Enkomi. This style continues on in the Phoenician world, especially in the Phoenician colonies.

25. The most notable differences have to do with the presence of beds/benches and the construction of the entrance. Mazar, *The Phoenicians in Achziv*, 77.

80   THE BURIALS OF CHILDREN IN ANCIENT ISRAEL

26. One other notable feature occurs in the vicinity of the shaft tombs. Vessels containing cremation burials were found placed in a natural crevice between two of the shaft tombs.
27. Mazar, "The Achziv Burials," 8.
28. At least one child was found in this type of pit burial wearing bracelets and beads. Mazar, "The Achziv Burials," 6.
29. E. Mazar, *The Phoenician Family Tomb N. 1 at the Northern Cemetery of Achziv (10th- 6th centuries BCE): Sam Turner Expedition, Final Report of the Excavations*, Cuadernos de Arqueología Mediterránea (Barcelona: Ediciones Bellaterra, 2004).
30. It appears that aside from T. N.1, the remainder of all tombs and their contents were cleared from this area and secondarily reburied to make room for the cremation cemetery. Mazar, *Phoenician Family Tomb N. 1*, 13. For details of the crematorium structure, its construction, and how it operated, see E. Mazar, *The Northern Cemetery of Achziv (10th- 6th c. BCE): The Tophet Site. Final Report of the Excavations (1992-2004)*, Cuadernos de Arqueología Mediterránea 19-20 (Barcelona: Bellaterra, 2013), 26-27, 186-200.
31. Mazar, *Northern Cemetery of Achziv*, 29.
32. The children were found in Urn 4, Urn 8, and Urn 9 respectively. In comparing the Achzib cremations to those of burial populations utilizing cremation in the wider Levant (Syria, Phoenicia, and Aramea), Smith et al. concluded that of the 300 burials examined, only two contained infants, and these were likely included in the cremations because they died at the time of childbirth. P. Smith and G. Kahila Bar- Gal, "Age Biases in Phoenician Funerary Practices," *Eretz-Israel: Archaeology, History, and Geographical Studies* 33 (2018): 169-70.
33. Mazar, *Northern Cemetery of Achziv*, 29.
34. On Phoenician religion and the afterlife, see the overview by López-Bertran, "Funerary Ritual," 293-309.
35. Mazar, *The Phoenicians in Achziv*, 157. See too M. Cradic, "Residential Burial and Social Memory in the Middle Bronze Age Levant," *NEA* 81 (2018): 191-201.
36. The excavations at 'Atlit occurred in the early 1930s, and the published reports are somewhat conflicted on the dating of the Iron II shaft tombs. I have found reports stating they were used in the 8th, 7-6th, and 5-4th centuries BCE. C. N. Johns, "Excavations at 'Atlit (1930-1)," *QDAP* 2 (1933): 41-104; C. N. Johns, "Excavation of Pilgrims' Castle, 'Atlit (1933): Cremated Burials of Phoenician Origin," *QDAP* 6 (1937/38): 135.
37. The first child (Burial ii) measured 80 cm / 2'7". According to height and age charts published by the World Health Organization, this length would fit an infant around eighteen months old. See sft_lhfa_boys_p_0_2.pdf (who.int). Even taking into consideration that the individual buried here may have been shorter in stature than modern children, the size indicates a very young individual buried in the shaft tomb. The identification of the second child comes by way of comparison: Burial ii "may be compared, for example, with one of the original burials in tomb 21 B, also the burial of a small girl, which had similar beads, bracelets and anklets, arranged in the same way." This child had a silver ankh pendant, a necklace of carnelian beads, a bead of gold, and various amulets (Johns, "Excavations at 'Atlit," 78; see too Johns, "Excavations at Pilgrims' Castle," 135). The burial items are found in Plates XXVI and XXXIII. Unfortunately, the preliminary report did not include images of the burial itself.
38. For example, John Green has demonstrated that jewelry, such as anklets and bracelets, was more a designation of age rather than gender in the Iron Age burials at Tel es-Sai'diyeh, Jordan. John Green, "Anklets and the Social Construction of Gender and Age in the Late Bronze and Early Iron Age Southern Levant," in *Archaeology and Women: Ancient and Modern Issues*, ed. S. Hamilton, R. D. Whitehouse, and K. Wright (Walnut Creek, CA: Left Coast Press, 2007), 283-311.
39. Johns, "Excavations at Pilgrims' Castle," 127.
40. See, for example, the burials listed as xi a, xi b, xi c. On ritually "killing" vessels, see B. Alpert Nakhai, "When Considering Infants and Jar Burials in the Middle Bronze Age Southern Levant," in *Tell It in Gath: Studies in the History and Archaeology of Israel. Essays in Honor of A. M. Maier on the Occasion of His Sixtieth Birthday*, Ägypten und Altes Testament 90, ed. I. Shai, J. R. Chadwick, L. Hitchcock, A. Dagan, C. McKinney and J. Uziel (Münster: Zaphon, 2018), 110-11.
41. Bloch-Smith, *Judahite Burial Practices*, 217.

BURIALS IN PHOENICIAN-INFLUENCED AREAS   81

42. Alexandre and Stern, "Phoenician Cremation Burials"; Aubet, "Phoenician Cemetery of Tyre," 144– 145; M. Aubet, F. J. Núñez, and L. Trelliśo, "La necropolis fenicia de Tiro- Al Bass: En el contexto funerano fenicio oriental," in *Huelra Arquelógica* 20 (Universitat Pompeu Fabra: Barcelona, 2003), 46–61.

43. While cremation may not have been understood by the Phoenicians as a specifically "Phoenician" burial style, Dixon notes, "It seems quite likely that Phoenician neighbors viewed the practice of cremation (and perhaps other aspects of the Phoenician mortuary system) as 'ethnically' Phoenician, even if the Phoenicians themselves did not." Dixon, "Phoenician Mortuary Practice," 541.

44. The cremation burials at Tell el-'Ajjul are only known through the plates published in the report. No narrative description accompanies them. The cremation burials in question are Cemetery J burials 1102, 1106, 1120, 1134, 1135–36, 1151, 1153, and Cemetery A burial 1160. With so many cremations, it is unfortunate that there is no description of their contents, nor any skeletal analysis (Culican, "The Graves at Tell er-Reqeish," *Australian Journal of Biblical Archaeology* 2 [1973]: 67 and 67 n. 3). I include Tell el-Ajjul in my list here because it is not impossible, based on other cemeteries from nearby Tell er-Reqeish and Tell el-Far'ah, that some of the urns might have contained infant or child burials.

45. Culican, "Graves at Tell er-Requeish."

46. A. Biran, "Tell er-Ruqeish to Tell er-Ridan," *IEJ* 24.2 (1974): 141–42; J. Ory, "Other Discoveries: 1 July 1928 to 30 June 1940," *QDAP* 10 (1944): 205.

47. Many of the jars contained Cypro-Phoenician bottles, and two jars contained two scarabs and beads of carnelian or blue glazed paste. Ory, "Other Discoveries," 205.

48. Culican, "Graves at Tell er-Reqeish," 68. C. N. Johns noted that the burial urns from Reqeish had decoration similar to those urns discovered at Achzib. C. N. Johns, "Discoveries in Palestine since 1939," *PEQ* 80.2 (1948): 88.

49. Culican, "Graves at Tell er-Reqeish," 68.

50. E. Stern suggests that er-Reqeish might be the Assyrian harbor, "closed Karum of Egypt," built by Sargon II. E. Stern, *Archaeology of the Land of the Bible*, vol. 2: *The Assyrian, Babylonian, and Persian Periods, 732–332 BCE* (New York: Doubleday, 2001), 21.

51. The grave goods for these unique burials included carnelian, ball and drop beads, bronze anklets, toe rings, earrings of gold, silver, an electrum, a bowl, gold earrings, and other beads. O. Tufnell, "Burials in Cemeteries 100 and 200," in *Beth- Pelet I (Tell Fara)*, ed. W. F. Petrie (London: British School of Archaeology in Egypt, 1930), 11.

52. Petrie, *Beth-Pelet I*, Plate LXVII.

53. Culican, "Graves at Tell er-Reqeish," 95–96; Petrie, *Beth-Pelet I*, 1–15.

54. Tufnell, "Burials in Cemeteries," 12.

55. Petrie, *Beth-Pelet I*, 13.

56. Statistics on infant mortality before age five in the nineteenth-century United States, Western Desert of Egypt, and Bedouin cemetery of Tell es- Hesi are listed as between 40% amd 50%. Smith and Bar-Gal, "Age Biases," 165.

57. Smith and Bar-Gal, "Age Biases," 170. However, the existence of tophets in the Phoenician colonies might argue against this conclusion.

58. Mazar, *Northern Cemetery of Achziv*, 214, 228.

59. Smith and Bar-Gal, "Age Biases," 170.

60. I myself have argued for a gradual entrance into full membership of the household based on age. K. H. Garroway, *Children in the Ancient Near Eastern Household*, EANEC 3 (Winona Lake, IN: Eisenbrauns, 2014), 239–46.

61. Aubet, "Cremation and Social Memory," 78.

62. J. Cerezo- Román, "Unpacking Personhood and Funerary Customs in the Hohokam Area of Southern Arizona," *American Antiquity* 80 (2015): 354.

63. See, for example, the reports from Achzib, Khaldé, and Tyre Al-Bass.

64. Mazar, *Northern Cemetery of Achziv*, 214, 228.

65. Aubet, "Cremation and Social Memory," 77–78; Michael Boyd, "Destruction and Other Material Acts of Transformation in Mycenaean Funerary Practice," in *THRAVSMA: Contextualising the Intentional Destruction of Objects in the Bronze Age Aegean and Cyprus*, ed. K. Harrell and J. Driessen (Louvain: Presses Universitaires de Louvain, 2015), 155–162.

82 THE BURIALS OF CHILDREN IN ANCIENT ISRAEL

66. On the relationship between shiny objects and protective measures, see Carol Meyers, *Rediscovering Eve: Ancient Israelite Women in Context* (Oxford: Oxford University Press, 2013), 154.
67. On bells and rattles as protection for children, see K. H. Garroway, "Rattle and Hum: A Reassessment of Closed-Form Rattles in the Southern Levant," *Journal of the American Oriental Society* 143 (2023): 173–94.
68. This point will be argued extensively for burials in Judah in Chapter 6.

4

Surveying Infant and Child Burials in Iron I Israel and Iron II Judah and Israel

This chapter concludes the overview of infant and child burials within the Iron Age by turning inland, where the burial picture becomes even more complex. While Iron I and II burials are found in the lowland sites, the area of the Central Highlands presents a much different picture. Moving chronologically, this chapter will first address the so-called invisible burials of the Iron I highlands, which contrast with the "family tombs" of the Iron II. It then moves to examine a sampling of other infant and child burials found in the Galilee, Jezreel Valley, Sharon Plain, and the Hill Country.

The "Missing" Tombs of the Iron Age I Central Highlands

The Central Highlands presents a special challenge to those studying Iron Age burials for the simple reason that the burial record goes relatively silent in the Early Iron Age, resurfacing again in the Iron II period. Moreover, reanalysis of the few burials that were labeled Iron I demonstrates that they might have been misdated.[1] Did the inhabitants abruptly stop burying their dead? Probably not. Why did burials again appear in the Iron Age II, this time in rock-cut tombs and caves, with benches and niches?

The general consensus is that the inhabitants of the Iron I highlands buried their dead in simple inhumations without grave goods.[2] Herein lies the rub. In the Late Bronze Age, the same region had a much lower population density, but a bountiful burial record. Comparatively speaking, Late Bronze Age tombs in the area were afforded a rich assortment of grave goods.[3] One might expect that when the population density rose in the Iron I, the visible burial record would, at the very least, mirror in number that of

The Dying Child. Kristine Henriksen Garroway, Oxford University Press. © Oxford University Press 2025.
DOI: 10.1093/9780197566718.003.0005

the previous period. Many reasons for a shift to "invisible" graves have been suggested. Raz Kletter suggests the Iron I society was much poorer, lacking a surplus of items for grave goods. Avraham Faust theorizes that the burials reflect not a social reality but an egalitarian ethos that is seen in other aspects of Iron I society as well.[4] Noting the collapse of the Late Bronze Age and the metal industry, David Ilan addresses the specific issue of missing grave goods, commenting that the scarcity of metal led people to cease burying their dead with jewelry as seen in other periods.[5] The implication is that individual burials in simple graves and without grave goods would be lost over time in the archaeological record.

There are a few places where burials from the Late Bronze II were thought to be reused in the Iron I. Kletter discounts many of these, asking whether the date should be "the crucial criterion for distinguishing between an Iron I and a Late Bronze tomb."[6] His question is whether we are to pay more attention to cultural shifts or dates. Seeing as how the movement from Late Bronze II to Iron I was long and complicated and occurred at different times throughout the Hill Country, cultural shifts might seem a more reliable indicator. Yet Rivka Gonen's study of the burials in the Late Bronze Age Hill Country offers fodder for some pushback. She noted that cave burials were the preferred burial in the Hill Country, calling them "indigenous" burials (as opposed to foreign) based on the fact that we find such burials carry over from previous time periods. Cave burials continued in use during the Iron II period as well, especially in the Hill Country outside of Judah. Unfortunately, in cases where caves were reused, bones remain either in poor condition or were deposited in such a way that makes assigning them to one period over another impossible.

Three things stand out with respect to these theories on the "missing" burial record. First, scholars are in agreement that the Iron I society of the Central Highlands did not abandon the dead. Second, the lack of visibility does not necessarily mean the cessation of mortuary activities. Third, and perhaps the most important aspect of the Iron I burial record, is that it treats everyone the same, *including infants and children*. To my knowledge, no one has stressed this point. Unlike other places and periods where we see infants or young children in jar burials, placed in intramural pits, separated from the adults in their burial community, or simply missing, we find the burial record for the residents of the Iron I Hill Country absent for all ages, and there is uniformity in the absence.

The "Family" Tombs of the Iron Age II in the Central Highlands

The mortuary record of the Iron II period is markedly different; burials appear again in the Central Highlands. Rock-cut tombs or caves with secondary burial pits and benches/niches have become synonymous with Judahite burials; however, such burials also appear in sites located within Samaria.[7] By the seventh to sixth c. these tombs regularly included bone repository pits. Unfortunately, repository pits are often found empty, and even when they do contain bones, the skeletal breakdown is not always taken into consideration. The discussion below is therefore limited by the available data. Sites with documented skeletal remains in Judah include Ketef Hinnom, Mt. Zion, Ma'alot in Jerusalem, Khirbet Beit Lei, and Tel 'Ira, as well as the border sites of Tel Hadid and Horbat Tittora South. The sites in Israel include remains found at Khirbet Shemsin, Khirbet el-Lauz, and Samaria.[8] While the number of sites with skeletal remains is low, the sample here does provide a litmus test for using the term "family tomb." Excavation reports and scholars have long used this term for bench tombs and tombs with repository pits with the assumption that they were family tombs. For example, the excavation report of Gibeon calls the burial there a family tomb, yet there are no bones; the "family" aspect is just assumed.[9] Scholars apply this nomenclature to tombs based primarily on their architecture. Since the majority of the tombs have no skeletal remains, the information collected below will help determine not only if there are infants and children buried in the tombs but also whether the term "family tomb" is accurate.[10]

Table 4.1 provides evidence for the presence of infants and children in the bench tombs of Judah.[11] In addition to the information given in the table, a few more details are important to note. All the reports said that the skeletal material was in poor condition, indicating that the total number of individuals may have been even greater than reported. This statement could be especially true for infants and children, whose bones are not fully developed and more friable to begin with. In addition, at each of these sites, children were intermingled with the adults. This is true for skeletal remains found on benches and in repository pits. At Mt. Zion, primary burials were removed, and the remains placed in two piles of long bones and skulls respectively. Notably, "All the material was mixed up without anatomical connection between the bones."[12] This signifies that the bones of children

Table 4.1 Rock-Cut Tombs in Judah with Benches/Repository Pits

Site	Source	Description
Ketef Hinnom (breakdown)	Barkay, 1994 Nagar, 2015	IA II bench tombs were discovered. Chamber 25 included 95 individuals and 1,000 + grave goods. Investigations of a repository identified individuals of all ages: 5 infants, 11 children 9–11 years old, 7 children 10–19 years old, and 24 adults.
Mt. Zion (long bones)	Arensburg and Yak, 1985 Kloner and Davis, 1994	7th c. tomb with two rooms and a variety of grave goods. MNI of 43 individuals: 26 adults and 17 juveniles, children and infants.[a]
North of Jerusalem, in the Ma'alot Dafnah neighborhood	Kloner, 2001, 95–97	8th–6th c. cave tomb with benches along the walls and a repository pit. The bones were highly deteriorated, and the report does not specify where each of the individuals was found. MNI 6 individuals: 3 adults, 1 "youth" 16–19 years old, 1 child 4–5 years old, 1 infant 1–2 years old.
Khirbet Beit Lei	Haas, 1963 Naveh, 1963	Two caves with bench tombs dated no later than the 6th c. Adults were found in Cave 1 placed on the benches surrounding the cave walls. Two of the benches held an adult female and a child. Cave 2 contained no benches, a male, 2 females, and a young child 5–6 years old. The latter three burials were all disturbed.
Tel 'Ira	Baron and Beith-Arieh, listed in Bloch-Smith, 1992, 203, 233[b] Beith-Arieh and Baron, 1999 Eshed, Wish-Barataz, and Hershkovitz, 1999	Tomb 15 is dated to the 10th–9th c. Chamber 1 has a MNI 23. At least 12 individuals were lying on benches, including adults and children. Chamber II contained an adult and child, while 11 individuals, adults and children alike, were identified in Chamber III. Tomb 13 contained 3 burial chambers and a small niche, which the excavators suggest many have been an infant burial. Twelve other burials of individuals 14+ years were discovered. Tomb 14 (8th–7th c.) contained a MNI of 10 individuals, 5 children and 5 adults. One of the children was a flexed burial of a 2-year-old on the floor.

[a] The age distribution was listed as 0–6 years old = 30%; 6–16 years old = 18%; 16–30 = 10%; 30–40 years old = 22%; 40–50 years old = 14%; and over 50 = 6%. The excavators note that "this age distribution differs from that of other assemblages of skeletons of the same period in which the proportion of adults of over 40 is greater and that of children under 6 is smaller." A. Kloner and D. Davis, "A Burial Cave of the Later First Temple Period on the Slope of Mount Zion," in *Ancient Jerusalem Revealed*, ed. H. Geva (Jerusalem: Israel Exploration Society, 1994), 110.

[b] Bloch-Smith, presumably following the language given in her sources, uses both "juvenile" and "subadult" to refer to children.

were not excluded, nor were they separated from the adult bones; they were treated in the same manner.

The most detailed and extensive Iron II cemetery is that of Tel 'Ira, where thirty rock-cut bench tombs have been identified.[13] It is also the most southern site in Judah, described as a stronghold in the Negev. The tombs were chamber tombs, some with benches and others with niches carved into the walls. While skeletal remains were not found in every tomb, the corpus collected is significant enough to draw some conclusions regarding how the living buried their dead. If the reports of Tomb 14 and Tomb 15 represent a pattern followed at Tel 'Ira, then it appears that infants and children were treated the same as adults; they are all found placed on benches and on the floor. Thus, age does not appear to be a factor in differentiating burial method or placement for these burials. The one possible differentiated burial would be the niche burial in Tomb 13, Chamber 104. Suggested as an infant burial, the niche has no parallel in any other excavated tomb.[14] However, without the presence of skeletal material in the niche, the excavators' conclusion remains speculation.

The physical anthropology report provides information on the skeletal population of the Tel 'Ira cemetery as a whole.[15] For example, Tomb 23, which was not described by the excavators, included the burial of a young child (up to five years old), older child (ten to fourteen years old), and adolescent (fourteen to eighteen years old), in addition to four adults. A total of ten tombs yielded a MNI of sixty-one individuals: thirty-seven adults and twenty-four children.[16] The category of children is further broken down as follows: thirteen young children (up to five years old), two children (five to ten years old), three slightly older children (ten to fourteen years old), and six adolescents (fourteen to eighteen years old). Statistically speaking, almost half of the children died before eighteen years of age. Of these children, about 21.3% died within the first five years of life.[17] If the burials do indeed represent family burials, then it is estimated that "in order to maintain zero population growth, a minimum of four children should be born to each family."[18] Such statistics are in line with what scholars who draw upon ethnography and paleo-demography suggest for Iron Age Israel.[19]

The site called "South of Ḥorbat Tittora" lies at the border of Judah and Israel.[20] There, Iron Age II burials were discovered in caves modified for burial and containing repository pits.[21] The skeletal remains were in relatively good condition, allowing for a physical anthropology report, the results of which are compiled in Table 4.2. Again, the site verifies the presence

88 THE BURIALS OF CHILDREN IN ANCIENT ISRAEL

Table 4.2 Skeletal Remains from the Caves South of Ḥorbat Tittora by Age

Location	0–4 years	5–9 years	10–14 years	15–17 years	17 + years	Unknown	Total
Cave 1 Room A	0	0	0	0	3	0	3
Cave 1 Room B	0	0	1	0	2	0	3
Cave 1[a] Room C	5	3	3	0	26	0	37
Cave 1 Room D	3	0	0	1	0	2	6
Cave 2	4	1	0	1	5	6	17
Cave 3	1	1	0	1	10	3	16
Cave 4	0	0	0	0	3	0	3
Cave 6	0	0	0	0	3	0	3
Total	13	5	4	3	52	11	88

[a] The burials here were listed as Iron II–Hellenistic. The report did not distinguish between skeletal remains in the different periods.

of all ages in the tombs. Of the seventy-seven aged individuals, children comprise 32.4% of the burial population, with children under five years old comprising 16.8%. These numbers are slightly lower than those of Tel 'Ira, but still suggest that they could be family tombs.

Northwest of Ḥorbat Tittora is the Iron II burial site at Tel Hadid, which lies at the edge of the highlands.[22] Estimated to have gone out of use sometime between 733 and 720 BCE, this site included a cave with benches and a repository pit. The skeletal remains were still on the benches, with additional bones found in the repository pit that were in a state of poor preservation. The skeletal remains on the benches were also in poor condition and were not collected or measured, but rather studied on site. Bones belonging to a child between one to one and a half years old and "a mature teenager" sixteen to nineteen years old were identified, in addition to teeth belonging to three other individuals who were four to six years old, fifteen to twenty years old, and forty-plus years old. While the skeletal remains were meager, it again appears as if this burial location was used for all ages.

Bench tombs were used during the Iron II in the highland region of Samaria as well, as attested to by sites such as Khirbet Shemsin, Samaria, and Khirbet el-Lauz.[23] Excavations of the capital city, Samaria, found seven burial caves with benches and repository pits. Here again, the bones were rather poorly preserved. The only identifiable remains were those of a thirteen- to fourteen-year-old individual laid out on a bench.[24] Khirbet Shemsin, on the western side of the Samaria Highlands, also contained identifiable skeletal remains.[25] A cut tomb included two caves reached by a central shaft. Cave 1 had benches on the south and north. The northern bench held an adult male, and the southern bench a female and two children. Adults and children alike were found placed on the floor to the eastern side in Cave 2. This cave had one more unique feature, two natural depressions in the ground that were covered with a stone slab. When the slab was removed, the remains of two infants were found, one in each niche. While the skeletal remains are somewhat limited for Judah and Samaria, it does appear that infants and children were not excluded by default from rock-cut bench tombs, making the moniker "family tombs" appropriate in these cases.

Additional Burials in Northern Regions

Outside of the highlands, Late Bronze Age burial methods again continue into Iron I. Sites such as Megiddo, Gibeon, Dothan, Tell el-Far'ah North, and Zeror use cist burials, pit burials, and rock-cut and chamber tombs. Along with the continuity in burial methods, there is also continuity between Late Bronze Age and Iron Age I ceramics. As David Ilan notes, "The Iron I material is often deposited in the same tombs as Late Bronze material; an expression of continuous use, likely by the same kin groups [making it] . . . difficult, or impossible, to isolate Iron I material from Late Bronze material."[26] In addition to the difficulties posed for the Iron I, there are sites that start in the Iron I and continue into the Iron II. Then there are reports that simply list a burial as "Iron Age," and other, older, reports that have Iron I materials that have been subsequently redated to other time periods. All this is by way of stating that the following discussion is by necessity somewhat limited with respect to the Iron I. The picture in the Iron II is a bit clearer as more information is available. The sampling of sites presented below begins in the north and moves south.

The Galilee

In 2004, a salvage excavation to the north of Tel Dan discovered a mix of burials dated to the seventh to sixth c., including burials laid on bedrock, cremations, jar burials, and a tomb.[27] Such a mix is reminiscent of the variety seen at Azor in the Iron I and later at Achzib. Notably, the burials on bedrock were covered with stones. Many of the individuals were identified as "young," between the ages of fifteen and twenty years. However, later in the report it lists the grave of an adult with two infants (ages one and a half years and six months) placed nearby. Two jar burials were also discovered. One was covered with a bowl, but the age of the individual was not given. The second was listed as a "juvenile," based on the size of the bracelet found inside the jar. It is thought that a standing stone nearby might have served as a *maṣṣebot*. The report also mentions adult cremations and a possible site where cremations took place.[28] The variety of burial methods is instructive, particularly the discovery of individuals placed on bedrock and in grooves. Such burials are rare but support the theory that many of the "invisible" burials in the archaeological record were indeed simple burials devoid of elaborate grave goods. With the case of infants and children, it is especially significant that infants were included within this burial group of differentiated burials, as well as burials used for other members of the community. Again, this furthers the conclusion that infants were afforded some degree of personhood. Moreover, it demonstrates a desire to bury infants close to other members of society.

Tel Kinnerot / Tell el-'Orēme is located on the western shore of the Sea of Galilee (Kinneret). Iron Age I burials were discovered inside and outside of the city walls. Of those burials discovered within the city walls, a few tombs stand out, such as a tomb placed under a house floor in which a twenty- to thirty-year-old female and a four-year-old child were found "placed lying on large, thick storage jar sherds."[29] Additional sherds covered the skeletons. Grave goods included a flask and a pierced seashell. While not a typical intermural jar burial, the description is nonetheless reminiscent of a deconstructed jar burial. Intramural burials are known from the Canaanite Bronze Ages, but they are increasingly rare in the Iron Age outside of the Philistine coast.[30]

Three sites in the vicinity of Nazareth were excavated as salvage digs, all of which uncovered caves from the Iron Age. The first was a series of four caves excavated near the Church of the Annunciation in Nazareth. These caves were first hewn in the Intermediate Bronze Age but reused again during subsequent periods. Cave D included skeletal remains and grave goods that were dated to the transition between Iron IB–IIA.[31] This cave is described as a family burial cave, with individuals ages six to eight, fifteen to twenty, twenty to thirty, thirty, and forty years old being identified.[32] A similar

Iron Age burial cave was discovered a little further south of the Church of the Annunciation in 1973.[33] This cave also had a repository pit similar to those found in rock-cut caves. Unfortunately, all the human remains were too fragmentary to undergo any meaningful analysis.[34] In Upper Nazareth, at Har Yona, a cave with a shaft entrance was excavated in 1998.[35] The cave appeared to be used for only a short time, as burials were all found in articulation, with no burials pushed to the sides. Individuals were laid supine with either head or feet pointing toward the entrance. Fourteen skeletons were discovered, including eleven adults, "one adolescent (10–18 years), one child (3–4 years) and one infant (about one year old)." Given the short duration of the cave's use and the inclusion of individuals of all ages, the tomb is thought to be a family tomb. The ceramic assemblage dates the burial to the Iron IB–IIA (eleventh to tenth c.).[36] Three bronze bracelets and six bronze rings were found in the burials; however, their dimensions are too large to fit on a child or infant.[37] Taken together, the Iron IB–IIA burials around Nazareth attest to the presence of family burials used for individuals of all ages.

The Jezreel Valley

The Iron Age burials at Megiddo are multifaceted and include intramural and extramural burials. Some appear within the site itself, while others are found extramurally. Within the site proper, the Late Iron I (Stratum VIA) included adult and infant burials.[38] Thirteen burials total were peppered throughout the domestic structures found of Area CC Squares Q9 and R9.[39] Two of the burials were intramural jar burials of infants. All the remaining burials were of adults. The inclusions of adults and children within the domestic sphere appears to be a continuation of methods used in earlier periods at Megiddo.[40] The houses among which they were found were "four-room" houses, with courtyards, stone and wood pillars, ovens, basins, querns, and so forth.

The extramural burials of Megiddo are also well documented and cover a long period of occupation at the site. Tomb 37 is particularly informative.[41] Multiple Early Iron Age burials were found within the cave. Tomb 37B was a rectangular grave with rounded corners dug into the rock floor into which an infant was placed in a supine position. Its grave goods included iron bracelets but no pottery. Tomb 37C comprised two connecting pits that were cut into the floor. The first pit, C1, held an infant in a supine position sans

92 THE BURIALS OF CHILDREN IN ANCIENT ISRAEL

grave goods. In the second pit, C2, an infant jar burial was discovered. The infant was under one year old, and grave goods included bronze bracelets, a shell bead, a necklace with seventy-eight beads of white and light-green faience, and cloth fragments.[42] The cloth fragments suggest that the infant was shrouded before being placed in the jar. The placement of the infants in pits carved into the floor is reminiscent of those found in the Iron II burials of Khirbet Shemsin in Cave 2. These burials also resemble earlier burials in the tomb, 37K4 and 37M, both of which were Late Bronze I infant jar burials placed in depressions on the floor.[43] The two other graves cut into the floor of Tomb 37 are also dated to the Early Iron Age, but neither of them held skeletal remains.[44]

In the site of Megiddo proper, the last area to merit mention is Schumacher's Temple Precinct, where some unusual burials were discovered. Referred to in the literature as Iron II cremation burials, they are often compared with other sites where cremations were found.[45] For example, John Abercrombie notes that the spouted jug and the pithoi used for the Megiddo burials find parallels at Tell er-Reqeish and Tell el-Far'ah South.[46] While Schumacher's 1908 report was sparse, it includes some shocking information. Unlike the other sites within ancient Israel or any of the Phoenician sites examined in the previous chapter, the cremated remains within the five Megiddo urns were listed as "sehr kleiner Kinder," in other words, infants.[47]

Schumacher's identification of the area as a temple appears to be based on the architecture, *maṣṣebot*, and small finds in the two "temple" rooms, including an idol of a white stone that broke when picked up, vases, plates, small jugs, a basalt grinding stone, a small stone column of limestone, and a three-footed basalt pot.[48] The cremation urns themselves were found in two locations within the "temple" area. The first location included a cluster of three or four urns of yellowish-gray material. These had no handles and were filled with sifted soil, ashes, and bones: "Die Urnen waren mit gesiebter Erde, Asche, und den Resten sehr kleinen Kinder angefüllt."[49] He then goes on to say that the skulls of the infants were found at the bottom of the urns with the knees bent at the top. He notes that only small fragments of the skulls remained, with a little more of the ribs, vertebrae, and thigh bones. There is nothing at this point specifically stating that the skeletons were burned in a cremation. The report states that the urns stood on fire debris one meter above the floor, implying that the urns were placed there after the temple had gone into decay or disuse.[50]

The final urn was found in a higher layer. This urn was a different shape, described as double-pointed. It contained the atomized bones of a young child. When discussing this urn, Schumacher states this one and the other three showed signs of burning.[51] It is not entirely clear from the report whether the bones were cremated or placed in the jars as infant jar burials and burned as a result of a subsequent fire. If these were cremations, then they are of a much different nature than those seen in the Phoenician homeland or on the coastal sites further south. Moreover, Megiddo would be the only site that used cremations exclusively for infants and that placed them within a building/temple complex, rather than in a cemetery complex. The closest contemporary parallel would be the placement of later child inhumations at the site of the crematorium in Achzib. If, however, they were jar burials, then the discovery of infants within a site is not out of the ordinary. Moreover, placement within a sacred space is not entirely without precedent, as seen with the infant jar burials under the pavement of the Middle Bronze Age High Place at Gezer.[52] However, placement in a building above ground is a bit strange for jar burials, especially if the building had gone out of use prior to their installation within it. Ultimately, whether infant cremations or infant jar burials, these differentiated burials attest to some measure of personhood and mortuary care given to very young members of the Megiddo society.

The Sharon Plain

Tel Zeror is located in the Sharon Plain, ten kilometers east of the Mediterranean. The cemetery included cist tombs, earthen (pit) graves, pits encircled by stones, and jar burials. Such an array is reminiscent of the variety seen at Azor to the south and at Achzib to the north.[53] The dating of the burials, however, is not clear. The report states that the burials date to the Late Bronze Age, Iron Age, and Hellenistic Period.[54] The cist graves are dated by Kiyoshi Ohata to the Iron I, while Meir Edrey suggests the ceramics demand an Iron II date.[55] The cist graves all had multiple interments, leading Ohata to conclude they were family burials.[56] In total, nine cist graves were discovered; however, no physical anthropology report was written. The only information on the remains comes from the field notes. Tomb I contained six bodies, with three in primary burial; two adults were lying extended with an infant placed beneath them. Additional burials were pushed to the side where bones and skulls were separated. Grave goods consisted of bowls and

94 THE BURIALS OF CHILDREN IN ANCIENT ISRAEL

a lamp. It is difficult to know whether the child and adults died at the same time. However, the one child buried here to the exclusion of other infants seems the exception that proves the rule; at Zeror infants and children did not merit inclusion in tombs.

The surprising find at the site belongs to the seemingly vast number of jar burials placed in the cemetery. Sixty-six jar burials and eleven pithos burials were discovered.[57] Most of the containers were covered by a bowl, preserving to some degree the remains inside. Ohata states that the jar and pithos burials belong to different periods. "Storage-jars and pithoi, of the Late Bronze and the Iron Ages and the Hellenistic Period[,] were unearthed."[58] The exact number of burials for each period is not given. However, the excavation report does state that only child and infant teeth were discovered in the jars/pithoi, meaning this type of burial was not used for adolescents or adults. Given the seeming lack of children and infants within the cist graves, it appears possible that the inhabitants of Zeror adapted the earlier Canaanite practice of infant jar burials. However, rather than burying the infants within the site, they now buried them extramurally.

The Samarian Highlands

Various cave and rock-cut tombs without benches were found in the Samarian Highlands. A survey found such tombs devoid of skeletal remains at Deir Abu Da'if, Baqa el-Gharbiya, 'Illar, and Yafit. Additional sites containing skeletal remains are seen in Table 4.3. The poor skeletal remains and brief reports do not specify much more regarding any infants and children found in the burials.

Table 4.3 Burials in the Samarian Hills

Site	Burial Type	Burial Contents
Et-Taiyba	Cave	Hundreds of bones were found; however, no specific skeletal analysis was given.
Khirbet Sirisya	Cave	Individuals of all ages (ages unspecified)
Horvat Zakur	Oval niche in kukar	An adult and child were placed in the niche. Ceramics (8th c.) and a bronze bracelet were associated with the burial.

Source: Compiled from Yezerski, "Iron Age Burial Customs," 72–98.

BURIALS IN IRON I–II JUDAH AND ISRAEL   95

Of all the burials in the Samarian Hills, Dothan provides the most data regarding infants and children. It is located due east of Zeror and sixty miles north of Jerusalem. No Iron II cemetery has been located at the site; however, jar burials, which seem more at home in the Middle Bronze Age than the Iron II, are found placed within domestic quarters.[59] These jar burials are securely dated to the eighth to seventh c. based on the typology of the storage jars.[60] Joseph Free lists a total of six infant jar burials, all found within a domestic context. Because the jar burials were not the only intramural burials, reference to the adult burials are included here for context. The first jar burial was found near two other burials, all in Area A.[61] The jar burial was found under a wall and is associated with an Assyrian bottle jar as well as an Iron II lamp.[62] One simple burial was unidentifiable but associated with an Assyrian palace ware bowl; the second simple burial was that of an adult with his back broken in two places. Free hypothesizes the person died in battle, but other explanations are also possible. For example, perhaps this person was paralyzed, understood as "other," and so given a burial outside of the cemetery. Dan Master et al. suggest this the man's back was not broken but the burial was disturbed.[63] A little further away in Area A, a third skeleton was found lying on a stone wall. Grave goods there included an Assyrian palace ware bowl and lamp.[64]

Area L was to the west of Area A. Here houses were again found built around a courtyard. Free calls the buildings at Dothan Assyrian style, while Master et al. identify them as Israelite.[65] The burials in Area L are a bit more varied, including a bathtub burial, a simple burial of a skeleton with the hands cut off and placed under the torso, and five jar burials.[66] The first three jar burials were found in House 13. One was on the pavement and two were on the walls. The two other jar burials were found under the floors of House 6.

Table 4.4 lists the gave goods associated with the burials as well as information regarding body deposition. Free understands all the burials to be related to the architecture and to the time period surrounding the Assyrian destruction of the site.[67] He further hypothesizes that the jar burials were Assyrian children, because he is tied to the idea that the Assyrians rebuilt the site. However, Master et al. interpret the burials to be unrelated to the destruction but date them as late eighth or early seventh c. burials that were cut into the ninth c. ruins, related to conflicts with Aram-Damascus and not with Assyria.[68] While both Free and Master et al. date the burials to late eighth or early seventh c., they disagree on whether the area in which the burials

96 THE BURIALS OF CHILDREN IN ANCIENT ISRAEL

Table 4.4 Intramural Burials of the Iron II Levels at Dothan

Burial	Area	Method	Field Notes on Location	Grave Goods
Jar Burial 1	Area A	Store jar	Under wall	Assyrian bottle jar, lamp
Adult Burial A	Area A	Simple grave	By wall	Assyrian palace ware bowl
Adult Burial B	Area A	Simple grave	Burial was disturbed, skeleton broken back	
Adult Burial C	Area A	Simple grave	Lying on stone wall	Assyrian palace ware bowl, lamp
Jar Burial 2	Area L	Store jar	Infant's head was east	Nine beads and an iron bracelet
Jar Burial 3	Area L	Store jar	n/a	An iron bracelet
Jar Burial 4	Area L	Store jar	n/a	None listed
Jar Burial 5	Area L	Store jar	n/a	None listed
Jar Burial 6	Area L	Store jar	n/a	None listed
Adult Burial D	Area L	Simple grave	Crushed burial, hands cut off (?), head facing south, feet facing north	Two fibulae and green stone on ring
Adult Burial E	Area L	Bathtub coffin	Near wall, contained two skulls and bones	Bowl, ring, metal pieces, and Assyrian bottle jar sherds

were located was inhabited at the time the individuals were interred. Neither Free nor Master et al. address the implications of this fact.[69] If the areas were not inhabited, then we have some randomly placed burials in houses and by walls that were in disrepair. Why would a population place individuals here? Is this an Iron II cemetery, or does it represent a desire to bury some infants and a few adults away from the rest of the society? If it is a cemetery, where is the rest of the population? On the other hand, if the areas were functioning as domestic quarters, then we see the continued practice of burying infants within domestic quarters.[70]

While it might be impossible to determine whether the houses were being reused during the later Iron II period, we can make some observations about the burial population. First, the only ceramics found were Iron II lamps and Assyrian-style ware. The bathtub coffin points to another Assyrian connection, as they begin to appear in the north after it is annexed to Assyria.[71] The jar burials, which are associated with the adult burials, would seem to belong to the same population as those burying individuals with Assyrian goods. Whether these ceramic items are the result of Assyrians who settled in the area, or were used by the local population using luxury items that came via trade to the area, is difficult to determine.[72] Nevertheless, these infants were cared for in death, placed in a jar, and afforded some degree of mortuary ritual.

Discussion of the Iron Age Burials in the Central Highlands

During the Iron I period, children and infants within the Central Highlands appear to face the same fate as the adults of their community. They are not buried within the settlement but outside the settlement. Like their adult counterparts, their burials remain invisible. In calling the Iron I burial population "invisible," studies emphasize the lack of burials. However, what they are really noting is that adults have disappeared from the mortuary record, for the majority of infants and children are never present in the mortuary record. As hinted at above, a more nuanced way of discussing the Iron I mortuary record is to note that now all individuals are treated the same, *including infants and children*. While it is possible that some Late Bronze tombs were reused, it seems most likely that all members of the Iron I highland societies buried their dead in simple graves. It is difficult to know whether the living left any temporary monument or marker of the burials, as with the passage of time piles of stones could have fallen over or been pushed aside.

The lack of a visible burial record has implications for how individuals were perceived. As discussed in the introduction, a marker of personhood carried into death was the need to protect the body from physical harm, that is, the provision of a burial. Along with this go the funerary rites associated with helping the dead body transition to its place in the afterlife. On the one hand, one could argue the silence of the burial record in the Iron I highland signals a drastic shift in the way that these societies perceived personhood. No burials, no personhood. However, most scholars agree that the Iron I society did not simply stop burying their dead.[73] Therefore, we might take to heart the idea that a lack of a visible burial record should not be equated by default with the lack of personhood. We simply lack data.

The Iron II period saw the rise of bench/niche tombs within the Central Highlands. This form was popular and well developed in Judah.[74] Such

98   THE BURIALS OF CHILDREN IN ANCIENT ISRAEL

tombs are often called family tombs. The study here collected data on the known skeletal remains from the tombs to determine whether the nomenclature is merited. As shown above, while many bones were in poor condition, all of the tombs examined contained either infants or children along with adults, and, in many cases, infants and children were both present; thus the moniker "family tomb" is apt.

Regarding personhood, we can look for markers of public rituals (burial rites) and protection from physical harm (tomb). If infants were intentionally excluded from the burial rites and protections accorded to other members of their family, it would suggest that infants had a personhood different from that of children and adults. It would also suggest the idea that infants held a different place in the household than the adults and children buried in the "family" tombs of Judah. Yet the extant data present the opposite picture: in the few cases we do have bones, there are also infants and children, meaning that burial in the family tomb was open to all ages. The one sticking point is that archaeologists do not always find as many infants and children in family tombs as ancient population demographics might suggest. It is possible that infant and child remains were overlooked by excavators or that they deteriorated over time, but it is also possible they were intentionally excluded from the family tomb. The implications of their inclusion with respect to their place in the family cult will be discussed further in the following chapters.

Other areas in the north, outside of Judah, present a more varied image. There burial methods from the Bronze Age, identified as Canaanite, persist and undergo some adaptations during the Iron Age I–II.[75] Jar burials, caves, tombs, cists, and pits continue to be used. While most northern sites employ only one or two burial methods, all of these methods are seen on the coast during the Iron II periods.[76]

Across all the sites examined, what stands out the most is the cessation of jar burials in Judah compared to the, albeit infrequent, sustained use in the north during the Iron Age. Individuals at Tel Dan North, Zeror, and Dothan interred some of their infants and children in jars, while infants at Megiddo were either interred in jars or cremated and then placed in jars. Added to these are the jar burials at sites in the realm of the Iron I Philistine and Iron II Phoenician lands. The jar burials themselves vary in location, with some found intramurally and others extramurally. While extramural jar burials are found in both Iron I and Iron II, apart from Tel Dothan, intramural jar burials appear to lose favor in the Iron II. As noted in Chapter 2, the use of jar burials to inter the youngest members of a society attests to a degree of personhood afforded through mortuary and funerary ritual. The implications of jar burials for personhood and the connection between jar burials, cremations, and the child's place in the Judahite cult will be addressed further in Chapter 7.

Notes

1. For Iron I burials see E. Bloch-Smith, *Judahite Burial Practices and Beliefs about the Dead*, JSOT Supp. 123, JSOT/ASOR Monograph Series 7 (Sheffield: JSOT Press, 1992), 168–69, 171, 177–78, 192; E. Bloch-Smith, "Resurrecting the Iron I Dead," *IEJ* 54 (2004): 77–91. For a reassessment of the dating see R. Kletter, "People without Burials? The Lack of Iron I Burials in the Central Highlands of Palestine," *IEJ* 52 (2002): 30–33. The site of Khirbet Nisya, near Ramallah, not addressed by Bloch-Smith or Kletter, was reported to have a two-chambered Iron I burial cave. A MNI of fifty people was established, comprised of eleven children and thirty-nine adults. The grave goods were jumbled and included bonze and iron bracelets, rings, pins, beads, seals, scarabs, shells, and ceramics. D. Livingston, "A MBA II and IA I Tomb (no. 65) at Khirbet Nisya," *'Atiqot* 43 (2002): 17–35.
2. Kletter, "People without Burials," 39; A. Faust, "'Mortuary Practices, Society, and Ideology': The Lack of Iron Age I Burials in the Highlands in Context," *IEJ* 54.2 (2004): 176; D. Ilan, "Iron Age Mortuary Practices and Beliefs in the Southern Levant," in *Engaging with the Dead: Exploring Changing Human Beliefs about Death, Mortality and the Human Body*, Studies in Funerary Archaeology 13, ed. J. Bradbury and C. Scarre (Oxford: Oxbow Press, 2017), 53.
3. R. Gonen, *Burial Patterns and Cultural Diversity in Late Bronze Age Canaan* (Winona Lake, IN: Eisenbrauns, 1992).
4. Faust, "Mortuary Practices," 180–83.
5. Ilan, "Iron Age Mortuary Practices," 53.
6. Kletter, "People without Burials," 33.
7. Rock-cut tombs are not a new invention. Rather, they are found in the lowland areas during the Late Bronze and make their way inland so that by Iron II they appear to be the preferred form of tomb. Gonen, *Burial Patterns*; Ilan, "Iron Age Mortuary Practices," 56; I. Yezerski, "Iron Age Burial Customs in the Samaria Highlands," *TA* 40.1 (2013): 92.
8. The delineation of Judah and Samaria follows the conclusions of Irit Yezerski, who examined markers in both culture and burials. Yezerski, "Burial-Cave Distribution and the Borders of the Kingdom of Judah toward the End of the Iron Age," *TA* 26 (1999): 253–70, esp. Figures 2 and 3.
9. H. Eshel, "The Late Iron Age Cemetery at Gibeon," *IEJ* 37.1 (1987): 1–17.
10. Unlike the previous two chapters, this chapter proceeds by presenting all the data first, reserving all observations until the discussion at the end of the chapter. Further analysis and conclusions pertaining to sites in Judah will be expounded in Chapter 6.
11. For a history of how the Judahite bench tomb developed and an overview and architectural plan of additional sites without skeletal remains, see M. Suriano, *A History of Death in the Hebrew Bible* (Oxford: Oxford University Press, 2018), 56–97.
12. B. Arensburg and Y. Rak, "Jewish Skeletal Remains from the Period of the Kings of Judah," *PEQ* 117 (1985): 30.
13. I. Beit-Arieh and A. G. Baron, "The Cemetery," in *Tel 'Ira: A Stronghold in the Biblical Negev*, Sonia and Marco Nadler Institute of Archaeology Monograph Series 15, ed. I. Beit-Arieh (Tel Aviv: Emery and Claire Yass Publications in Archaeology, Institute of Archaeology, Tel Aviv University, 1999), 129–69.
14. Beit-Arieh and Baron, "The Cemetery," 147.
15. V. Eshed, S. Wish-Baratz, and I. Hershkovitz, "Human Skeletal Remains," in Beit-Arieh, *Tel 'Ira*, 495–510.
16. Eshed et al., "Human Skeletal Remains," Table 17.1.
17. Eshed et al., "Human Skeletal Remains," Table 17.2.

100 THE BURIALS OF CHILDREN IN ANCIENT ISRAEL

18. Eshed et al., "Human Skeletal Remains," 500.
19. See C. Meyers, *Rediscovering Eve: Ancient Israelite Women in Context* (Oxford: Oxford University Press, 2013), 110; I. Hershkovitz, "The Effect of Mating Type on Growth and Development of Children in South Sinai Bedouin Isolates" (PhD dissertation, Tel Aviv University, 1984).
20. Following Yezereski's reconstruction, the site would be in the area of Samaria. Yezereski, "Burial-Cave Distribution," Figure 2.
21. E. Kogan-Zehavi, "Tombs and Installations from the Iron Age II to the Byzantine Period from S. Ḥorbat Tittora," *'Atiqot* 72 (2012): 13–92 (in Hebrew).
22. E. Yannai and Y. Nagar, "A Burial Cave from the Iron Age II and Early Roman Period North of Tel Hadid," *'Atiqot* 70 (2012): 1–20 (in Hebrew).
23. Yezerski, "Iron Age Burial Customs." No remains were listed for Khirbet el-Lauz.
24. Yezerski, "Iron Age Burial Customs," 84. For an overview of the earlier excavations by K. Kenyon and E. Sukenik, see Bloch-Smith, *Judahite Burial Practices*, 197. Here it is mentioned that Tomb 103 had drains and pits like those dated to an earlier period in Ugarit.
25. Yezerski, "Iron Age Burial Customs," 75–76; N. Aizik and Y. Peleg, "An Iron Age IIb Burial Cave to the East of Khirbet Shemsin," in *Excavations and Discoveries in Samaria*, Judea and Samaria Publications 9, ed. I. Yezerski (Jerusalem: IAA, 2009), 201–4 (in Hebrew).
26. Ilan, "Iron Age Mortuary Practices," 52; Kletter, "People without Burials," 29–35; Bloch-Smith, *Judahite Burial Practices*, 152–59.
27. These materials have only been recorded in a preliminary report. M. Hartal, "Tel Dan (North)," *Hadashot Arkheologiyot* 118 (2006), https:// www.hadas hot- esi.org.il/ report _ det ail_ eng. aspx?id = 342.
28. Only one cremated individual was aged. Found in a hole-mouth krater, this individual was over twenty years old.
29. S. Wolff and G. Edelstein, "The 1964 Excavation at Tell el-'Orēme," in *Kinneret II: Results of the Excavation at Tel el 'Orēme in 1994– 2008*, vol. 1, Ägypten und Altes Testament 120, ed. W. Zwickel and J. Pakkala (Münster: Zaphon, 2024), 610–11.
30. See Chapter 1 for an overview of burials in earlier time periods.
31. Y. Alexandre, "Burial Caves from the Intermediate Bronze Age, Middle Bronze Age, and Iron Ages at Nazareth," *'Atiqot* 93 (2018): 42.
32. Alexandre, "Burial Caves," 7. See also Table 1 on page 7, prepared by Yossi Nagar.
33. F. Vitto, "An Iron Age Burial Cave in Nazareth," *'Atiqot* 42 (2001): 159–69.
34. Vitto, "Iron Age Burial Cave," 160.
35. Y. Alexandre, "An Iron Age IB/ IIA Burial Cave at Har Yona, Upper Nazareth," *'Atiqot* 44 (2003): 183–89.
36. Ceramics included three store jars with dipper juglets placed inside, additional juglets, a lamp, and bowls. No Philistine or Phoenician pottery was included in the burial (Alexandre, "Iron Age IB/IIA Burial," 184, Plan 1).
37. Alexandre, "Iron Age IB/IIA Burial," 187, Plan 3.
38. T. P. Harrison, *Megiddo 3: Final Report on the Stratum VI Excavations*, OI Publications 127 (Chicago: Oriental Institute, 2004), Appendix A, 109–11.
39. Harrison, *Megiddo 3*, 19–20.
40. M. Martin, M. Cradic, and R. Kalisher, "Area K: Intramural Pit and Jar Burials (Level K-10)," in *Megiddo VI: The 2010– 2014 Seasons*, ed. I. Finkelstein and M. Martin (Winona Lake, IN: Eisenbrauns, 2022), 224–91.
41. This cave was used as a dwelling, workshop, and burial location from the Early Bronze I to the Iron Age. P. L. O. Guy, *Megiddo Tombs* (Chicago: University of Chicago Press, 1938), 74–79, 138.
42. Harrison, *Megiddo 3*, 72–73.
43. Gonen, *Burial Patterns*, 46.
44. Guy, *Megiddo Tombs*, 79, 81.
45. Bloch-Smith, *Judahite Burial Practices*, 244–45.
46. J. R. Abercrombie, "Palestinian Burial Practices from 1200 to 60 BCE" (PhD dissertation, University of Pennsylvania, 1979), 304–5.
47. G. Schumacher, *Tell et Mutesellim: Bericht über die 1903 bis 1905 mit Unterstützung SR. Majestät des deutschen Kaisers und der Deutschen orient Gesellschaft vom Deutschen Verein zur Erforschung Palästinas veranstalteten Ausgrabung* (Leipzig: Ruldof Haupt, 1908), 122.
48. Schumacher, *Tell et Mutesellim*, 110–23.

49. Schumacher, *Tell et Mutesellim*, 122.
50. The implication is that children were not sacrificed specifically to a deity and then placed before it.
51. Schumacher, *Tell et Mutesellim*, 122.
52. R. A. S. MacAlister, *The Excavation of Gezer, 1902–1905 and 1907–1909*, vol. 2 (London: Palestine Exploration Fund, 1912), 402–4; David Usshishkin, "On the History of the High Place at Gezer," in *Timelines: Studies in Honor of Manfred Bietak*, vol. 2, ed. E. Czerny (Peeters: Leuven, 2006), 411–16.
53. D. Ben-Shlomo, "The Cemetery of Azor and Early Iron Age Burial Practices," *Levant* 40.1 (2008): 29–54.
54. K. Ohata, *Tel Zeror III: Report of the Excavation Third Season, 1966* (Tokyo: Society for Near Eastern Studies in Japan, 1970), 71–74. Based on ceramic finds, it seems that the pit graves belong to the Late Bronze Age, while the jar burials are Iron Age. Pottery outside of the cist graves dates from the Late Bronze through the Hellenistic Period. K. Ohata, *Tel Zeror II: Preliminary Report of the Excavation Second Season, 1965* (Tokyo: Society for Near Eastern Studies in Japan, 1967), 40.
55. M. Edrey, E. Arie, H. May, and A. Yasur-Landau, "The Iron Age Tombs of Area E, Tel Achziv," *IEJ* 68 (2018): 166 n. 4; Ohata, *Tel Zeror II*, 36–41.
56. Ohata, *Tel Zeror II*, 41.
57. Ohata, *Tel Zeror III*, 71.
58. Ohata, *Tel Zeror III*, 74.
59. While no Iron II cemetery was found associated with the site, a Late Bronze II / Iron I cemetery (1400–1000 BCE) was discovered on the western side of the tell. Three tombs were excavated. Unfortunately, despite the hundreds of burials, the bones were in very poor condition. In the Iron I layer, a single infant skull was identified in Tomb I, a cave tomb that had multiple round chambers and included a "feeding channel" that opened to the outside. Storage jars and dipper juglets were associated with the channel, suggesting some sort of libation practice. The channel is reminiscent of drinking shoots identified in two built tombs in Achzib's Southern Cemetery. A cistern tomb included an adult and infant along with eighty-nine ceramic items, some bronze objects, and a knife. No identifiable remains were found in the shaft tomb. R. Cooley and G. Pratico, "The Western Cemetery, with Comments on Joseph Free's Excavations, 1953–1964," in *Preliminary Excavation Report: Sardis, Bir Umm Fawakhir, Tell el-'Umeiri, the Combined Caeserea Expeditions, and Tell Dothan*, ed. W. Dever (Winona Lake, IN: Eisenbrauns, 1995), 147–90.
60. D. Master, J. Monson, E. Lass, and G. Pierce, eds., *Dothan I: Remains from the Tell (1952–1964)* (Winona Lake, IN: Eisenbrauns, 2005), 68.
61. J. P. Free, "The Second Season at Dothan," *BASOR* 135 (1954): 18.
62. Master et al., *Dothan I*, 112; Free, "Second Season at Dothan," 18.
63. Master et al., *Dothan I*, 112–13.
64. J. P. Free, "The Third Season at Dothan," *BASOR* 139 (1955): 8.
65. J. P. Free, "The Seventh Season at Dothan," *BASOR* 160 (1960): 9; Master et al., *Dothan I*, 68. Free's identification was based on a comparison to the Assyrian style buildings in Megiddo Stratum III, a comparison with which Master et al. do not agree (*Dothan I*, 87).
66. J. P. Free, "The Sixth Season at Dothan," *BASOR* 156 (1959): 24–26; Free, "Seventh Season at Dothan," 9; Master et al., *Dothan I*, 112–13.
67. Free, "Third Season at Dothan," and Free, "Sixth Season at Dothan."
68. Master et al., *Dothan I*, 68.
69. Master et al. do note that Area A could have been used as a cemetery in the eighth c. BCE. But for what population? They assert that new architecture was not found until the Hellenistic Period, implying that Area A was abandoned after ninth c. destruction (*Dothan I*, 77). However, in discussing area L they state: "The next notable occupation of the site likely came after the conquest of the Assyrians" (*Dothan I*, 115).
70. Earlier infant and child burials both in pits and in jars were seen in the Middle Bronze Age levels (Master et al., *Dothan I*, 53).
71. L. Singer-Avitz, "The Pottery of Megiddo Strata III_II and a Proposed Subdivision of the Iron II Period in Northern Israel," *BASOR* 372 (2014): 1123–45; Ilan, "Iron Age Mortuary Practices," 57; E. Stern, *Archaeology of the Land of the Bible*, vol 2: *The Assyrian, Babylonian, and Persian*

102 THE BURIALS OF CHILDREN IN ANCIENT ISRAEL

Periods 732–332 BCE (New York: Doubleday, 2001), 33. It should be noted; however, that a re-examination of the bathtub coffins suggests they may actually be large tubs related to the textile industry that are in secondary use. In this analysis, their Mesopotamian origin is questioned. L. Mazow, "The 'Bathtub Coffin' from Tel Qitaf: A Re-examination of Its Context and Function," *PEQ* 146.1 (2014): 31–39; L. Mazow, "Throwing the Baby Out with the Bathwater: Innovations in Mediterranean Textile Production at the End of the 2nd / Beginning of the 1st Millennium BCE," in *Textile Production and Consumption in the Ancient Near East Archaeology, Epigraphy, Iconography*, Ancient Textile Series, ed. M. L. Nosch, H. Kofoed, and E. Anderson Strand (Oxford: Oxbow Press, 2013), 213–21.

72. For the possibility of Assyrian settlement in Israel, see N. Na'aman, "Population Changes in Palestine following the Assyrian Deportation," *TA* 20 (1993): 116; Stern, *Assyrian, Babylonian, and Persian*, 42–43.

73. Ilan, "Iron Age Mortuary Practices," 53; Kletter, "People without Burials," 35–36.

74. Norma Franklin suggests that necropoli with bench tombs did not reach the same proportions in the Kingdom of Israel they reached in the Kingdom of Judah due to the Assyrian destruction of the north. For example, Samaria had a necropolis similar to that of Jerusalem, but Samaria was established later and destroyed earlier. N. Franklin, "The Tombs of the Kings of Israel—Two Recently Identified 9th-Century Tombs from Omride Samaria," *ZDPV* 119 (2003): 1–11; Ilan, "Iron Age Mortuary Practices," 57.

75. For a delineation of borders between Samaria and Judah, see I. Yezerski, "Burial- Cave Distribution."

76. See Chapter 3.

PART II

INTERPRETING THE BURIALS OF CHILDREN IN ANCIENT ISRAEL

5

Memorializing Death

Memorials serve as a way to continue the functional immortality of the deceased. In memorializing an individual, the community or family engages in a public ritual that provides a visible way for societies to acknowledge an individual's personhood.[1] Memorials can take the form of written memorials or structural memorials. Written memorials are perhaps most familiar, as much has been written about funerary inscriptions on adult graves.[2] Most well known are those West Asian inscriptions related to the burials of the royal steward Katumuwa, Panamuwa I and Panamuwa II, and King Ahiram. Structural memorials encompass those physical monuments made for death, including everything from memorial pillars, to *maṣṣebot*, to the actual tomb. These monuments can be a locus of postmortem rituals that continue the relationship between the living and the dead. Families may gather here to say prayers, pour out libations, recite the names of the deceased, or offer food to those who have passed on. In doing so, they build bridges between the households of the living and the dead. However, not everyone was memorialized, and certainly not every infant or child.[3] The chapter first examines the relatively limited number of written memorials for children before moving to the more expansive corpus of structural memorials.

Written Memorials

Written memorials have power and a purpose, as attested in those found in adult tombs. The duties of the ideal son, links to kinship ties, ancestors, and the continuance of the family name are just some of the different ways in which written memorials are related to the functional immortality of the deceased.[4] Children did not receive elaborate funerary inscriptions. This is not surprising, since such inscriptions are limited to the royal, adult, male realm. However, this does not mean that children were not the recipients or beneficiaries of written memorials. Turning from an adult-centric to a child-centric gaze reveals written memorials in unexpected places.

The Dying Child. Kristine Henriksen Garroway, Oxford University Press. © Oxford University Press 2025.
DOI: 10.1093/9780197566718.003.0006

106 INTERPRETING THE BURIALS OF CHILDREN

Consider again the stillborn children from the Gilgamesh Epic. As it stands, Gilgamesh's children "live on" through the narrative. The narrative in this sense functions as a memorial to the children. Without it we the readers would not know of the deceased children. In light of this fact, we might reconsider the definition of functional immortality with respect to children.[5] Did children, who had no legacy, require some kind of memorial, a written or physical marker of their life, in order to obtain functional immortality? And if so, was this memorial a part of a cult for the dying child? It is hypothesized here that children's functional immortality could be extended via the different kinds of memorials provided for them. The three examples given here include writing on a burial jar, tomb, and amulet, providing not only a basis for thinking about memorializing children in cults of the dead, but for thinking more broadly about the corpus of written memorials and their function.

An Inscribed Burial Jar

During the Iron I, residents of Ashkelon show a preference for burying infants in simple pit burials. This fact alone makes the jar burial labeled Burial 375 stand out. Even more surprising is that it is not a common Levantine store jar, but an inscribed Egyptian store jar. Why was an Egyptian jar used? Is there any Egyptian connection to this burial? Perhaps, as Kathleen Birney and Brian Doak suggest, the jar was chosen because of its larger capacity or the exotic nature of the design.[6] It is also possible that the reused domestic object was meant to process the grief of the living by facilitating "'continuing bonds' between the dead and those burying them."[7]

The osteological report of the jar burials at Ashkelon did not list any abnormal pathologies, except for this burial. This infant had a bifurcated rib, which is more prominent in males.[8] It does seem rather prescient that an Egyptian jar was buried out of sight at the same time the Egyptian presence at Ashkelon was itself removed from the area. Was this a family who had shaky Egyptian connections, connections they did not wish to make known, but did wish to pass on to their infant in death? Or is there nothing to be made of the store jar? This population was not wealthy; they reused and recycled.[9] Given the fact that the population of Grid 38 is described as poorer, the choice to use a jar as a coffin rather than to continue using it for daily life seems significant.

The two images found on Burial 375 add to its mystique.[10] The image on Side A has been interpreted as a four-legged animal, likely a jackal deity. It is associated with Upwawet, whose image is found on a group of grave stelae from tombs at Asyut in Egypt.[11] The dedicants in this Egyptian tomb group were male and female, from a variety of professions, and both wealthy and commoners. The image on Side B is perhaps a stylized standard for the animal or an offering table with bread. Unlike the monumental funerary inscriptions given to rulers, the image found on this jar was not meant to be visible to those who passed by the infant's burial. The burial was a private, not a public affair, lending some insight into how a particular family practiced their own form of household religion. While the inscription on the jar would have been hidden from the living, this does not mean that the inscription was insignificant for the deceased. Upwawet, like Anubis, was a soul-guider, a psychopomp. It seems no small matter that such an image would be included on a jar used for an infant burial. In fact, one wonders whether the jackal deity was depicted to help guide the infant in the process of rebirth.[12] While such ideas are simply ideas, they do not negate the fact that a unique jar, manufactured in Egypt, and inscribed with Egyptian symbols was used to bury an infant—not a child or adult—at Ashkelon.

The Inscriptions at Khirbet Beit Lei

Khirbet Beit Lei presents another unusual case of inscription and burial. While the tomb was used, the complex was left unfinished, and no repository was created. It appears that the builders had intended to do more. However, the dead were not left unprotected; the inscriptions speak to the reality that the dead were collectively placed under divine care, which apparently needed to last into eternity as the secondary burial rituals customary to this time period were, for whatever reason, never carried out.

The epigraphic remains found at the tomb were inscribed on the walls of Room 1. Because the writings do not directly refer to the deceased, death, or afterlife, some have suggested that the writings belong to a later phase of the tomb when it was reused as a hiding place for refugees.[13] Recent reanalysis of the inscriptions and the tombs puts to rest this idea, demonstrating that the tomb is best understood as a single-period tomb whose inscriptions are at home within an Iron Age funerary context.[14] The inscriptions are prayers and curses related to deliverance, placed in a dark space where individuals

108   INTERPRETING THE BURIALS OF CHILDREN

coming into the tomb would understand their intended meaning.[15] Alice Mandell and Jeremy Smoak point out the importance of where the inscriptions are placed, namely on the antechamber leading into the bench rooms, which is a place of transition and boundary marking.

Most significant for the current study are the undisturbed remains of Tomb 1. The remains included not only adults but also children laid in primary burial. If the inscriptions were meant, as Mandell and Smoak suggest, as boundary markers, demarcating areas of impurity and purity, the space carved out for the deceased and that where visitors might leave offerings, then we must apply the demarcation not only to the adult burials but to the child burials as well.[16] Furthermore, the inscriptions themselves refer to Yahweh, the God of the hills of Judah and the God of Jerusalem. The connection between the divine and the space in which the tomb is located (the Judean foothills) "link the divine name with the physical space of the tomb" and further "draw upon a stock of protective language."[17] This language was meant to protect those in the tomb, which included children. In addition to the protective language, the language of *BLei 6* (Inscription B)[18] is suggestive of transgenerational language. If the text reads, "Attend (to us) Yah, O gracious God! Acquit Yah, O Yahweh!" it finds resonance with the epithet "gracious God," used in Exodus 34:6–7.[19]

> The implication of *BLei 6*, and its use of this specific set of verbs (נקה and פקד), is that Yahweh's sovereign power extends across generations and is inclusive of the dead. Its binding force allows a people, here an unidentified kinship group, to align itself across generations through modes of identification that are tied to the tomb.[20]

Not only are the generations abstract groups of people reaching into the past and future, but the inscription refers to the generations currently present in the tomb, as represented by the adults and their children. Just as we saw with the bench tomb repositories, children are again brought into the collective generational sphere, this time through words.

The Ketef Hinnom Amulets

Uncovered in 1979, the two silver amulets from Ketef Hinnom contain the oldest reference to the texts of the Priestly Blessing found in Numbers

6:24–26.[21] The amulets are dated to the seventh century BCE through their paleography and the remains with which they were discovered.[22] Like the inscriptions at Beit Lei, these amulets refer to Yahweh and invoke the protective nature of Yahweh on behalf of the dead.[23] Jeremy Smoak has drawn comparisons between these silver amulets and Phoenician silver amulets. Like the Phoenician amulets, the Judahite ones also begin with a personal name, meaning the protection was initially requested for a particular individual.[24] Matthew Suriano stresses the importance of the name being preserved in death: "To preserve one's name was also to preserve one's memory."[25] The ideology at play is fascinating, for there was a call to remember the individual within a collective repository. Furthermore, the scrolls were rolled up, so that the writing was hidden from both the wearer and those observing the wearer. Not only this, but the writing was rather difficult to read. It is almost as if a game of hide and seek is occurring in the amulets.

Smoak turns our attention instead to the materiality of the objects; they were silver, highlighting their "ritual function as 'hidden' texts that were not made to be seen, but to communicate through their materiality and design."[26] He demonstrates how silver's shiny properties act as a physical, visible, representation of God's countenance shining upon the wearer and how the refining process of obtaining pure silver echoes the Judahite beliefs surrounding the process of removing evil from oneself.[27]

That these amulets were meant to be worn seems likely. Numbers 6:23 states that the priestly benediction in Numbers was to be uttered aloud by Aaron and his sons, and in doing so "They will put my name on the children of Israel, and I will bless them" (Numbers 6:27). The amulets appear to be a reinterpretation of what it meant to place God's name on someone. Given the ritual importance of these amulets, we can ask: How do these amulets shed light on Judahite children within the cult of dead kin? We might answer this question in two ways. First, the size of the amulets is important. The larger amulet measures 97 × 27 mm when unrolled. The smaller one measures 38 × 11 mm; it is no wider than a thumbnail. Given that the two amulets were personalized by name, one wonders if they were tailored to the recipient's body size as well. Was the larger one for an adult and the smaller for a child?[28] Even though this suggestion is conjecture, it is not entirely far-fetched to think that a child would be given an amulet, likely by the parents. Such protective baubles are often associated with infants and young children and meant to protect them from harm.[29] Shiny objects were used in the house

110   INTERPRETING THE BURIALS OF CHILDREN

as a means of warding off evil.[30] With silver in particular, its luminescent nature might be reminiscent of the shine and protection of the moon, which provided light in the dark.[31] The command to protect children with written words, to inscribe the words of the covenant upon one's heart, is echoed in Deuteronomy 6:6–7.[32]

Here too, we might think about the process of giving and receiving amulets. Ethnographic and archaeological data suggest that amulets of many sorts were placed on living children as a means of protecting them.[33] Included in a burial, such an amulet given by a parent to a child would be a tangible link between generations, unifying them both in life and in death. While we do not know the exact circumstances surrounding the small Ketef Hinnom amulet, it is not unreasonable to hypothesize the same unifying motivations were in play with this amulet. We might even take this one step further and stress that if this were the case for the Ketef Hinnom amulet, then what we see is the power of the inscribed Priestly Blessing covering the entire family first in the household of the living and then in the household of death.

The second way of answering the question is to think about where the amulets were found; both silver amulets were discovered in the repository of Chamber 25. While we might not be able to talk in definitive terms about the original wearer of the amulets, it is possible to talk about the "secondary wearers." I argue in the following chapters for the inclusive nature of repository pits. Inasmuch as we can talk about partible personhood as related to ceramics, so too is it possible to perceive personal items functioning in the same collective manner. In this way, the amulet functions in death not only for the original, individual wearer but also, through the materiality of the object, for the secondary, collective "wearers" that it touches in the repository. And here we are on surer ground when we include children, because children and infants were found in the repository.

Written Memorials and Children in Cults of the Dead Kin

The three instances of child burials associated with inscriptions are different in form, yet they share a single element in common: the inscriptions were part of the burial, not visible to those passing by; they were meant for the dead. Each example is important because each example attests to a different way in which children were included within the various cults of the dead kin. The jar burial attests to markings being used in an infant Levantine burial that was not Judahite. It suggests a specialized meaning imbued in the burial of the infant, with the proposed jackal figure functioning as a psychopomp for the deceased infant. The inscriptions on the Khirbet Beit Lei inscription, on the other hand, were meant to protect the family as a whole. Since the inscription was not personalized, any individual buried within the family tomb would benefit from the inscription. The Ketef Hinnom amulets are again slightly different for they were initially meant for a single individual yet could also have imparted their protective properties to all those that were found with them as they entered the repository collective. Because memorials aid in the remembrance/functional immortality of an individual, the infants and children touched by these inscribed memorials had some degree of personhood that extended into death.

Structural Memorials

Within the Southern Levant, two types of structured memorials stand out, infants interred in jar burials or in pits under house floors, and infants and children buried in bench tombs. The bench tomb, with its so-called tree shape, resembles the structure of the four-room house.[34] In thinking about the relationship between space and the people who inhabit it, Matthew Suriano states, "This form of access could indicate the central authority of a family leader," while Avraham Faust and Shlomo Bunimovitz, argue the opposite, that the four-room house plan "expresses a more egalitarian spirit," allowing anyone to have access to all areas of the house.[35] Melissa Cradic notes that in societies that have dividual and fractal personhood, such as those of ancient Israel, the head of the household acts as an entity or corporate person.[36] In such societies, the interests of the household are facilitated by and through the paterfamilias, who has achieved full personhood in life and will become an ancestor in death. As Chapter 6 will argue, the intermingling of ancestor and non-ancestor bones in the repositories becomes an act of integrating individuals of different ages and statuses together in the family collective.

Whereas the bench tombs are found in Judah and reflect a concept of an afterlife that continues the family and kin group into a household of the dead as mediated by an ancestor, the infant jar and intramural burials present a different picture. These latter burials are prevalent in the Bronze Age, continuing into the Iron Age in areas outside of Judah. Whether found on the

112 INTERPRETING THE BURIALS OF CHILDREN

Philistine coast or in the areas of the Northern Kingdom, such infant burials emphasize the individual over the collective in death. Due to the differential burial style and separation from the family, one might view these individuals as having no personhood or a personhood that is erased. However, rather than arguing for the elimination of an infant's personhood, such burials can also be understood as commemorating infants. As will be demonstrated, it is possible that intramural infant burials actually extended the memory of the infant, giving members of the living household opportunities to interact with the infant not just when a tomb was opened, but on a daily basis.

The jar burials of the Philistine coast, particularly those at Ashkelon and Ekron, provide the best examples of a possible integration of infant burials and social memory. Some of the intermural jar burials at Ashkelon were ringed with stones. This practice could be a form of commemoration.[37] It is notable that the floors in Ashkelon Grid 38 are littered with pits. Adam Aja characterized the pits as "hidden installations," including bowl-lamp-bowl foundation deposits, infant burials, and animal bone deposits.[38] He stresses the visibility, or lack of visibility, as it were, of the deposits. "The subfloor and sub-wall installations could not have served a practical function similar to that of visible installation and would likely have been known only by those people who participated in the practice of laying the deposits in the pits."[39] This observation is a good point and can be pushed even further. Paula Hesse and Deirdre Fulton comment as follows: "Considering the inhabitants of Grid 38 also lived with buried human infants, puppies, complete limbs and partial skeletons, it would seem they had a high tolerance for a malodorous environment. Nasty smells did not discourage burial behaviors."[40]

What Aja, Hesse, and Fulton are highlighting is the almost absurd number of things buried under the floors of Grid 38. Combing through the various reports on the grid, what is even more amazing is that the deposits at lower levels are not regularly cut into by pits in higher levels. Given the number of items hidden in the ground, it seems nigh impossible to avoid running into something. In order for disturbances not to occur on a regular basis, it would appear that some form of above-ground marker must have been used to indicate where an item was deposited. The idea that the deposits simply vanished from sight and would have no impact on the living society post-deposition does not seem viable.[41]

It is possible that the stone- or sherd-encircled jar burials, such as those found at Ashkelon, represent one kind of marker. We can hypothesize that

MEMORIALIZING DEATH 113

this marker was more permanent than other markers, say a pot or a textile that might have eventually been moved, and therefore they remain in the archaeological record. A more permanent marker of space for a burial would seem appropriate if the family wished to remember the deceased infant. Along these lines, the construction of new floors might also be considered an intentional marker of space, such as Ashkelon Burial Pit 962, which included two infant burials and was placed in the southeast corner of the room. Coincidentally, a new floor layered with shells was also placed in the southeast corner of the room. So too the Ekron burial in Room 16 Field I NE was placed under the cobbles in the room. Other visible spatial markers should also be considered. In Ekron INE burials were found among bricks placed against a wall, in a thin layer of brick material on the surface of a floor, and inside a fire installation. While these architectural features are certainly not out of the ordinary, they do serve as markers that would remain visible to the inhabitants of the dwellings.

Marking infant burials with permanent architectural features, such as floors, installations, and bricks, or placing them in corners or under thresholds suggests that the living were engaged in the process of place-making and commemoration. The practice of intramural place- making is also seen in other sites outside of Iron I Philistine Pentapolis cities. For example, Iron I Megiddo (Stratum VIA) included thirteen burials within the domestic area, including adults and children. While the practice of intramural burial for all ages is nearly unique within Israel, it is not out of the ordinary for Megiddo.[42] Jar burial Tomb 1776 in Area CC Square Q9 appears to have been buried by a wall.[43] While walls can serve as place markers, the more interesting jar burial is Tomb 1763, found in Area CC Square R9. A mass of broken store jars appears to be placed at the infant's head.[44] Based on the report of Area CC, it seems that the jars were not intentionally broken in association with the infant's burial, but more likely that they were destroyed in the same conflagration that destroyed Stratum VIA.[45] Given the relative distance between the jar burial and the store jars, it could be possible that the store jars served as a place marker for the burial below. This is not to argue that the store jars were *maṣṣebot* of any kind or that they were intentionally set up as markers but rather to encourage us to think about the way in which temporary above-ground items could serve as surface markers for the burials below. Every time members of that household entered the store jar space, they might be prompted to remember the infant buried below.

114 INTERPRETING THE BURIALS OF CHILDREN

When we move to the Iron II period, a few intramural infant burials again stand out. The single infant found at Timnah was placed under a stone floor, which was likely part of a building that abutted the city wall. Unfortunately, the discussion of this individual is lacking, so we are left to try to put together pieces of the puzzle.[46] The stratigraphy chapter does not mention a burial in this area, while the skeletal remains report makes it clear that an entire skeleton of a two-year-old was found. Since neither report referenced a jar burial or constructed burial, it seems likely the child was buried in a pit. Without a destruction layer, it would be rather odd to leave a child lying on the ground. If it was a pit burial, it is in line with intramural burials near walls and liminal spaces. A lack of grave goods also fits the pattern seen in other burials at the time. While the stratigraphy report does not mention the child or any details of a burial, it does provide us with another piece of the puzzle. The building and locus listed in the skeletal report puts the infant burial in Building 737, which is also known as the *LMLK* Jars Building. To repeat for emphasis, the location of the one intramural infant burial was in a building that stored inscribed store jars. Given the relationship between clay, birth, jars, and so forth, it may be that the burial of in the infant in this building held special significance. The floor was built over in the subsequent stratum, meaning that the marked space, and potentially the memory of the infant buried there was erased.

The Iron II intramural burials found at Ashdod included mass burials and individual burials. These burials come on the heels of the Assyrian campaign in the region. Adults and children alike were included in the pits found throughout the site. The excavators surmise that the bodies of the deceased were gathered shortly after their deaths, placed in the pits, and covered with offerings, after which the entire area was sealed with a lime-plastered floor.[47] Of note is the location of the burial pits found in a potters' quarter. Three of the pits are within twenty-five meters of each other as the crow flies. The location of the fourth mass burial is difficult to determine from the final report.[48] The link between clay, creation, and birth might explain the choice of the potters' quarter for burying individuals who may still have been understood to have a place within the household of the living.[49] Newer studies on childbirth in the ancient Near East (ANE) use a materiality approach to discuss the ceramic paradigm and the importance of clay's physical properties in shaping the ritual landscape.[50] Locating the deceased in a place linked with creation and birth may have been another link to the ritual landscape and an attempt to commemorate the lives cut short.

The Tomb as Womb

On a structural level, burial receptacles serve as a visual physical memorial to the deceased. Tombs in general have often been compared to a womb, with chamber and rock-cut tombs specifically being compared to the female reproductive system: "burial chamber / jar = womb; entry = cervix; corridor, shaft or dromos = birth canal."[51] A mapping of the reproductive system onto the layout of tombs is not surprising given that death is often understood as a return to Mother Earth, from which humans were created. The appearance of headrests within some bench tombs has also fueled the conversation regarding death and rebirth.[52] I will return to this idea below.

Regarding creation from dust or clay, consider biblical conceptions of human creation (Genesis 2:7, Job 10:9, 33:6, and Psalms 103:14), or those found in Mesopotamian and Egyptian creation myths. The latter two describe the genesis of humans in various ways, yet, among the different methods, clay is always included. For example, in the Atrahasis Epic, Nintu-Mami, the divine midwife, mixes clay and blood, or clay and saliva, and pinches off the wet clay to form humans.[53] And in Egyptian mythology Khnum, a master potter, fashions humans out of clay on his potter's wheel.[54]

As for death and a return to the earth, clay imagery is used not only in the Hebrew Bible but also in ANE texts.[55] In the Descent of Ishtar, Ereshkigal, the goddess of the Underworld, describes her existence in terms of death and clay: "I eat clay for bread, I drink muddy water for beer." Right after this she talks of people who died before their time, including the infant child who was miscarried.[56] In the "Poem of the Righteous Sufferer," Marduk is credited with restoring life from the grave, life that is described as "bits of clay Aruru pinched off."[57]

The structure of a jar burial also lends itself to a similar understanding of death and rebirth. Infants were found in the fetal position, often with the head toward the opening of the jar, as if waiting to be birthed.[58] The shape of many store jars furthers the comparison with the reproductive system: jar body = womb; the elongated neck of the jar = birth canal; circular opening = cervix. I have hypothesized elsewhere that jar burials may have been chosen as a symbolic way of returning the infant to the mother's womb, where it was safe, protected, and nurtured.[59] I further suggested that a return to the womb might also have been envisioned as returning the infant to a place where it could be rebirthed. Ethnographic parallels from various

116   INTERPRETING THE BURIALS OF CHILDREN

cultures hold that particular types of burial foster infant rebirth. Tribes in Malaysia and Borneo hope that burying infants under house floors will encourage them to be reborn into the house.[60] West African tribes, as well as the Huron Native Americans, buried infants in the road so that when a woman walked over them, "they may secretly enter her womb, and . . . she may give them life again."[61] A closer parallel is found in ancient Egypt, where various goddesses were envisioned as mothers who welcomed the dead back to their wombs.[62] Most prevalent in this theology are the goddesses Mut, Nut, and Hathor.[63] The womb of the goddess is intangible, an aspirational destination for the deceased. However, newer studies of Egyptian pot burials argue for them as the physical representation of the womb.[64] Moreover, these studies suggest that the shape of the pot is related to the shape of the egg. Placing the deceased in a pot symbolically returned the deceased to the womb, where it would be rebirthed.

More recent approaches in materiality may help further the link between jar burials, the womb, and rebirth. The "material turn," or, as some have called it, the "(re)turn to material," focuses on the place of an object's materiality as agentic.[65] It is "both a turning towards the material and ontological, away from a postmodern emphasis on the discursive and epistemological, and the moment in which the material takes its turn."[66] Applied to jar burials, the "material turn" encourages a focus on the relationship between the space, shape, and ceramic nature of the burial receptacle.

Using a materialist approach, Kerry Sonia has drawn the connection between clay and procreation in the biblical and ANE mind.[67] Her insights demonstrate the parallels between a woman's womb and ceramic pots. For example, in Gilgamesh, Enkidu, and the Netherworld, a woman who has not given birth is likened to a pot that has been cast aside.[68] The analogy is between the unused ceramic pot and the unused womb, both of which find no place within society. The analogy also aligns with how Kevin McGeough characterizes the way that clay and ceramics conceptualized the "formation of person, household, and other social networks."[69] The very nature of clay and the links it has with creation and death provide a natural connection with the households of the living and dead. Sonia further points to the case of the Sotah woman in Numbers 5 to draw parallels between ceramic vessels and the womb. She notes: "The vessel is the medium by which the priest creates and enacts the sterilizing curse against the woman's womb, effectively turning her into a cursed vessel."[70] The woman's womb and the ceramic vessel become interchangeable.

With the connection between clay and womb established, a materiality approach further asks what additional insights can be gleaned from the use of a *clay jar*, as opposed to a container of alabaster, reeds, sticks, pitch and bitumen, et cetera. This question becomes especially important when thinking about the differences between infants buried in jars, under house floors, and infants included in Judahite rock-cut burials. Clay is porous, permeable, so much so that the biblical text places it in a special category. Biblical texts concerned with ritual purity note that ceramic vessels or ovens (tabun ovens) that come into contact with unclean animals must be destroyed.[71] They are so susceptible to contamination that regular purification rituals are useless.[72] Dead bodies are one such contaminate. Their impurity was so severe that the Israelite high priest was not allowed to encounter a dead body lest he be ineligible for service (Leviticus 21:1–17). According to Numbers 19:11–16, a dead body contaminates not only the people that touch it but the space it inhabits. The tent/house that holds a dying body is unclean. Any open vessels within the tent/house are also unclean. Anyone currently in the tent/house or who comes into the tent/house is unclean. The dying body contaminated, and to stop the contamination from spreading, it needed to be buried as soon as possible.

A materiality approach can be a useful corrective and provide new insights when thinking about Israelite religion.[73] Rather than starting with the text, one should start with the material that the text is describing. In the case of burials, this means asking how burials might inform our understanding of the biblical text. While the biblical texts discussing the contaminating impurity of dying bodies can be dated to the Iron III / Persian Period at their earliest, they appear to be in conversation with an older known practice, namely, burial in family tombs. At the risk of stating the obvious, Judean tombs are not built tombs made of brick; rather they are carved caves or rock-cut tombs.[74] From a materiality perspective, the absence of brick tombs, and more importantly, jar burials within Iron Age Judahite areas might be related to the properties of stone versus ceramics.[75]

Pottery cannot be purified, but the biblical text states that metal can be purified with fire or water (Numbers 31:31–32), and wood, cloth, skin, and sackcloth can be purified with water (Leviticus 11:32–33, 15:12; Numbers 31:19–20). However, nothing is said about stone. The increased use of stone in building projects and common household items within the Second Temple Period suggests that Jews understood silence in the matter of stone to mean that stone could not become impure.[76] This may have been seen as one

118   INTERPRETING THE BURIALS OF CHILDREN

benefit for the use of stone in bench tombs.[77] The impurity caused by death would be contained within the stone walls; it would not seep out.

Returning to the tomb-to-womb theory, I noted that the tomb layout and reproductive overlay works for both jar burials and tombs. However, the materiality approach applied above highlights differences in the analogy when thinking about the materials used in the burials. Stone functions to keep things in, not to let them out. Accordingly, stone would represent a sterile womb from which no being could be rebirthed. By the same token, a materiality approach would argue that jar burials could well represent a return to a fertile womb and perhaps even indicate a belief in rebirth. Clay is porous and associated with procreation, and, unless sealed, things can pass in and out of it.[78] It seems not insignificant, then, that Iron Age jar burials are found outside of Judah, not within.

If jar burials, especially those placed within the house, were associated with rebirth, they would have no place in a Judahite household.[79] A few reasons support this conclusion. First, the archaeological picture shows Judahite burials are always found outside of cities (not in homes). This is likely due to the impurity associated with death. Second, death in ancient Israelite texts is always associated with sleep, not rebirth (Psalms 13:3, 90:5; Job 7:21, 14:10–12). Upon death one goes to "sleep" or "lies down with" with the ancestors (Deuteronomy 31:16; 2 Samuel 7:12; 1 Kings 2:10, 11:43, 14:20). The extended position of corpses on "beds" in stone bench tombs correlates better with the biblical text's description of death as sleep rather than with a belief in rebirth.[80]

Jar burials, however, present a different picture. They are most often reserved for infants, who are placed in a fetal, knees-to-chin, position. Gabriel Barkay argues that outside of Judah, "such (fetal position) burials are common and are taken to be clear representations of the concept of death equals rebirth."[81] Indeed, jar burials are found on the coastal plain and in the areas associated with the northern Israelite Kingdom. Placed in a porous container, where things can seep out as well as in, and under house floors, a jar burial, it is not too far-fetched to think, held some sort of ritual significance. Perhaps burying the infant in an intermural jar burial expressed the wish for that particular infant to join the household permanently. The burial within the household may then have a double function; it literally held the infant's dead body in the house in order to encourage rebirth into the same house.[82] Given the underrepresentation of infant burials within burial populations, maybe it was only deceased firstborn infants who received such burials.[83] While there is yet no way to prove this hypothesis, it is nonetheless an intriguing possibility.

Discussion

Burial memorials, both written and structural, attest to different ways that Iron Age inhabitants in the land of ancient Israel recognized the personhood of infants and children. The corpus of memorials examined is quite broad and covers a wide geographical span: an inscribed jar burial from Ashkelon, a tomb inscription from Beit Lei, silver amulets from Ketef Hinnom, jar burials outside Judah, and bench tombs within Judah. Though each of the different memorials should be understood in its own cultural location, the various memorials point to an overarching belief that threads its way through each memorial: living adults actively worked to bring dying children into a collective generational space through the process of commemoration and place-making.[84] That each memorial can be understood in this light further highlights three things. First, it demonstrates the active place of children within the households of the dying. Second, it furthers our understanding of ways in which children fit into the cult of the dead kin. Finally, that generational ties involve linking the living and the dead, the young and the old, persons past and future, reaffirms that infants and children were perceived to have some measure of personhood. If infants and children had no personhood, or if it was erased in death, there would be no need to engage them, protect their bodies, or memorialize them.

Excursus: while the biblical text does not advocate for a belief in rebirth, it is nonetheless possible that those living in Judah would have been familiar with the concept given ongoing Egyptian influence within the Southern Levant.[85] Not only were Egyptians present in the lands of Judah and Israel, but Egyptian items are found within burials, such as scarabs, which represent rebirth and renewal, and amulets with Egyptian themes.[86] The relationship between Egypt and Judah extended into the religio-political realm as well. Christopher B. Hays has argued that the covenant with death, described in Isaiah 28, is actually a covenant with the Egyptian goddess Mut. "Mut certainly could have been familiar to a Judean intellectual who had contact with Egyptians in the eighth or seventh century. Most scholars would agree that at least Isa 28:7–22 is a response to Judah's seeking Egyptian support under the Neo-Assyrian threat."[87] Mut is known for many things. She is connected

120 INTERPRETING THE BURIALS OF CHILDREN

with the throne and a guarantor of covenants. However, it is her links to the underworld and her motherly aspects that are of most interest for infant burials. She is the protector of the dead in the underworld, a mother goddess, a divine wet-nurse, and her cult is full of lotus imagery—a flower associated with rebirth.[88] The polemic in Isaiah 28 may point to more than just a political covenant with Egypt, which was ratified with or reflected in ritual actions undertaken by the populace. The polemic against a covenant with Mut could also be a condemnation of her cult, a cult that had links to a belief not sanctioned by Isaiah or the cult of Yahweh, or reflected in the death rituals of Judah, namely rebirth. Isaiah's chastisement hints that from his perspective, something was rotten in Judah. Judahites were not following "official Yahweh-centric" religious practices; they were turning their beliefs to foreign deities.[89]

Notes

1. C. Fowler, *The Archaeology of Personhood: An Anthropological Approach* (London: Routledge, 2004), 45; T. M. Lemos, *Violence and Personhood in Ancient Israel and Comparative Contexts* (Oxford: Oxford University Press, 2017), 11.
2. A. Mandell and J. Smoak, "Reconsidering the Function of Tomb Inscriptions in Iron Age Judah: Khirbet Beit Lei as a Test Case," *JANER* 16 (2016): 192–245; S. L. Sanders, "Appetites of the Dead: The Language of the New Zincirli Stela and the History of a West Semitic Funerary Tradition," *BASOR* 369 (2013): 85–105; D. Pardee, "A New Aramaic Inscription from Zincirli," *BASOR* 365 (2009): 51–71; J. D. Scholen and A. Fink, "New Excavations at Zincirli Höyük in Turkey (Ancient Sam'al) and the Discovery of an Inscribed Mortuary Stele," *Bulletin of the American Schools of Oriental Research* 365 (2009): 1–13; M. Suriano, "Breaking Bread with the Dead: Katumuwa's Stele, Hosea 9:4, and the Early History of the Soul," *JAOS* 134 (2014): 385–405; M. Bauks, "Soul-Concepts in Ancient Near Eastern Mythical Texts and Their Implications for the Primeval History," *VT* 66 (2016): 181–93; K. Sonia, *Caring for the Dead in Ancient Israel*, ABS 27 (Atlanta: SBL Press, 2020), 44–50 and sources therein.
3. As with discussions of the tombs themselves, discussions of other structural memorials have centered on adults, such as the pillars erected by Absalom (2 Samuel 18:18) and for Rachel (Genesis 35:20).
4. Sonia, *Caring for the Dead*, 50; M. Suriano, *A History of Death in the Hebrew Bible* (Oxford: Oxford University Press, 2018), 33. See the ancient inscriptions and the literature on them, inter alia, Duties of the Ideal Son in the Aqhat Epic (*KTU* 1.17 i. 26b–34); Ahiram's Sarcophagus (*KAI* I); Panamuwa I inscription (*KAI* 214); Eshmunazar inscription (*KAI* 14); the KTMW stele; C. B. Hays, *A Covenant with Death: Death in the Iron Age II and Its Rhetorical Uses in Proto-Isaiah* (Grand Rapids, MI: Eerdmans, 2011), 110–11, 128–31; D. Bonatz, *Das syro-hethitische Grabdenkmal: Untersuchungen zur Entstehung einer neuen Bildgattung in der Eisenzeit im nordsyrisch-südostanatolischen Raum* (Mainz: van Zabern, 2000); M. Pope, "Cult of the Dead in Ugarit," in *Probative Pontification in Ugaritic and Biblical Literature: Collected Essays*, ed. M. S. Smith (Münster: Ugarit-Verlag, 1994), 225–50; T. Lewis, *Cults of the Dead in Ancient Israel and Ugarit*, HSM 39 (Atlanta: Scholars Press, 1989), 59–65.
5. Refer to the introduction for a fuller discussion of functional immortality as related to legacy.
6. K. Birney and B. R. Doak, "Funerary Iconography on an Infant Jar Burial from Ashkelon," *IEJ* 61.6 (2011): 47.
7. R. Power and Y. Tristant, "From Refuse to Rebirth: Repositioning the Pot Burial in the Egyptian Archaeological Record," *Antiquity* 90. (2016): 1483–84; D. Klass and T. Walter, "Processes of

MEMORIALIZING DEATH   121

Grieving: How Bonds Are Continued," in *Handbook of Bereavement Research: Consequences, Coping and Care,* ed. M. Stroebe, R. Hansson, W. Stroebe, and H. Schut (Washington, DC: American Psychological Association, 2001), 431–48; and C. Renfrew, "Towards a Theory of Material Engagement," in *Rethinking Materiality: The Engagement of Mind with the Material World,* ed. E. DeMarrais, C. Gosden, and C. Renfrew (Cambridge: McDonald Institute for Archaeological Research, 2004), 23–31.

8. This condition occurs in only 1.2% of humans. One rib bone on one side is split in two at the sternal end. M. K. Rathinasabapathi and H. K. Perumallapalli, "Bifid Rib: A Rare Anomaly," *Medical Journal DY of Patil University* 8.5 (2015): 607– 71, https:// doi.org/ 10.4103/ 0975-2870.164952; W. Song, S. Kim, D. Park, and K. Koh, "Bifid Rib: Anatomical Considerations in Three Cases," *Yonsei Medical Journal* 50.2 (2009): 300– 303, https:// doi.org/ 10.3349/ ymj.2009.50.2.300.

9. Consider, for example, the poorly constructed mud bricks. They included recycled sherds and large inclusions. A. Aja and D. Master, "Conclusion: Uncovering Philistines," in *Ashkelon 7: The Iron Age I,* ed. L. Stager, D. Master, and A. Aja (University Park, PA: Eisenbrauns, 2020), 860.

10. A full description of the images and discussion of the jar can be found in Birney and Doak, "Funerary Iconography," 32–53.

11. T. DuQuesne, *The Salakhana Trove: Votive Stelae and Other Objects from Asyut* (London: Darengo, 2009).

12. Whether the carvings were done specifically for the burial is impossible to know. However, if they were, then the proposed interpretation regarding rebirth would be strengthened.

13. For a full overview of the refugee perspective and the relationship between the drawings and the inscriptions, see Z. Zevit, *The Religions of Ancient Israel: A Synthesis of Parallactic Approaches* (London: Continuum, 2001), 435–37; J. Naveh, "Old Hebrew Inscriptions in a Burial Cave," *IEJ* 13 (1963): 89–92.

14. Mandell and Smoak, "Reconsidering the Function," 192–245; Suriano, *History of Death,* 78–80, 117–23. The tomb and its inscriptions are dated to the late Iron II or early Iron III period. For dating, see the extensive bibliography in Mandell and Smoak, "Reconsidering the Function," 194 n. 8.

15. Noting that most individuals were illiterate, Mandell and Smoak emphasize the reliance upon ancient individuals' cultural knowledge. People familiar with tombs and inscriptions would know the basic "gist" of what the inscription meant, even if they could not clearly read it. The inscriptions and graffiti held more of a semiotic function. Mandell and Smoak, "Reconsidering the Function," 206–7, 234.

16. Boundary markers functioning in this way are found in other Iron Age tombs, most notably at the Tomb of the Royal Steward, as well as later burials. Mandell and Smoak, "Reconsidering the Function," 207–8; Sanders, "Appetites of the Dead," 89–90.

17. Mandell and Smoak, "Reconsidering the Function," 242.

18. Naveh, "Old Hebrew Inscriptions," 73, Figure 3.

19. Translation by Matthew Suriano following the reconstruction of André Lemaire. Suriano, *History of Death,* 118; A. Lemaire, "Prières en temps de crise: Les inscriptions de Khirbet Beit Lei," *Revue Biblique* 83 (1976): 558–68. For comparisons with Exodus 34 see P. Miller, "Psalms and Inscriptions," in *Israelite Religion and Biblical Theology: Collected Essays,* JSOT Supp. 267 (Sheffield: Sheffield Academic Press, 2000), 210–32.

20. Suriano, *History of Death,* 120.

21. G. Barkay, "The Priestly Benediction on Silver Plaques from Ketef Hinnom in Jerusalem," *TA* 19 (1992): 148–51.

22. Scholars have gone back and forth regarding their dating; however, the consensus is now firmly on the side of the seventh century. See the debate and bibliography in J. Smoak, "You Have Refined Us Like Silver Is Refined (Ps 66:10): Yahweh's Metallurgic Powers in Iron Age Judah," *AABNER* 1.3 (2021): 83–84, 83 n. 2.; Suriano, *History of Death,* 123 n. 71; S. Aḥituv, "A Rejoinder to Nadav Naʾaman's 'A New Appraisal of the Silver Amulet from Ketef Himmom,'" *IEJ* 62 (2012): 223–32.

23. Suriano points out the similar function of the *Qom 1* inscription. Suriano, *History of Death,* 125.

24. For a reconstruction of the inscriptions, see J. Smoak, *The Priestly Blessing in Inscription and Scripture: The Early History of Numbers 6:24– 26* (New York: Oxford University Press, 2016), 18–42.

25. Suriano, *History of Death,* 125.

26. Smoak, "You Have Refined Us," 84.

122   INTERPRETING THE BURIALS OF CHILDREN

27. Smoak, "You Have Refined Us."
28. Many thanks to Jeremy Smoak for suggesting that size might be correlated to age. Personal communication.
29. Light, either by lamps or reflective surfaces, was used to protect infants' rooms. Ethnographic studies show the Albanian Muslims and Moroccan Berbers keep their children's rooms lit. C. Meyers, *Rediscovering Eve: Ancient Israelite Women in Context* (Oxford: Oxford University Press, 2013), 154–55. In Bagdad ethnographic literature notes that a shiny knife or dagger might be kept in the room to ward off evil. E. Drower, "Women and Taboo in Iraq," *Iraq* 5 (1938): 110.
30. Meyers, *Rediscovering Eve*, 154.
31. Smoak argues this point in "You Have Refined Us," 105.
32. See, too, Exodus 13:9; Deuteronomy 11:18; Proverbs 6:21; Isaiah 3:20.
33. K. H. Garroway, *Growing Up in Ancient Israel: Children in Material Culture and Biblical Texts*, ABS 23 (Atlanta: SBL, 2018), 111–36.
34. A. Faust and S. Bunimovitz, "The Judahite Rock-Cut Tomb: Family Response at a Time of Change," *IEJ* 58.2 (2008): 161–62; Suriano, *History of Death*, 91–97.
35. Suriano, *History of Death*, 94; A. Faust and S. Bunimovitz, "The Four Room House: Embodying Iron Age Israelite Society," *NEA* 66.1–2 (2003): 28.
36. M. Cradic, "Transformations in Death: The Archaeology of Funerary Practices and Personhood in the Bronze Age Levant" (PhD dissertation, University of California, Berkeley, 2017), 41–42; Fowler, *The Archaeology of Personhood*, 48–52.
37. The use of jar burials, pit burials under floors, and burials that are ringed or somehow marked with stones, sherds, or shells is also found in the Aegean world. It should be noted that the practice of encircling a jar with stones or sherds is not limited to jar burials. Other so-called sunken jar installations (e.g., installations in Building 667) at Ashkelon also exhibit this behavior. Aja, "Grid 38," in Stager, Master, and Aja, *Ashkelon 7*, 85.
38. A. Aja, "Philistine Domestic Architecture in the Iron Age I," (PhD dissertation, Harvard University, 2009), 380–400.
39. Aja, "Philistine Domestic Architecture," 400.
40. P. Hesse and D. N. Fulton, "Faunal Remains," in Stager, Master, and Aja, *Ashkelon 7*, 723.
41. Aja argues that the item would have meaning only for the people burying the item/individual.
42. The inhabitants of Megiddo buried intramurally for many hundreds of years. M. Martin, M. Cradic, and R. Kalisher, "Area K: Intramural Pit and Jar Burials (Level K-10)," in *Megiddo VI: The 2010–2014 Seasons*, ed. I. Finkelstein and M. Martin (Winona Lake, IN: Eisenbrauns, 2022), 224–91. The use of intramural burials in Megiddo society and the place of social memory in the Middle Bronze Age has been explored by M. Cradic, "Residential Burial and Social Memory in the Middle Bronze Age Levant," *NEA* 83 (2018): 191–201; Cradic, "Transformations in Death."
43. The final report cobbles together older excavation notes from the 1940s, and it is difficult to situate the jar burial among the other finds in the square. The observations above are based on a photo. T. Harrison, *Megiddo 3: Final Report of the Stratum VI Excavations* (Chicago: Oriental Institute of the University of Chicago, 2004), Figure 77.
44. Observations based on Harrison, *Megiddo 3*, Figure 87.
45. Harrison, *Megiddo 3*, 19–20.
46. B. Arensburg, "Human Skeletal Remains from Tel Batash," in *Timnah (Tel Batash) III: The Finds from the 2nd Millennium BCE*, Qedem 45, ed. N. Panitz-Cohen and A. Mazar (Jerusalem: Hebrew University, 2006), 313; A. Mazar, "Areas A and D," in *Timnah (Tel Batash) I: Stratigraphy and Architecture*, Qedem 37, ed. A. Mazar (Jerusalem: Hebrew University, 1997), 189, 199.
47. M. Dothan, *Ashdod II–III: The Second and Third Seasons of Excavations 1963, 1965: Soundings in 1967* (Jerusalem: Department of Antiquities, 1971), 92–93.
48. N. Haas includes a note that some of these remains belong to the first season of excavation and were found near Wall 1106. N. Haas, "Anthropological Observation on the Skeletal Remains Found in Area D (1962–1963)," in *Ashdod II–III: The Second and Third Seasons of Excavation 1963, 1965*, ed. M. Dothan (Jerusalem: 'Atiqot IX–X, 1971), 212–14. The main report of Area D in *Ashdod II–III* does not include these burials.
49. Among others, see Genesis 2:7; the "Enuma Elish," COS 1.111; "Atrahasis," COS 1.130; the Berlin "Hymn to Ptah," COS 1.14 n.8; "The Legend of Isis and the Name of Re," COS 1.22; "The Ba'lu Myth," COS 1.86 n. 206.
50. K. Sonia, "Thinking with Clay: Procreation and the Ceramic Paradigm in Israelite Religion," *JNEAR* 21 (2021): 185–207. While Sonia's article specifically addresses Israelite religion, the

MEMORIALIZING DEATH 123

widespread use of clay in various ANE, Egyptian, and Greek creation myths attests to similar understandings in other cultures.

51. D. Ilan, "Mortuary Practices at Tel Dan in the Middle Bronze Age: A Reflection of Canaanite Society and Ideology," in *The Archaeology of Death in the Ancient Near East*, Oxbow Monographs 51, ed. S. Campbell and A. Green (Oxford: Oxbow Press, 1995), 135. A tomb-to-womb understanding of the entire tomb complex does not negate the association of the rock-cut tombs with the house, as discussed previously. The two understandings may exist simultaneously.

52. O. Keel, "The Peculiar Headrests for the Dead in First Temple Times," *BAR* 13.4 (1987): 50, 52–53; G. Barkay, "Burial Headrests as a Return to the Womb—a Reevaluation," *BAR* 14 (1988): 48–50.

53. The Atrahasis Epic (COS 1.130). See also COS 1.145–47: "Let us create a figure of clay and impose the toil on it," or "Enki and Ninmah," (COS 1.159). Compare this with the way creation is described in the Enuma Elish, where Marduk uses the blood of a divine being to craft the first humans (COS 1.111).

54. The "Instruction of Amenemope" (COS 1.47) describes humans as built by the divine from clay and straw. The "Legend of Isis and the Name of Re" (COS 1.22) notes that the creator animates lifeless clay into humans.

55. Genesis 3:19; Song of Solomon 3:2; and Job 4:17–2.

56. COS 1.108.

57. COS 1.153.

58. K. H. Garroway, *Children in the Ancient Near Eastern Household*, EANEC 3 (Winona Lake, IN: Eisenbrauns, 2014), 241.

59. Garroway, *Children*, 241.

60. G. Appell and L. Appell, "Death among the Rungus Momogun of Sabah, Malaysia: The Dissolution of Personhood and Dispersion of the Multiple Souls and Spiritual Counterparts," in *Journeys of the Soul: Anthropological Studies of Death, Burial, and Rebirth Practice in Borneo*, Borneo Research Council Monograph 7, ed. W. Wilder (Philips, ME: Borneo Research Council, 2003), 41–121; M. Amster, "Gender Complementarity and Death among the Kelabit," in Wilder, *Journeys of the Soul*, 251–308.

61. A. Mills and R. Slobodin, *Amerindian Rebirth: Reincarnation Belief among North American Indians and Inuit* (Toronto: University of Toronto Press, 1994), 46; J. E. King, "Infant Burials," *Classical Review* 17.1 (1903): 83.

62. J. Assmann, *Death and Salvation in Ancient Egypt*, trans. D. Lorton (Ithaca, NY: Cornell University Press, 2005), 165–73; J. Assmann, "Death and Initiation in the Funerary Religion of Ancient Egypt," in *Religion and Philosophy in Ancient Egypt*, Yale Egyptiological Studies 3, ed. J. P. Allen et al. (New Haven: Yale University Press, 1989), 139–40.

63. A comprehensive study on the relationship between the theology of rebirth found in Job as influenced by the Egyptian funerary corpus was undertaken by C. B. Hays, "My Beloved Son, Come and Rest in Me": Job's Return to His Mother's Womb (Job 1:21a) in Light of Egyptian Mythology," *VT* 62 (2012): 607–21.

64. Power and Tristant, "From Refuse to Rebirth." On Egyptian awareness of reproductive physiology see L. Meskell, *Private Life in New Kingdom Egypt* (Princeton: Princeton University Press, 2002), 68.

65. For an overview of religion, archaeology, biblical text, and the material turn, see inter alia A. Mandell and J. Smoak, "The Material Turn in the Study of Israelite Religions: Spaces, Things, and the Body," *Journal of Hebrew Scriptures* 19, Article 5 (2019): 1–42; Z. Crossland, "Materiality and Embodiment," in *The Oxford Handbook of Material Culture Studies*, ed. D. Hicks and M. C. Beaudry (Oxford: Oxford University Press, 2010), 386–405; R. Joyce, "Life with Things: Archaeology and Materiality," in *Archaeology and Anthropology: Past, Present and Future*, ed. David Shankland (London: Routledge, 2012), 119–32; S. Hazard, "The Material Turn in the Study of Religion," *Religion and Society* 4.1 (2013): 58–78; F. Stavrakopoulou, "Religion at Home: The Materiality of Practice," in *The Wiley Blackwell Companion to Ancient Israel*, ed. S. Niditch (Malden, MA: Wiley-Blackwell, 2016), 346–65.

66. L. G. Canevaro, "Review Article, Materiality and Classics: (Re)turning to the Material," *Journal of Hellenic Studies* 139 (2019): 223.

67. Sonia, "Thinking with Clay."

68. A. Gadotti, *"Gilgamesh, Enkidu, and the Netherworld" and the Sumerian Gilgamesh Cycle*, UAVA 10 (Boston: de Gruyter, 2014), 114; Sonia, "Thinking with Clay," 193.

69. K. McGeough, "Birth Bricks, Potter's Wheels, and Exodus 1:16," *Biblica* 87 (2006): 309; Sonia, "Thinking with Clay," 197.

124 INTERPRETING THE BURIALS OF CHILDREN

70. Sonia, "Thinking with Clay," 191.
71. Leviticus 11:33, 11: 35. Sonia posits that other purification rituals using ceramics do so because the ceramic vessel is easily broken and disposed of after the ritual is done (Leviticus 14:5, 14:50; Numbers 19:17). Sonia, "Thinking with Clay," 191–93.
72. Sonia, "Thinking with Clay," 191.
73. Mandell and Smoak, "Material Turn."
74. For multiple examples of the distribution of bench tombs and mudbrick built tombs, see the catalog in E. Bloch-Smith, *Judahite Burial Practices and Beliefs about the Dead*, JSOT Supp. 123, JSOT/ASOR Monograph Series 7 (Sheffield: JSOT Press, 1992).
75. The logic here is that if ceramic jars were available, why not use them? A materiality answer is that impurities can seep out through clay, while stone holds them in.
76. Y. Adler, "Watertight and Rock Solid: Stepped Pools and Chalk Vessels as Expressions of Jewish Ritual Purity," *BAR* 47 (2021): 44–51. Stuart Miller sees the use of stone and chalk in daily wares as a byproduct of the Herodian stone building industry. He argues the popularity of stone in daily ware was heightened by its non-contaminating properties. S. Miller, *At the Intersection of Texts and Material Finds: Stepped Pools, Stone Vessels, and Ritual Purity among the Jews of Roman Galilee* (Göttingen: Vandenhoeck and Ruprecht, 2019), 153–83. Celia Wassén disagrees, arguing that purity had nothing to do with stone's rise in popularity among Jews. C. Wassén, "Stepped Pools and Stone Vessels: Rethinking Jewish Purity Practices in Palestine," *BAR* 45 (2019): 52–58.
77. I am not arguing that the availability of stone was the main reason for creating bench tombs. Rather, we must consider how the materiality of the burial's construction might have correlated with the ritual beliefs held by those who used the tombs.
78. Note that during the Bronze Age it was common to find bowls covering jar burials. Yet the bowls were not sealed tightly over the jars with bitumen or the like. Rather, bowls may have been left purposely unsealed. While it is conjecture, they perhaps could have been understood to serve the same purpose as a mucus plug, releasing the child for (re)birth.
79. Assuming that Judahites adhered to some measures found in the Hebrew Bible.
80. Barkay, "Burial Headrests," 48–50. However, caution needs to be taken so as not to read the biblical text as describing a singular belief system and/or the belief system driving every single Judahite burial. For example, as Hays points out, Job 1:21 suggests a conception of death as re-birth. Looking to the archaeological record, he interprets the omega-shaped "Hathor Headrests" found in the St. Étienne tomb complex as a clear indication of both knowledge (and borrowing) of Egyptian afterlife beliefs and a reference to the tomb as womb within a Judahite rock cut bench tomb. Hays, "My Beloved Son," esp. 618–21.
81. Barkay, "Burial Headrests," 49.
82. The idea of jar burials as rebirth does not negate the possibility suggested in Chapter 2 that they also functioned as sympathetic magic. Ritual actions can have more than one meaning.
83. A. H. Goodman and G. J. Armelagos, "Infant and Childhood Morbidity and Mortality Risks in Archaeological Populations," *WA* 21 (1989): 225–43.
84. Wilk and Rathje's position that transmission was an important part of the household dynamic focused on the "transfer of rights, roles, land, and property between generations." R. Wilk and W. Rathje, "Household Archaeology," *American Behavioral Scientist* 25.6 (1982): 677. The connection to family burials in this regard is important.
85. On the Egyptian influence in Canaan and the wider Levant during the Late Bronze Age, see E. Cline, *1177 B.C. The Year Civilization Collapsed* (Princeton: Princeton University Press, 2014), and Hays, *A Covenant with Death*, 281–355.
86. For an overview of burials that included scarabs during different phases of the Iron Age, see Bloch-Smith, *Judahite Burial Practices*, 84. Other Egyptian amulets appear in burials, including the Eye of Horus, Bes, Isis, Bast, and so forth. Bloch-Smith, *Judahite Burial Practices*, 83, 83 n. 2, 144.
87. C. B. Hays, "The Covenant with Mut: A New Interpretation of Isaiah 28:1–22," *VT* 60 (2010): 217.
88. Hays, "The Covenant with Mut"; C. B. Hays, "The Egyptian Goddess Mut in Iron Age Palestine: Further Data from Amulet and Onomastics," *JNES* 71 (2012): 299–300.
89. The book of Isaiah is not alone. Jeremiah also laments the influx of foreign religious practices, most notably in the passages concerning the Queen of Heaven (Jeremiah 7 and 45).

6

Children and Infants in Judahite Family Tombs

Death is relational, and representations of death in the mortuary record paint an idealized picture.[1] The Iron Age burials described in the previous chapters provide proof that what is considered ideal can vary from one community to the next. Yet it is possible to see three overarching patterns in the burial record. First, outside of Judah there are the burials that are specific to the youngest members of society, namely jar burials. Even though a few adults appear buried this way, as a whole, the phenomenon of jar burials remains primarily linked to infants and very young children. Second, burials on the coast and in the north lean more toward individualized burials. This trend begins in Iron I and continues into the Iron II period. Infant jar burials, bathtub coffins, simple inhumations, pits, cists, and cremations all appear outside of Judah. Finally, after Iron I, when the mortuary record in Judah becomes visible again, a specific pattern appears: the population of Judah used bench or rock-cut tombs, that is, "family tombs."[2] In this way, burials seen in Judah present a certain unified picture of death. The current chapter delves into this unified image, asking why it appears in Judah and how infants and children fit into the picture.

Households of Life and Death

Infants, children, and adults alike were eligible for burial within the Judahite family bench tomb; the family that lives together, dies together.[3] The decision of the living to bury their dead infants and children within the family tomb is significant. It speaks to the role of infants and children within the household of the dead. However, before exploring their potential role, it is necessary to understand the relationship between the households of the living and the dead within Judah.[4]

The Dying Child. Kristine Henriksen Garroway, Oxford University Press. © Oxford University Press 2025.
DOI: 10.1093/9780197566718.003.0007

126 INTERPRETING THE BURIALS OF CHILDREN

Most of the population of the Southern Levant was engaged in subsistence agriculture. The cities and villages, and the mortuary remains associated with them, represent a smaller urban contingency.[5] Yet both populations, urban and rural, constructed houses built on the four-room house plan, suggesting a common understanding of the household structure; their households were based on the *bet 'av*.[6] As noted in the introduction, households comprise three different components: the physical space, the activities within that space, and the people who populate the space.[7] The similarities between the physical structure of the household of the living (the four-room house) and the household of the dead (the bench tomb) has been explored most recently by Matthew Suriano.[8] Drawing upon older studies, he demonstrates that the layouts of the house for the living and of the house for the dead are spatially similar. Both the tomb and the house follow what household archaeologists have called the egalitarian "tree shape" pathway of access, versus what might be seen in Canaanite-Phoenician dwellings that followed a more prohibitive access of a "railroad"-style layout.[9] Suriano notes that central access is of utmost importance in studies of houses and calls attention to its importance in the tombs as well. Central access allows anyone entering the tomb to have access to all areas of the tomb. In other words, access to space and the individuals within those spaces was not guarded.

The spatial use of houses, however, does not map directly onto the spatial use in tombs. For example, houses have spaces for weaving, cooking, food preparation, eating, housing animals, storage, conducting family economic business, and so forth. Sleeping areas were thought to be on the second story of the house. These same activities are not all present in households of the dead, or if they are, they are not necessarily done in the same places. I would, however, point out that even though the use of the spaces by the living does not directly map onto spaces of the dead, we can still draw parallels in spatial use between tombs and houses. For example, rooms in houses had primary and secondary uses, and this seems to be the case with bench tombs as well. Second, like houses, the bench tombs had spaces assigned for specific uses. In the case of the tombs, these were spaces for bone repositories, benches for bodies, communal gathering space in entryways, and collection areas for the ceramic grave goods used in the mortuary rituals. Additionally, there is a loose parallel between the two main activities associated with the house: eating and sleeping. Finally, the people who populate the households of the dead and households of the living are also similar. Both the four-room

CHILDREN AND INFANTS IN JUDAHITE FAMILY TOMBS 127

house and bench tomb are used by a multigenerational family. Generations live together in life and in death respectively.

The following analysis of infants and children within the Judahite family tomb relies upon anthropological theories, archaeological data, and the texts of the Hebrew Bible. For cultures like ancient Israel, which hold a belief in an afterlife, dying involves a three-part transition. The first stage of dying is biological death, where the body becomes a corpse. The second stage, or liminal stage, is represented by the time in the tomb, when an individual has no fixed state of being. As is common to liminal phases, this is the time when a dying individual needs the most care and protection. Since interment and preservation can differ for individuals, the personhood question remains relevant. The final phase occurs when the individual transitions to the afterlife. In this last phase, the age and personhood of the individual determine how the individual enters the afterlife. Previous studies have examined how this process might unfold for adults, thereby providing a theoretical steppingstone for envisioning how the dying process might unfold for children in Judah.[10] The remainder of the chapter examines the tripartite dying process, investigating the Judahite child in the corpse phase, liminal phase, and afterlife.

The Corpse of the Judahite Child within the Household of the Dead

Given the comparisons between the four-room house and tomb, an emphasis on family tombs during the tumultuous Iron Age II period may have been a means of maintaining the household of the living in the household of the dead. If, as Avraham Faust and Shlomo Bunimovitz hypothesize, the bench tomb was meant as a counter-symbol to the rapid rise in urbanization and the changing social dynamics within the urban center, this might explain the use of bench tombs in locations that are close to urban areas.[11] City life that decentralized the family and loosened ties to the larger kin network was countered by tombs that preserved the family ties. This conclusion is reminiscent of the way that Early Bronze II–III charnel tombs and Middle Bronze II built tombs were associated with urbanization.[12] Suriano concludes that "the rock-cut design of the bench tomb imitated the plan of the typical Judahite house in order to create a house for dead bodies."[13]

However, there may be more to this layout than just creating a house for the dead. The adoption of a particular house-style tomb could also be related

128   INTERPRETING THE BURIALS OF CHILDREN

to social memory and memory making.[14] The common tomb becomes a place to be visited and revisited, drawing connections between the living and the dead and (re)constructing social identities. Given the political turmoil (as witnessed by various wars) and competing ideologies Judah faced (as expressed in the Hebrew Bible), the Judahite tomb could function as a means of confirming ethnic identity.[15] Indeed the tomb could function as a means of continuity and stabilization during times of turmoil and change. As Kerry Sonia has pointed out: "Both the family and the state are in a constant process of making and unmaking themselves, always losing and gaining new members."[16] With respect to infants and children, burial in the family tomb became a way of stabilizing loss by marking the dying children as Judahite and including them in the collective household of death.

The desire to mark infants and children as Judahite seems to be part of a larger movement within the Iron II–III. Two other practices echo the desire to tie the youngest members of the household to Judean society. The first practice is that of circumcision. As practiced by different ancient Near Eastern (ANE) cultures, circumcision was undertaken around adolescence as a rite of passage.[17] Texts speak of the ceremony in relation to rituals, fertility, and impending marriages.[18] For example, the Ugaritic corpus (*KTU* 1.23 and *KTU* 1.24) speaks of circumcision in mythological marriage. In the Hebrew Bible, Shechem must undergo circumcision before marrying Dinah (Genesis 34:14–17), and King David brings back foreskins of the Philistines as a bride-price for his marriage to King Saul's daughter (1 Samuel 18:25). Yet, according to Leviticus 12:3, circumcision did not happen during adolescence but on the eighth day. Genesis 17 provides the etiology for this practice, laying out the link between circumcision and membership in the covenant:[19] "For the Israelites, circumcision was transformed from a ceremony marking social maturity and virility to a ceremony quite literally marking the member as a part of a fertile covenantal line."[20] Failure to circumcise resulted in an individual being cutoff from the community (Genesis 17:14). If Genesis 17 was penned by the Priestly writer who was writing in exile, then infant circumcision could be a way to ensure that the Judahites in the Diaspora maintained their covenantal group identity from the moment a son was born.[21]

While it is impossible to know how widely the Priestly laws of Leviticus 12 and Genesis 17 were practiced, it is important to note the specific role of infants in maintaining Judahite group identity with respect to exile and death. According to the biblical text, for those Judahites in exile, the marker of group identity is to be inscribed upon the body before death.[22] Moreover,

CHILDREN AND INFANTS IN JUDAHITE FAMILY TOMBS   129

it appears to be essential that all males be marked this way, not just adolescent males. Why this shift? Not only did many infants die young, but war, exile, and potential slavery could also mean that children might die young. It seems reasonable to infer that Judahites in exile would wish to make sure that others knew very early on that they were Judahite. In doing so, they retained their identity within a cosmopolitan setting.

According to the biblical text, group identity was important not only for maintaining one's place in the land of the living but also in the society of the dead. The belief that circumcision determines one's experience in the afterlife is most clearly expressed in another exilic text. Ezekiel 32:17–31 discusses the death of Israel's enemies and says they shall go down to the pit and lie in death with the uncircumcised.[23] The particular pit in question here is the repository for all manner of unsavory, non-Judahite individuals, that is, the uncircumcised. Such a belief would provide an impetus for circumcising one's son as an infant so that he did not endure a horrible, shameful existence in the afterlife should his own life be cutoff at an early age.[24] Notably, the concern here would be with the afterlife of sons and not daughters.[25]

If residual trauma inflicted by Babylonian exile might have encouraged infant circumcision, pressure in the previous Iron II period where the *potential* exile loomed heavy might by the same token have encouraged the inclusion of infants and children within bench tombs. Noting that previous periods saw infants excluded from family burials, placed in jars or simple inhumations within the settlement, or under house floors, a shift to including the youngest members of a household in a family burial could be a conscious ideological statement: infants and children were Judahite persons or Judahite persons *in potentia*; they were an important part of the Judahite household. Unlike circumcision, the corpses of both the dying male and female child would be marked as Judahite by their burial.

The other practice related to infants/children and ethnic identity is the use of Judean pillar figurines (JPFs). JPFs, like rock-cut bench tombs, appeared in different areas in the early Iron II period, but became popular within Judah during the eighth to seventh c. BCE. Ian Wilson hypothesizes that JPFs' increased use during this time was a direct result of the ever-expanding hold of the Neo-Assyrian empire. He suggests that JPFs were part of a late Iron Age discourse to uphold and/or construct Judahite identity. As noted, bench tombs are understood in the same way. While JPFs might be an ethnic identity marker, their exact use and what they represent are a little harder to discern. Found everywhere from large public buildings, to houses, to streets,

130 INTERPRETING THE BURIALS OF CHILDREN

refuse pits, and even a few tombs, the large-breasted females have been identified as a goddess or icon of family or popular religion.[26] Scholars think they may have been used as a fertility mediatrix, or more likely in exorcistic or apotropaic rituals related to the health of the family.[27] All means of illness or harm could befall the most vulnerable members of the household, from SIDS, to malaria, to dysentery, to malnutrition, et cetera.[28] Given the importance of children to the health of the nation (among other things, they would eventually be needed to serve in the army in case of war), their well-being within the household served not only familial needs but national needs as well. If used as scholars suggest, then JPFs would be another way in which infants and children are connected both to an item marking ethnic identity and to an item potentially linked with childhood death.

Infants and children have not always been included in discussions about Judahite markers of ethnic identity.[29] Yet, as these examples have demonstrated, infants and children are important to the discussion of Judahite identity. Moreover, as set out here, Judahite identity was not only fostered in life but also formed in relationship to the (potential) death of the infant or child. The conclusions here argue for understanding infants and children as having a degree of personhood in life that was extended into death. If understood as Judahite, then it would stand to reason that the physical body of the infant or child would be cared for in a Judahite manner as it went through the transitional dying phase, when the corpse moved through the de-fleshing period to its final, skeletal form.

Betwixt and Between: The Dying Child in the Liminal Phase

In anthropological terms, the dying process can be understood as a transitional ritual. Victor Turner, drawing upon Arnold van Gennep, emphasized the liminal experience that took place in a rite of passage.[30] During this time the individual was betwixt and between, neither in one state nor the other, but transitioning. The liminal space is something of a paradox. It both separates and joins individuals. On the one hand, the individual is separated from society as part of the transitioning phase. At the same time, a liminal individual is drawn into a shared space with others in the liminal phase. Turner describes this phenomenon as *communitas*.[31]

The liminal, or transitional, phase is particularly important for the dying body. As neither one thing nor another, the dying body was in

CHILDREN AND INFANTS IN JUDAHITE FAMILY TOMBS   131

need of specific ritual protection.[32] What exactly was being protected as it transitioned is a sticky topic, as it brings to the fore the question of how the ancient Israelites understood the relationship, if any, between the body and soul.[33] This study embraces the concept of functional immortality.[34] Immortality as understood by the Hebrew Bible and other ANE literature was the "preservation and endurance of one's legacy."[35] Preservation and endurance of one's legacy has been understood as pertaining to the dead *adult*. Preserve the *dead adult's* legacy. Legacy involves one's inheritance, reputation, name, and things passed down. This understanding of functional immortality means the living need to preserve all these things that were related to the now-deceased adult for future generations to come. But legacy can also refer to children. If we reread "preservation and endurance of one's legacy" with children in mind, then additional possibilities arise. First, it could mean keeping children safe and alive so that they might reproduce and in doing so carry on the deceased adult's lineage. Suriano links this understanding to the ideology found in the Epic of Gilgamesh, Tablet XII in the conversation between Gilgamesh and his dead friend Enkidu. As they go back and forth with question and answer, Gilgamesh inquires about the dead man with one, two, three, four, five, six, and seven (living) sons. The more sons one had, the epic recounts, the greater a father's joy, and the easier a father's afterlife existence became and the more a father's chances for a lasting legacy increased.[36] Such a view of functional immortality demonstrates a deep concern for children.

So far, these understandings of functional immortality have assumed the deceased was an adult. Yes, sons bury their fathers, but fathers also bury their children. What happens to the definition of functional immortality when the deceased is a child? A child obviously does not have children, but does a child have a legacy to pass on or preserve? Can a child transition to the afterlife in the same manner as adults, or does something else happen to children? The Epic of Gilgamesh provides another thought- provoking example via the question Gilgamesh poses to Enkidu regarding his own children. "Did you see my little stillborn children who never knew existence?" "I saw them." "How do they fare?" "They play at a table of gold and silver, laden with honey and ghee."[37] Gilgamesh's stillborn children were in the afterlife, sitting at a table befitting their royal status, enjoying the best food and drink possible. Not only does the Gilgamesh epic attest to the afterlife and the importance of legacy, but it demonstrates the preservation of the same household structure in life as in death.[38] These were royal children receiving a royal place in the afterlife. The reference to eating and drinking in the afterlife is also significant.

132 INTERPRETING THE BURIALS OF CHILDREN

These are activities done while one is living and also by the adults in the afterlife. The Gilgamesh narrative therefore provides a neat explanation for the relationship of children to the concept of functional immortality. But are these ideas also seen in ancient Israel? I would argue yes. The Gilgamesh epic hints at the possibility that children, like adults, had a certain status, but more importantly, needed food and drink in the afterlife. Similar arguments have been made to explain the presence of ceramic goods alongside adults in tombs, and Judahite bench tombs provide a great deal of evidence for arguing that children also needed certain items to reach functional immortality.

Judahite Bench Tombs and Grave Goods

Most bench tombs were found empty, making those tombs that do contain both skeletal and ceramic remains all the more important for reconstructing the burial record.[39] When grave goods are found near bodies laid out in primary burial, they are usually arranged around the body.[40] Lamps were placed by the head or in small niches next to headrests or in the walls, as evidenced by residual soot.[41] Notably the lamps that were found by heads or as grave goods did not show evidence of use, leading to the conclusion that they were for symbolic rather than practical use.[42] Other ceramic items included those used for food preparation or storage, such as cooking pots, bowls, jars, and juglets.[43] In some cases, seals, simple rings, beads, or other jewelry accompanied the burials.[44] When the corpse was ready for secondary burial, the items that accompanied the body would be removed, along with the bones, and placed in the repository pit or deposited on the floor of the tomb. Consider the intact repository pit found at Ketef Hinnom, which contained items of glass, metal, ivory, and bone. These objects were more personal in nature, including seals, toiletry items, and jewelry.[45] The ceramics found in the pit included juglets, perfume bottles, lamps, and decanters. Such pottery "is typical of burial caves, with no storage or cooking vessels."[46]

Knowing whether infants and children were given grave goods has an impact on how we understand the way the living adults processed their deaths. When grave goods were deposited, the question then becomes, what was meant by the deposition of these grave goods? Theories of grave goods in bench tombs suggest that grave goods were needed by the dying corpse only to help it on its journey to the afterlife. The objects once visible become invisible to the living, remaining only "present" for the deceased.[47] Once the

CHILDREN AND INFANTS IN JUDAHITE FAMILY TOMBS 133

corpse had decomposed and the social being entered its next stage in the afterlife, travel provisions were no longer necessary. Rather than a functionalist approach that sees skeletal remains and grave goods removed from benches simply to make more room, the approach here takes into consideration the transitional nature of death and the process of dying.[48] Burials are done with intention and placement of objects and individuals is done for a reason. This idea goes to the heart of the mortuary ritual *process*. A burial and the rites conducted are often thought of as a one-time occurrence; however, they happen over a period of time, be it months, weeks, days, or even hours.[49] It is a sequence of transformative acts that are connected to the biological, social, and spiritual transformations understood to occur at death.[50] Within this process the grave goods take on an important role as symbols within the transformative process.[51] As symbols, the grave goods are meant to communicate.[52] Moreover, the message an object communicates may differ from one context to another.[53] Returning to the aforementioned lamps, I would point out that, in addition to a practical use, providing light, a lamp might have one meaning when found in a domestic context and a different meaning in a funerary context.

Revisiting the idea of intention, even the removal of items to a repository pit needs to be considered. Why were individuals and items included and not excluded from the pit? Children and infants, like adults, were included. Personal items, jewelry, perfume bottles, and small luxury items were also included. Were these objects placed in the pit because they were impure due to contact with the deceased? Removed because they ceased functioning when the body decomposed? Or perhaps because they still held a connection to the deceased or were inextricably bound to the beings with whom they were deposited? These questions will be explored in the case study below.

Tel 'Ira: A Case Study in Grave Goods and Partible Personhood

The most complete picture we have of infant and child burials in bench tombs comes from the cemetery at Tel 'Ira (see Table 6.1). Piecing together the physical anthropology report and field notes allows one to make some observations about the grave goods deposited in the tombs.[54] Eight of the ten tombs excavated contained infant or child remains. The physical anthropology report discusses only those remains that were complete enough to analyze. However, the field report attests to the presence of many more bones

134 INTERPRETING THE BURIALS OF CHILDREN

Table 6.1 Ages of Individuals in the Bench Tombs at Tel 'Ira

Tomb Number	0–5 years old	5–10 years old	10–14 years old	14–18 years old	Over 18 years old
3	1	0	1	0	0
4	1	0	0	0	3
5	3	1	0	0	2
8	0	0	1	0	3
9	0	1	0	1	2
14	5	0	0	1	4
15	1	0	0	1	3
23	1	0	1	1	3
Total number of burials	12	2	3	4	22

in poor condition, some of which might have belonged to additional infants and children. Following the pattern of many eighth to seventh c. bench tombs, secondary burials were removed to the floor and not to a repository pit.[55]

With the exception of Tomb 23, the burials date to the ninth/eighth to the seventh c. BCE.[56] In every tomb listed, bones were found gathered on the floor and ceramic objects dispersed throughout. The ceramic items include bowls, jugs, chalices, juglets, strainers, lamps, and kraters. Adornment and personal items including earrings, bracelets, necklaces, and rings were found in Tombs 13, 14, 15, and 23.

When we cross- examine both the field notes and the physical anthropology report, a few of the tombs in particular stand out. Tomb 3 is noteworthy because all the skeletal remains were found deposited in a corner.[57] This means that the remains of the child and teenager were found intermingled together with those of adults. Likewise, in Tomb 4 the bones were intentionally gathered in a single area, specifically near the southwest bench. The single infant was found among the adults, along with twenty-five pottery sherds. Tomb 14 is significant because in addition to the seven bodies on the floor, there was a flexed burial in a corner, as well as the remains of a two- year- old.[58] Since a primary burial was found on a bench, it is possible that those remains found on the floor, including the two- year- old, were all secondary burials.

CHILDREN AND INFANTS IN JUDAHITE FAMILY TOMBS   135

Primary bench-burials were found in Tombs 5, 13, 14, and 15. However, in only one of these, Tomb 15, were children identified on a bench. Tomb 15 comprises three chambers: the entrance chamber (locus 115), the north chamber (locus 119), and the west chamber (locus 120). In locus 115, the left bench held a woman and her seven- to eight-year-old child.[59] The woman appeared to be cradling the child in her arm. On the right bench of this tomb, ten individuals were found, five of whom were juveniles.[60] The bones on the floor of Tomb 15 included a fully formed skull of a fetus, suggesting that even fetuses were given a burial.[61] Two burials were found on the bench in locus 120. One of these burials belonged to a juvenile, who had black fabric adhering to the skull, perhaps remnants of a burial shroud.[62] Scattered bone and iron were also on the bench. The ceramic finds for this tomb were extensive in comparison to the other tombs. However, the finds are presented in a list, making it difficult to know whether they were associated with a specific bench or floor deposit. The grave goods included four bowls, four jugs, one chalice, seven juglets, two jugs, one strainer, three lamps, four jars, one arrowhead, one strainer jar, one bronze item, and one alabaster pyxis.[63]

The mix of personal grave goods and ceramic wares, and the variety of burial styles and ages deposited over time in Tomb 15, present a complex mortuary picture. The interment of children on benches along with adults is suggestive. It would appear that the woman and child laid out in primary burial in locus 115 may have died around the same time. However, what of the ten burials on the other bench? Did they too die at the same time? Or were they all family members who might have died before the previous inhabitant of the bench had fully decomposed and been transformed? Did the bench serve as a means of keeping a lineage together? If so, it would appear that children were considered to have enough personhood to merit burial with their kin and were afforded the same mortuary rites as the adults. The inclusion of all ages in the tomb, including a two-year-old and a fetus found on the floor, argues for degrees of personhood being recognized in even the youngest members of society, for all ages were afforded a good burial in death.

Discussion of Tel 'Ira

What mortuary rites might entail for Iron II Judahites has been the topic of many studies.[64] Certainly their Canaanite predecessors engaged in a cult of the dead, and while the biblical text protests against such a cult, it

136 INTERPRETING THE BURIALS OF CHILDREN

is impossible to ignore all of the references suggesting it existed.[65] The cult construed broadly involved caring for dead kin.[66] Part of this care was a proper or good burial.[67] If the cemetery at Tel 'Ira is representative of Judahite bench tomb practice in general, then we see that those communities who buried in bench tombs made sure to provide their infants and children with good burials.[68] A good burial included not only interment in the family tomb but deposition with grave goods. Here the concept of partible personhood, which will be discussed more below, becomes significant.[69]

In cases where it is impossible to determine what grave goods were associated with which individuals, it is perhaps more useful to look to the places where grave goods and skeletal remains were intermingled. Indeed, for the current investigation of children and infants, this remains the best way to view grave goods. Investigating the relationship of individuals and material culture is necessary for reconstructions of personhood in an archaeological context.[70] If we understand grave goods to be placed with intention around a primary burial, through the materiality of the object, a chain of events takes place.[71] First, individuals placing the grave good impart some of their personhood to the object.[72] Here the concepts of divisibility and partible personhood are important.[73] Note that with partibility, "Parts of oneself originate in and belong to others. These can be identified as objects and extracted."[74] In the current context the objects are grave goods, which leads to the second point, that grave goods are in relationship with the dying body. Third, regardless of when the grave good ceases to function, the relationship of the dying body with the grave good means that the dying body imparts some of its own personhood onto the object. Finally, given that personhood is partible and permeable, this means that when the skeletal remains and grave goods are moved into a secondary burial space and intermingled with older burials, many personhoods become intermingled. This is not to say things become a meaningless, complicated mess. To the contrary, the intermingling of the personhoods imparted on individuals and objects both past and present creates new bonds, thereby reinforcing social memory and kinship bonds.

Based on this analysis, the placement of infants and children in areas of tomb floors, and/or their deposit into repository pits in areas where the adults of their community were placed along with grave goods, takes on special meaning. The living members of a society actively chose not only to include their infants and children in bench tombs but also to collect their remains and intermingle them with adults and "adult" grave goods. As referenced in Table 4.1, this is seen in the repository pit at Ketef Hinnom,

CHILDREN AND INFANTS IN JUDAHITE FAMILY TOMBS   137

where over ninety-five individuals of all ages were found along with over one thousand objects.[75] So too, in the bench tomb of Mt. Zion, where the bones of infants, children, and adults were separated not by age, but by type. Long bones were in one pile and skulls in a second pile, and grave goods were scattered throughout.[76] Rather than excluding infants and children or placing them in a slightly different area, they were fully incorporated into the household of the dead, where they are given functional immortality.

Feeding the Dead in Light of Texts and Grave Goods

Many ancient West Asian cultures believed that part of the cult of the ancestors or cult of the dead kin included feeding or feasting with the ancestors.[77] Some, like the Mesopotamians, had a robust definition of what rations should be offered to those dwelling in the afterlife. As Seth Richardson states: "Food offerings might go well beyond bread to include fruit, spice, salt, tortoises, turtles, chaff, sheep, or mouthfuls of locust fat (yes: disgusting)."[78] The Ugaritic texts and the Epic of Aqhat include lines that reference feasting with the dead or on behalf of the dead.[79] The archaeological record also connects death and food, and Late Bronze Age tombs from Ugarit are known for having covering stones with holes in them.[80] The holes are referred to as "drinking tubes," through which, it is thought, libations could be poured into the tombs.[81] Feasting or offering food is seen in the Phoenician world near funeral pyres, while monumental evidence from Sam'al (Iron II) suggests that feeding the dead coincided with feeding the gods.[82]

A few biblical texts (Deuteronomy 26:14; Isaiah 56:6; Jeremiah 16:7; Hosea 9:4; Job 21:25; Psalms 106:28) have presented a challenge to interpreters who understood them to say that food (for various reasons) was prohibited within Judahite mortuary rituals.[83] Others, however, see these verses as attesting to the very fact that food offerings were a part of the death rituals.[84] Indeed, the ceramic corpus from Judah itself attests to the fact that food was commonly included in bench tombs. The question for Iron II Judah, then, is not whether food was a part of the mortuary ritual but how the food in the ritual functioned. Was the food that was placed in the tomb thought to feed the deceased or to sustain the corpse as it went through the transitional phase?[85] Perhaps these ceramic dishes were deemed no longer fit for common use, as they were used in a meal associated with the dead, and so they were buried with the deceased. Or, as seen in other societies, it may be

138 INTERPRETING THE BURIALS OF CHILDREN

that the ceramic items within the tomb were meant to function symbolically, placing the dying corpse in *communitas* with the living who were eating.[86]

Matthew Suriano points to the primary burials at Khirbet Beit Lei Tomb 1, where no grave goods were placed on the benches. He suggests that since we know grave goods were eventually placed close to the corpse, the grave goods were placed later, "during the intermediary stage between primary and secondary burial," rather than during the initial phases of burial.[87] This possibility raises some questions. First, was the mortuary practice seen at Khirbet Beit Lei the standard practice? If Suriano's suggestion is correct for Khirbet Beit Lei, did *all* individuals receive grave goods related to feasting, or only some? If only some, then what were the qualifications? Age, status in the community of the living, status in the community of the dead, rank, something else, or a combination of things? Without direct information, one can only speculate on the myriad of possibilities and the implications therein. For example, it is possible that the younger the individual, the less food was needed.[88] Consider that the funeral kit for a Canaanite jar burial generally contained a juglet, likely because an infant drank only milk.[89] Because we do not have much information linking ceramics to infant and child burials in bench tombs, it is difficult to know how many items they received in comparison to the adults in the tomb. Yet, unless Judahites held to a completely different standard, breaking not only with past Canaanite tradition but also with the traditions seen in the individual graves of infants and children in surrounding lands, it is reasonable to infer that infants and children alike were afforded some number of vessels for food items.[90]

Since all of the suggestions in the previous paragraphs seem possible, it is difficult to come to a single conclusion regarding the intended function of the grave goods.[91] Ultimately, however the ceramic dishes were meant, however many were deposited directly with infants and children, they, like the bones, underwent both a primary and a secondary deposition. And, in this secondary deposition, ceramic items, adults, children, and infants were intentionally intermingled and then gathered into the household of the dead.

A Child's Personhood in the Liminal Phase

Care for the dying body through the transitional phase is related to ritual activities carried out at the tomb.[92] The condition of the body and any protection afforded during the liminal phase was dependent upon those burying

CHILDREN AND INFANTS IN JUDAHITE FAMILY TOMBS   139

the body. In this way, "The ritual actions that resulted in the burial of the dead were meaningful."[93] This observation is particularly important in the discussion of children as it pertains to their personhood. As noted, the living had an important role in the preservation of the dead; the living present the dead as they wish them to be seen and as they wish them to be preserved.[94] I have argued in this chapter that the intentional preservation of children either in individual or in family burials is related to the kind of personhood a society placed on that child. For Judahite children buried in family bench tombs, care would have indicated their place within Judahite society, as members in both the household of the living and the household of the dead.[95]

Rather than individualized, as personhood is understood in contemporary Western societies, personhood in the lands of ancient Israel was partible. Partible personhood extends not only to the skeletal remains but to the grave goods that were given. Focusing on the materiality of objects made and given, we should understand part of the personhood of the living members was passed on to those receiving the goods. In turn, when grave goods were collected along with skeletal remains and deposited in a common area, either a repository pit or gathered with other skeletal remains in the tomb, the personhoods of all individuals connected to the grave goods would intermingle.

Examining grave goods through the lens of partible personhood provides a new way of thinking about grave goods, especially those grave goods found in repository pits or heaped together. Sometimes the process of time has caused goods to form an amalgam of items stuck together. When this happens, especially with bones, excavation reports will say the bones were "undefinable," seemingly dismissing the remains as having any lasting significance or as beyond the bounds of analysis. Ironically, time and climate conditions have perhaps done what societies intended all along: collected the remains together, incorporating the individual into the group. The individual has been "gathered to the ancestors" so much so that it is impossible to distinguish one from another. Most important, within Judean bench tombs, infants and children alike were intentionally brought into this collective.

Navigating a New Relationship: Children in the Cult of Ancestors / Cult of the Dead Kin?

The introduction presented the many different studies that have concentrated on what has been called the cult of the dead. Within these studies, there are

140 INTERPRETING THE BURIALS OF CHILDREN

those who argue for a cult of the ancestors. Such a cult would have involved the veneration of ancestors. Scholars disagree as to whether the ancestors would have been able to provide blessings or benefits to the living community and whether necromancy played a role in the cult.[96] Who could become an ancestor and the ancestor's role within the larger household of the living and the dead is a question often danced around. Studies will discuss the ancestors without directly saying who they are. For example, Rüdiger Schmitt states that "the 'ābōt are thought to have comprised a collective, to whom the deceased were 'gathered' . . . or next to who they 'laid' themselves . . . thus reflecting family coherence even in post-mortem existence."[97] It appears that the ancestor was a named dead person with living kin and descendants. To be an ancestor, one must have a biological child or have adopted a child; those who die childless are not candidates for ancestor-hood.[98] I would further add that in societies where only dominant males can achieve full personhood, it is the dominant male, here the paterfamilias, who could become an ancestor.[99] As members of the natal or extended family, other adults or children could be buried with the paterfamilias. Taking this to the logical conclusion, children and infants would not fulfill the requirements needed to be an ancestor; however, they do fit within the larger cult of the dead kin.[100] As such, they are cared for in the same manner as other members of their community.

If infants and children were not transitioning into ancestors, then we can ask what they were transitioning into. In those areas outside of Judah, infants and children seem to have a different relationship to the rest of the household of the dead. In these regions, we often see individual infants and children buried in cemeteries or even within tombs next to adults in their community. Additionally, many of the sites examined retained older practices of cave burials, similar to those found in Canaanite times. While infant or child burials in cave tombs or cemeteries are in the same general location as adults, this does not necessarily indicate similar status or a similar relationship to the other members of the dying community. In fact, it appears to be the opposite. In places like Tell el-Far'ah South there are tombs with common burial areas, shallow graves, and cremations.[101] Tell el-'Orēme attests to cist burials inside the settlement as well as simple graves and modified jar burials within the site.[102] And at Megiddo Tomb 37, various styles were used within a single tomb for burials.[103]

This picture is also different on the Phoenician coast, for example, where one finds a variety of burial methods, with infants and children often buried

CHILDREN AND INFANTS IN JUDAHITE FAMILY TOMBS   141

differently than other members of their society. At places like Tyre and Tel Bira, where adults of the community are cremated, children and infants are not. When infants are found in urns or cremation burials, these occur not in houses, but in cemeteries or tombs ('Atlit). The Philistine coast again shows a mixed trend, where sometimes the youngest are included in cemeteries (Ashkelon), while other times the youngest are removed from the rest of the burial population and placed in intramural infant jar burials (Ashkelon, Timnah, Miqne-Ekron) or absent entirely from the burial record (Yavne-Yam). It is possible that in these other areas, the household of the dead is constructed differently than it is within Judah.

Through their physical architecture, use of space, and the materials present within, cave tombs and Judahite bench tombs emphasize the collective, the family. Because family burials continue the household into death, it is suggested that Judahite children, who have established some social relationships and are buried similarly to adults in their community, are transitioning into their place as family members in the afterlife. This appears especially true for the burials in Judahite bench tombs. The inclusion of grave goods suggests that while children and infants may not have been part of the cult of the ancestors, they received care and were part of the general cult of the dead kin. Just as feeding or caring for the defunct soul was important for adults, so too was it for children and infants.

Personhood is also a key issue in determining what children transform into. Again, the ideas of differentiated and partible personhood are essential. While infants and children were not transitioning into ancestors, it might be that specific children, especially male children, may have been understood as ancestors *in potentia* in the same way that we understand a crown prince to be king *in potentia*. While skeletal analysis does not allow for sex differentiation in subadults, it is reasonable to suggest that in a patriarchal society, children buried with adults may have been males and received preferential treatment due to their potential for full personhood. Such children may also have had a privileged place within the larger kinship network. Infants, on the other hand, who have few social connections and are buried differently from the members in their society, are not ancestors *in potentia*. This is not to say that infants are not afforded personhood but that their degree of personhood was not great enough for them to be considered a possible ancestor. In this case, infants remain infants within the household.

142 INTERPRETING THE BURIALS OF CHILDREN

Notes

1. Death as idealized and relational is argued in the introduction.
2. For an additional overview and historical analysis of the bench tomb and burials in surrounding areas, see M. Suriano's discussion of the Judahite Bench Tomb in *A History of Death in the Hebrew Bible* (Oxford: Oxford University Press, 2018), 91–97. It should be noted that while some bench tombs and cave burials have been discovered in areas outside of Iron II Judah, they appear not to the exclusion of other burial styles.
3. See Chapter 4.
4. It is possible that the conclusions drawn here for the societies using bench tombs in Judah might apply equally to the areas in Samaria that also have burials in bench tombs. Since our understanding of bench tombs in Samaria is limited, and the skeletal remains there even more so, the discussion here remains focused on Judah.
5. See the discussion of burial caves around Jerusalem and their relationship to the inhabitants in A. Kloner, "Iron Age Burial Caves in Jerusalem and its Vicinity," *BAIAS* 19–20 (2001): 113–14.
6. C. Meyers, *Rediscovering Eve: Ancient Israelite Women in Context* (Oxford: Oxford University Press, 2013), 112–13; S. Bender, *The Social Structure of Ancient Israel: The Institution of the Family* (beit 'ab) *from Settlement to the End of the Monarchy* (Jerusalem: Simor, 1996); W. Dever, *The Lives of Ordinary People in Ancient Israel: Where Archaeology and the Bible Intersect* (Grand Rapids: Eerdmans, 2012), esp. 47–105.
7. R. Wilk and W. Rathje, "Household Archaeology," *American Behavioral Scientist* 25.6 (1982): 618; C. Foster and B. Parker, "Introduction: Household Archaeology in the Near East and Beyond," in *New Perspectives in Household Archaeology*, ed. C. Foster and B. Parker (Winona Lake, IN: Eisenbrauns, 2012), 1.
8. Suriano, *History of Death*, 93–97.
9. A. Faust and S. Bunimovitz, "The Four Room House: Embodying Iron Age Israelite Society," *NEA* 66.1–2 (2003): 28. See the helpful diagram in Suriano, *History of Death*, 94, Figure 12.
10. For example, H. C. Brichto's "Kin, Cult, Land, and Afterlife—a Biblical Complex," *HUCA* 44 (1973): 1–54. M. Suriano's *History of Death*, and K. Sonia's *Caring for the Dead in Ancient Israel* (Atlanta: SBL Press, 2020) examine adult death in text and archaeology. Books such as T. Lewis's *Cults of the Dead in Ancient Israel and Ugarit*, HSM 39 (Atlanta: Scholars Press, 1989), B. B. Schmidt's *Israel's Beneficent Dead: Ancestor Cult and Necromancy in Ancient Israelite Religion and Tradition* (Winona Lake, IN: Eisenbrauns, 1996), and F. Stavrakopoulou's *Land of Our Fathers: The Roles of Ancestor Veneration in Biblical Land Claims*, LHBOTS 473 (New York: T & T Clark, 2010) analyze the death and afterlife of adults from a textual perspective.
11. Faust and Bunimovitz argue for the bench tomb as a means of solidifying the *bet 'av* in stone and discuss the nonverbal language of objects and what the four-room house/tomb symbolized. A. Faust and S. Bunimovitz, "Judahite Rock-Cut Tomb: Family Response at a Time of Change," *IEJ* 58.2 (2008): 150–70. See also the discussion of their argument in Suriano, *History of Death*, 95–96.
12. M. Chesson, "Libraries of the Dead: Early Bronze Age Charnel Houses and Social Identity at Urban Bab edh-Dhra, Jordan," *JAA* 18 (1999): 137–64; R. Hallote, "Mortuary Archaeology and the Middle Bronze Age Southern Levant," *Journal of Mediterranean Archaeology* 8.1 (1995): 93–122.
13. Suriano, *History of Death*, 96.
14. A. Boutin, "Crafting a Bioarchaeology of Personhood: Osteobiographical Narratives from Alalakh," in *Breathing New Life into the Evidence of Death: Contemporary Approaches to Bioarchaeology*, ed. A. Baadsgaard, A. T. Boutin, and J. E. Buikstra (Santa Fe, NM: School for Advanced Research Press, 2011), 111; J. Osbourne, "Secondary Mortuary Practice and the Bench Tomb: Structure and Practice in Iron Age Judah," *JNES* 70.1 (2011): 47; M. Cradic, "Transformations in Death: The Archaeology of Funerary Practices and Personhood in the Bronze Age Levant" (PhD dissertation, University of California, Berkeley, 2017). Note also the passages in the Hebrew Bible that use the word בת (house) meaning קבר (grave): Isaiah 14:18; 1 Samuel 25:1; Qoheleth 12:5; and Psalms 49:12.
15. While they do not go so far as to include infants and children in their discussion, Faust and Bunimovitz argue that the tomb acts as a counter-symbol to the fact that the social meaning of the family (*bet 'av*) was threatened during the later Iron II (Faust and Bunimovitz, "Judahite Rock-Cut Tomb," 161–62).

CHILDREN AND INFANTS IN JUDAHITE FAMILY TOMBS 143

16. Sonia, *Caring for the Dead* 207.
17. The Egyptian record includes tomb reliefs of a group circumcision ceremony from Ankh-mahor's tomb (ca. 2355–2343 BCE). The context seems to be one of ritual purity. The biography of Uha (ca. 2011 BCE) relates his circumcision was also done in a group setting. M. A. Roth, *Egyptian Phyles in the Old Kingdom: The Evolution of a System of Social Organization*, Studies in Ancient Oriental Civilization 48 (Chicago: University of Chicago Press, 1991), 65–72. Jeremiah 9:25–26 states that Canaanites, Ammonites, Moabites, Edomites, Phoenicians, and Arameans all circumcised their males.
18. For a discussion of ancient texts, ethnographic texts, and a list of archaeological finds related to circumcision, see K. H. Garroway, *Growing Up in Ancient Israel: Children in Material Culture and Biblical Text*, ABS 23 (Atlanta: SBL Press, 2018), 141–50; A. Faust, "The Bible, Archaeology, and the Practice of Circumcision in Israelites and Philistine Societies," *JBL* 134 (2015): 273–90.
19. As a sign of the covenant with God, Abraham and Ishmael are both circumcised when they become fertile (Genesis 17:24–25). Isaac, however, is circumcised at eight days (Genesis 21:4), which becomes the fulfillment of Genesis 17:12.
20. Garroway, *Growing Up*, 151.
21. N. Wyatt, "Circumcision and Circumstance: Male Genital Mutilation in Ancient Israel and Ugarit," *JSOT* 33 (2009): 409–10.
22. As opposed to those Judahites living pre-exile who may have been circumcised at adolescence.
23. The enemies listed include Egypt, Edom, Elam, and Sidon (Phoenicia), peoples that Jeremiah 9:25–26 claims did circumcise. Their place with the uncircumcised is meant as an insult.
24. Ironically, circumcision is an alteration of the flesh, one of the first things to decompose. It appears that the author of Ezekiel is concerned less with the decomposition process and final physical form of the dying body than with the markers of ethnic identity that would be present upon primary burial. However, the passage might point to further insights about the timing of when a person was thought to enter the afterlife. One might envision the physical body fading down into the earth and reappearing in the afterlife in the same shape/form it had in the land of the living. Bones left behind then represent a link to the land of the living. Of course, this is all conjecture.
25. The Hebrew Bible prescribes no physical transformation to mark a daughter's body as a member of the covenantal line. Given the patriarchal structure of society, this is not surprising. Questions as to whether a daughter's place in the afterlife was ever in peril are not raised in the Hebrew Bible. One could interpret this fact in contradicting ways: a daughter had no place in the afterlife (hence it was not even worthy of mention) or a daughter's place was assured in the afterlife (it was a given, so no need to reference it).
26. Erin Darby's succinct overview offers an overview of scholarship on the JPFs: "Judean Pillar Figurines (JPFs)," in *Archaeology and History of Eighth-Century Judah*, ANEM 23, ed. Z. Farber and J. Wright (Atlanta: SBL Press, 2018), 401–14. For a more in-depth analysis see E. Darby, *Interpreting Judean Pillar Figurines: Gender and Empire in Apotropaic Ritual*, FAT 2, Reihe 69 (Tübingen: Mohr Siebeck, 2014); and R. Kletter, *The Judean Pillar Figurines and the Archaeology of Asherah*, British Archaeological Reports 636 (Oxford: Tempus Reparatum, 1996). The number of JPFs found in tombs is very small. Within the greater Jerusalem area, eleven were found, and of these hardly any are in undisturbed graves. See Darby, *Interpreting Judean Pillar Figurines*, 233–36, which collects the tomb data from various excavations. She concludes, "The evidence that remains from undisturbed tomb assemblages does not suggest that pillar figurines in Jerusalem were commonly interred with the dead or used in tomb contexts" (236).
27. Darby, "Judean Pillar Figurines," 405–10; K. Sonia, "Thinking with Clay: Procreation and the Ceramic Paradigm in Israelite Religion," *JANER* 21 (2021): 204–5.
28. Garroway, *Growing Up*, 241–45, and sources therein.
29. Such discussions tend to focus on the state and the network of the kingdom. See, for example, discussion of the *lmlk* jar stamp impressions: O. Lipschits, O. Sergi, and I. Koch, "Royal Judahite Jar Handles: Reconsidering the Chronology of the *lmlk* Stamp Impressions," *TA* 37 (2010): 3–32; I. Koch, "Judahite Stamped and Incised Jar Handles: A Tool for Studying the History of Late Monarchic Judah," *TA* 38 (2011): 5–41; N. Na'aman, "The *lmlk* Seal Impressions Reconsidered," *TA* 43 (2016): 111–25.
30. V. Turner, *The Ritual Process: Structure and Anti-structure* (Chicago: Aldine, 1969); V. Turner, *The Forest of Symbols: Aspects of Ndembu Ritual* (Ithaca, NY: Cornell University Press, 1967); A. van Gennep, *Rites of Passage* (Chicago: University of Chicago Press, 1960).

144 INTERPRETING THE BURIALS OF CHILDREN

31. Turner, *The Ritual Process*, 96–97; van Gennep, *Rites of Passage*.
32. On ritual and practice, see P. Bourdieu, *Outline of a Theory of Practice*, trans. R. Nice (Cambridge: Cambridge University Press, 1977); C. Humphrey and J. Laidlaw, *The Archetypal Actions of Ritual: A Theory of Ritual Illustrated by the Jain Rite of Worship* (Oxford: Clarendon Press, 1994); C. Bell, *Ritual Theory, Ritual Practice* (Oxford: Oxford University Press, 1992).
33. Matthew Suriano has tackled this subject in depth in his study of death and the dying body (*History of Death*, 1–35, 133–54). Others have assumed a relationship between the soul and body that is based more on anthropological societies, or an understanding of death and the division of the body and soul like that of the Greeks. See, for example, Osbourne, "Secondary Mortuary Practice," 38–47. Such ideas are anachronistic, making Suriano's understanding even more compelling.
34. Suriano, *History of Death*, 6–11.
35. Suriano, *History of Death*, 6.
36. http:// etcsl.ori nst.ox.ac.uk/ secti on1/ tr1 814.htm, accessed 2 March 2020; Suriano Prolegomenon, 7.
37. http://etcsl.orinst.ox.ac.uk/section1/tr1814.htm, accessed 2 March 2020.
38. See Suriano's lengthy discussion of functional immortality as it relates to memorials and death (*History of Death*, 200–216).
39. Suriano, *History of Death*, 41, 42 n. 4.
40. For a description of corpse placement on benches, and benches with headrests, see the overview in Kloner, "Iron Age Burial Caves"; A. Kloner and D. Davis, "A Burial Cave of the Later First Temple Period on the Slope of Mount Zion," in *Ancient Jerusalem Revealed*, ed. H. Geva (Jerusalem: Israel Exploration Society, 1994), 107–10; G. Barkay, "Burial Headrests as a Return to the Womb—a Reevaluation," *BAR* 14 (1988): 48.
41. See the examples in Suriano, *History of Death*, 48; and Kloner and Davis, "A Burial Cave," 108.
42. Suriano, *History of Death*, 48 and 48 n. 27, Osbourne, "Secondary Mortuary Practice," 42.
43. For an overview of ceramic forms with images see E. Nagar and Y. Nagar, "A Burial Cave from the Iron Age II and Early Roman Period North of Tel Hadid," *'Atiqot* 70 (2012): 1–20 (in Hebrew); L. Freud, "Iron Age," in *Tel 'Ira: A Stronghold in the Biblical Negev*, Emery and Claire Yass Publications in Archaeology, ed. I Beit-Arieh (Tel Aviv: Institute of Archaeology, Tel Aviv University, 1999), 189–289.
44. One can see this array most easily at Ketef Hinnom in Jerusalem. G. Barkay, "Excavations at Ketef Hinnom in Jerusalem," in Geva, *Ancient Jerusalem Revealed*, 95–105.
45. Barkay, "Excavations at Ketef Hinnom," 95–105.
46. Barkay, "Excavations at Ketef Hinnom," 98–99. Due to the limited number of remains found in situ it is difficult to tell whether all infants and children received these burial goods. However, as will be shown below, grave goods have meaning beyond their direct association with an individual.
47. Suriano, *History of Death*, 48; F. Ekengren, "Contextualizing Grave Goods: Theoretical Perspectives and Methodological Implications," in *The Oxford Handbook of the Archaeology of Death & Burial*, ed. S. Tarlow and L. N. Stutz (Oxford: Oxford University Press, 2013), 186.
48. Osbourne, "Secondary Mortuary Practice," 38.
49. Ekengren, "Contextualizing Grave Goods," 175–79.
50. Bell, *Ritual Theory, Ritual Practice*; S. Tarlow, *Bereavement and Commemoration: An Archaeology of Mortality* (Oxford: Blackwell, 1999), 178.
51. E. Hallam and J. Hockney, *Death, Memory and Material Culture* (Oxford: Berg, 2001); P. Uko, "Ethnography and Archaeological Interpretation of Funerary Remains," *WA* 1 (1969): 262–80.
52. I. Hodder, *The Present Past: An Introduction to Anthropology for Archaeologists* (London: Batsford, 1982), 139–40, 206–9.
53. M. Parker Pearson, *The Archaeology of Death and Burial* (College Station: Texas A&M University Press, 1999), 33; C. Fowler, *The Archaeology of Personhood: Anthropological Approach* (London: Routledge, 2004), 41–42.
54. I. Beit-Arieh and A. Baron, "The Cemetery," in Beit-Arieh, *Tel 'Ira*, 129–69; V. Eshed, S. Wish-Baratz, and I. Hershkovitz, "Human Skeletal Remains," in Beit-Arieh, *Tel 'Ira*, 495–520.
55. Repository pits rose in popularity during the seventh to sixth centuries. Osbourne, "Secondary Mortuary Practice," 40.
56. Tomb 23 was dated to the sixth c. BCE. However, it did not use a repository pit but removed bones and items to the floor. Tomb 15 was used in the ninth to eighth c. BCE.
57. Beit-Arieh and Baron, "The Cemetery," 132–33.

CHILDREN AND INFANTS IN JUDAHITE FAMILY TOMBS   145

58. Beit-Arieh and Baron, "The Cemetery," 149–50.
59. The physical anthropology report did not include skeletal remains for an individual of this age range. These notes come from the field report. Beit-Arieh and Baron, "The Cemetery," 152–53. The discrepancies between the field report and the physical anthropology report could be due to the fact that not all bones were sent for analysis.
60. Beit-Arieh and Baron, "The Cemetery," 153.
61. Beit-Arieh and Baron, "The Cemetery," 152.
62. Beit-Arieh and Baron, "The Cemetery," 154.
63. Beit-Arieh and Baron, "The Cemetery," 151–59.
64. See introduction.
65. The following scholars have also argued for some form of a cult of the dead kin: G. von Rad, *Old Testament Theology*, vol. 1: *The Theology of Israel's Historical Traditions* (Louisville, KY: Westminster John Knox, 2001) (German orig., 1957); Brichto, "Kin, Cult, Land"; W. F. Albright, *Yahweh and the Gods of Canaan* (Winona Lake, IN: Eisenbrauns, 1968); K. Spronk, *Beatific Afterlife in Ancient Israel and in the Ancient Near East*, Alter Orient und Altes Testament 219 (Neukirchen- Vluyn: Neukirchener Verlag, 1986); Lewis, *Cults of the Dead*; M. Pope, "Notes on the Rephaim Texts from Ugarit," in *Essays on the Ancient Near East in Memory of Jacob Joel Finkelstein*, Memoirs of the Connecticut Academy of Arts and Sciences 19, ed. M. de Jong Ellis (Hamden, CT: Archon Books, 1977), 163–82; M. Pope, "The Cult of the Dead at Ugarit," in *Ugarit in Retrospect: Fifty Years of Ugarit and Ugaritic*, ed. G. D. Young (Winona Lake, IN: Eisenbrauns, 1981), 159–79; M. Smith and E. Bloch-Smith, "Death and Afterlife in Ugarit and Israel," *JAOS* 108 (1988): 277–84; C. B. Hays, *A Covenant with Death: Death in the Iron Age II and Its Rhetorical Uses in Proto-Isaiah* (Grand Rapids, MI: Eerdmans, 2011).
66. Sonia, *Caring for the Dead*; R. Schmitt, "Care for the Dead in the Context of the Household and Family," in *Family and Household Religion in Ancient Israel and the Levant*, ed. R. Albertz and R. Schmitt (Winona Lake, IN: Eisenbrauns, 2012), 429–73.
67. A good death is associated with burial and postmortem care. Sonia, *Caring for the Dead*, 1–24, 195; K. H. Garroway, "The Anthropology of Death in Ancient Israel," in *T&T Clark Handbook of Anthropology in the Hebrew Bible*, ed. E. Pfoh (London: Bloomsbury T & T Clark, 2022), 462–63; Stavrakopoulou, *Land of Our Fathers*, 2–18; S. Olyan, "Some Neglected Aspects of Israelite Interment Ideology," *JBL* 124 (2005): 603–7.
68. The remains from other bench tombs would indicate that the Tel 'Ira sample is representative. While other bench tombs might have fewer skeletal remains, the general picture aligns with what is seen in the Tel 'Ira data set.
69. For a definition of partible personhood see introduction. See also Boutin, "Crafting a Bioarchaeology," 110; and Cradic, "Transformations in Death," 34–71.
70. C. Fowler, "From Identity and Material Culture to Personhood and Materiality," in *The Oxford Handbook of Material Culture Studies*, ed. D. Hicks and M. C. Beaudry (Oxford: Oxford University Press, 2010), 352–85; J. I. Cerezo- Roman, "Unpacking Personhood and Funerary Customs in the Hohokam Area of Southern Arizona," *American Antiquity* 80 (2015): 353–75.
71. L. Quick, *Dress, Adornment, and the Body in the Hebrew Bible* (Oxford: Oxford University Press, 2021); J. Smoak and A. Mandell, "The Material Turn in the Study of Israelite Religion: Spaces, Things, and the Body," *Journal of Hebrew Scriptures* 19 (2019): 1–42; E. Casella and K. Croucher, "The Materiality of Personhood," *Feminist Theory* 12.2 (2011): 209–17.
72. On individuals imparting personhood onto gifts see K. H. Garroway, "The Case of Joseph's Coat: Giving Gifts to Children in the Hebrew Bible," *AVAR* 1.2 (2022): 190–92; M. Strathern, *The Gender of the Gift: Problems with Women and Problems with Society in Melanesia* (Berkeley: University of California Press, 1998); M. Mauss, *The Gift: Forms and Functions of Exchange in Archaic Societies*, trans. Ian Cunnison (New York: Norton, 1967).
73. Refer to the introduction for more on divisible and partible personhoods.
74. Fowler, *The Archaeology of Personhood*, 5.
75. Barkay, "Excavations at Ketef Hinnom," 96; Y. Nagar, "Skeletal Remains from the Excavation at Ketef Hinnom, Jerusalem," *'Atiqot* 80 (2015): 55–58 (in Hebrew).
76. B. Arensburg and Y. Rak, "Jewish Skeletal Remains from the Period of the Kings of Judah," *PEQ* 117 (1985): 30–34.
77. See, inter alia, M. Bayliss, "The Cult of Dead Kin in Assyria and Babylonia," *Iraq* 35 (1973): 115–25; K. van der Toorn, *Family Religion in Babylonia, Ugarit, and Israel: Continuity and Changes in the Forms of Religious Life* (Leiden: Brill, 1996); K. van der Toorn, "Second Millennium West Asian Family Religion," in *Household and Family Religion in Antiquity*, ed. J. Bodel and S. Olyan

146 INTERPRETING THE BURIALS OF CHILDREN

(Oxford: Blackwell, 2008), 20–36, esp. 25–28; B. Brown, "Kingship and Ancestral Cult in the Northwest Palace at Nimrud," *JANER* 10 (2010): 1–53; Hays, *A Covenant with Death*, 34–132.

78. S. Richardson, "Thy Neighbor's Ghost: Ideal Types, Stereotypes, All Types," *Metatron* 2.1 (2022), published in *Metatron* (scholasticahq.com). While these items might be part of the rite of *kispum*, Richardson goes on to say he knows of no place where the rite actually took place at the grave. *CAD K*: 425–27.

79. Sonia, *Caring for the Dead*, 31–38; Lewis, *Cults of the Dead*, 80–95. Christopher B. Hays gives a history of scholarship concerning the interpretation of the Aqhat Epic and the Ugaritic *marziḫu*. Hays, *A Covenant with Death*, 110–21, 163–66.

80. W. Pitard argues that the tombs and drinking tubes were originally misinterpreted by Shaeffer and are instead domestic drains carved for use in houses. W. Pitard, "The 'Libation Installations' of the Tombs at Ugarit," *BA* 51 (1994): 20–37.

81. Such tombs often include a jar or jars below the "shoot" or drinking tube (Ugaritic *gngn*) thought to catch the libation remains. See Chapter 3. The Phoenician ashlar chamber tombs in the Southern Cemetery at Achzib also include drinking shoots. E. Mazar, *The Phoenicians in Achzib, the Southern Cemetery: Jerome L. Joss Expedition, Final Report of the Excavation, 1988–1990* (Barcelona: Laboratorio de Arqueología, Universidad Pompeu Fabra de Barcelona, 2001), 75–76. Drinking pipes / libation tubes (*arūtu*) are also found in Mesopotamian architecture: *CAD A II*: 324.

82. See the reconstructed Phoenician funeral sequence by Aubet in "The Phoenician Cemetery of Tyre," *NEA* 73 (2010): 144–55. Monuments referencing food and the dead include the Katumuwa Stele and Hadad Statue. Sonia, *Caring for the Dead*, 44–46; M. Suriano, "What Did Feeding the Dead Mean? Two Case Studies from Iron Age Tombs at Beth-Shemesh," *AABNER* 1.3 (2021): 135–38; D. Bonatz, "Katumuwa's Banquet Scene," in *Remembrance of Me: Feasting with the Dead in the Ancient Middle East*, ed. V. Rimmer Herrmann and J. D. Scholeon (Chicago: Oriental Institute of the University of Chicago, 2014), 39–44.

83. J. Blenkinsopp, "Deuteronomy and the Politics of Post-mortem Existence," *VT* 45 (1995): 1–16; Toorn, *Family Religion*, 208–10. R. Schmidt argues that we do not have a lot of information in support and what we do have seems to argue against feeding the dead (Schmitt, "Care for the Dead," 455–57). The "prohibition," however, was meant to separate the care and feeding of Yahweh from the care and feeding of dead kin (Suriano, "Feeding the Dead," 137–38).

84. Brichto, "Kin, Cult, Land," 28–29; Hays, *A Covenant with Death*, 163–65; Suriano, *History of Death*, 158–73; Suriano, "Feeding the Dead," 117–42; Lewis, *Cults of the Dead*, 99–170.

85. Schmitt argues that because Israelite burials contained a relatively consistent number of grave goods, we should understand them to function for the short term, during the transition process. This thought is the most popular one among scholars. Schmitt, "Care for the Dead," 454–55.

86. In *The Archaeology of Personhood*, C. Fowler gives multiple examples spanning Neolithic Britain to Melanesia showing how a feasts or meals are eaten cyclically with the dead. We may see reference to this in the biblical text as well, where David begs an absence from Saul's table with the excuse that he is involved in a commemorative feast with his family (1 Samuel 20:5–6).

87. Suriano, *History of Death*, 157.

88. That individuals needed different amounts of food based on their age is well attested in ration lists. See, for example, I. E. Gelb, "The Ancient Mesopotamian Ration System," *JNES* 24 (1965): 230–43; H. Waetzoldt, "Compensation of Craft Workers and Officials in the Ur III Period," in *Labor in the Ancient Near East*, ed. M. A. Powell (New Haven: American Oriental Society, 1987), 132–35; R. Harris, *Gender and Aging in Mesopotamia: The Gilgamesh Epic and Other Ancient Literature* (Norman: University of Oklahoma Press, 2000), 6.

89. For an analysis of the relationship between grave goods and infants and children from the Early Bronze I to Iron II, see K. H. Garroway, *Children in the Ancient Near Eastern Household*, EANEC 3 (Winona Lake, IN: Eisenbrauns, 2014), 228–38, esp. 235.

90. See the previous chapters for examples of graves where infants and children are found with ceramic food vessels.

91. Therefore, it is more productive for the current enterprise to stick with the information that we do know. I am less concerned with the question of how to understand the presence of food in the mortuary ritual because if we cannot come to a consensus for adults, how much more impossible is it to say for infants/children, whom we know less about?

92. See the work by Sonia, *Caring for the Dead*; Schmitt, "Care for the Dead," 433–34; S. Olyan, *Biblical Mourning: Ritual and Social Dimensions* (Oxford: Oxford University Press, 2004).

93. Suriano, *History of Death*, 10.

CHILDREN AND INFANTS IN JUDAHITE FAMILY TOMBS   147

94. Pearson, *Archaeology of Death*, 103.
95. This idea stems from the observation made by Lewis that "cultural attitudes dictate where and how infants and children are buried, when they assume their gender identity, whether they are exposed to physical abuse, and at what age they are considered adults." M. Lewis, *The Bioarchaeology of Children: Perspectives from Biological and Forensic Anthropology* (Cambridge: Cambridge University Press, 2007), 1.
96. For example, B. B. Schmidt argues that necromancy was not a part of cult of the ancestors, while J. Tropper argues that it was. Schmidt, *Israel's Beneficent Dead*; J. Tropper, *Nekromantie: Totenbefragung im Alten Orient und im Alten Testament*, AOAT 223 (Kevelaer: Neukirchen-Vluyn, 1989).
97. Schmitt, "Care for the Dead," 432. Matthew Suriano has argued for a more nuanced understanding of *'ābōt* in the phrase "gathered to his fathers," as it appears in royal epilogues in the books of Kings and Chronicles. He sees *'ābōt* as the royal dead, as opposed to the *'ammîm*, which is more closely related to individual kinship and collective identities. M. Suriano, *The Politics of Dead Kings: Dynastic Ancestors in the Book of Kings and Ancient Israel* (Tübingen: Mohr Siebeck, 2010), 165–71. I would argue that those using the bench tombs of the Judahite elite are concerned with their lineage and their specific class of ancestors in the same way Suriano argues the authors of Kings and Chronicles were concerned with portraying royal ancestry (Suriano, *Politics of Dead Kings*, 171–72).
98. K. Teinz, "How to Become an Ancestor— Some Thoughts," in *(Re)- constructing Funerary Rituals in the Ancient Near East: Proceedings of the First International Symposium of the Tübingen Post-Graduate School "Symbols of the Dead" in May 2009*, Qaṭna Studien Supplementa 1, ed. P. Pfälzner, H. Niehr, E. Pernicka, and A. Wissing (Wiesbaden: Harrassowitz Verlag, 2012), 239–42.
99. Here I follow T. M. Lemos's conclusion that within ancient Israel, only dominant males achieved full personhood. T. M. Lemos, *Violence and Personhood in Ancient Israel and Comparative Contexts* (Oxford: Oxford University Press, 2017). One might also hypothesize that in matriarchal families, adult women became ancestors.
100. For issues with the term "ancestor cult," see Sonia, *Caring for the Dead*, 7–8.
101. W. F. Petrie, *Beth-Pelet I (Tell Fara)* (London: British School of Archaeology in Egypt, 1930).
102. S. Wolff and G. Edelstein, "The 1964 Excavation at Tell el-'Orēme," in *Results of the Excavation at Tel el 'Orēme in 1994–2008*, Kinneret II/1, ed. W. Zwickel and J. Pakkala (Münster: Zaphon, 2024), 610–11.
103. P. L. O. Guy, *Megiddo Tombs* (Chicago: University of Chicago Press, 1938); T. P. Harrison, *Megiddo 3: Final Report on the Stratum VI Excavations*, OI Publications 127 (Chicago: Oriental Institute, 2004).

7

The Death of Children in the Hebrew Bible

Child Sacrifice, Personhood, and Judahite Ideals

Whereas the previous chapters have addressed the archaeological record of ancient Israel, this chapter moves to the biblical text to address the intersection of text and archaeology with respect to the death of children. Among the references to child death in the Hebrew Bible, child sacrifice is perhaps the most disturbing. Biblical texts about children highlight their vulnerability, and this is particularly true with texts of utmost violence. The violence done to children via child sacrifice has also been used to argue that children and infants did not have personhood.[1] Whether or not child sacrifice actually occurred, the texts are based on the idea that child sacrifice was conceivable. The rhetoric surrounding child sacrifice in the Hebrew Bible, especially the texts concerned with passing a son/daughter through fire, is reassessed here. The chapter begins by using an anthropological lens to address the issues of sacrifice and personhood, after which it moves to discuss the archaeological evidence for child sacrifice in the region. The chapter suggests that cremated burials were represented in the biblical text by children who were "sacrificed," that is, "passed over the fire." In reaching this conclusion, it brings together data presented in the previous chapters and argues that the biblical prohibition against child sacrifice is related to a concern that Judahite children continue to be buried with their families, in family tombs.

In framing the discussion of child sacrifice, it is important to note that no evidence of widespread child sacrifice has been found in the archaeological record of ancient Israel. This fact is a bit surprising considering the numerous times that child sacrifice is referenced in the Hebrew Bible. Abraham and Jephthah sacrifice their children as·a measure of devotion (Genesis 22; Judges 11), while kings and mothers sacrifice their children in times of desperation (2 Kings 3:26–27, 6:24–30).[2] And the Torah itself has Yahweh asking for the sacrifice of first fruits/ firstborn (Exodus 13:1–2, 22:28).[3] Yet other texts condemn child sacrifices undertaken for any reason (Deuteronomy 18:10; Leviticus 18:21, 20:2–4; 2 Kings 23:12; Isaiah 57:5; Jeremiah 32:25).

The Dying Child. Kristine Henriksen Garroway, Oxford University Press. © Oxford University Press 2025.
DOI: 10.1093/9780197566718.003.0008

DEATH OF CHILDREN IN THE HEBREW BIBLE   149

Many scholars have tried to square this circle. Some argue that child sacrifice was meant as a polemic against foreign nations; it offered a critique of a practice that was considered inappropriate and pagan.[4] Others suggest that child sacrifice was an integral part of Israel's hoary past.[5]

A major issue with the texts on child sacrifice is that the language is often vague.[6] Rather than using firm terms such as שחט "slaughter" or זבח "ritually slaughter," the texts commonly use euphemisms. Children are "offered up" (עלה), "passed/burned with/through (fire)" (שרף + באש / עבר + באש/העביר), or "given" (נתן). Yet we should not be surprised at the ambiguous language. The Hebrew Bible frequently talks around practices. Consider all the ways it describes sexual intercourse: "to lie with" (שכב), "to take" (לקח), "to go in" (בא), or "to know" (ידע) someone. "Whether the practice is a distant memory or itself the victim of an elaborate cover-up operation, one thing seems evident: the biblical authors were highly concerned with Israelites engaging in child sacrifice."[7]

Given the fact that no clear evidence of child sacrifice has been found in ancient Israel, but that texts are highly concerned with the practice, can anything more be said? The answer is yes. First, the issue of personhood looms large. On the one hand, it is possible to argue that the rhetoric around the violence done through child sacrifice neither revokes nor erases the personhood of children and infants but indicates that it was never there to begin with.[8] Yet, on the other hand, why would individuals sacrifice something that had no personhood? Would it still have value? Furthermore, while the *absence* of burials with remains of child sacrifice has been noted, the relationship between the extant burial record—a record that indicates some infants and children were cremated or buried in urns—and the biblical texts describing sacrifice has not been discussed in full. Looking first at the intersection of personhood and child sacrifice and then at how the burial record might inform what the biblical authors were concerned with, this chapter argues in favor of a measure of personhood belonging to children. It concludes that the biblical texts had a specific understanding of how that personhood should be incorporated into the household of death.

Religious Anthropology and Sacrifice

Approaching child sacrifice from an anthropological perspective provides an entry point for thinking about the aspects of personhood represented in

150 INTERPRETING THE BURIALS OF CHILDREN

child sacrifice and the burial record. Depending on the culture, human sacrifice could take various forms and have different meanings. In the Americas, the sacrifice of children was undertaken as a plea to the divine for fertility or to aid the gods in their process of procreation and maintaining the world structure.[9] The deposition of sacrificial victims in ritual pits or specific burials suggests that the sacrificed individuals were understood to have some measure of personhood.[10] Consider the Maya: they did not sacrifice children because they were lesser, marginal, or without personhood. Rather, children were one of the most precious types of sacrifices because they were considered close to the ancestors.[11]

Religious anthropology defines sacrifice as a plea to the divine. A plea can either be a plea for separation or a plea for communication.[12] If one desires to communicate with the divine, then the sacrifice takes the form of an offering. Offering sacrifices generally occurs on a regular basis and at a set, sacred place.[13] Ritual killings, or eliminatory sacrifices, are used to dispel evil. Unlike the offering sacrifice, eliminatory sacrifices occur on an ad hoc basis away from sacred spaces.[14] Examples of these within ancient Near East literature might be the death of Tiamat in the Enuma Elish, or the scapegoat ritual in Leviticus 16:10–22. Eliminatory sacrifices can also be used for the purposes of transformation and reintegration.[15] Rituals become popular when there is a need to establish order, be it political, social, cultural, or religious.[16] As these definitions demonstrate, "Ritualization is the interrelationship of action and meaning within a specific setting."[17]

As for the victims of sacrifice, they are not chosen at random but are selected with care. The victim is a stand-in for the sacrificer, so the closer the victim is to the individual offering the sacrifice, the better.[18] For example, due to the time and care put into domestication, a domesticated sheep would be a better sacrifice than a wild ram.[19] The biblical text adheres to this hierarchy as well. Consider the preference placed on sacrificing a stall-fed calf. This calf is not a lean, free-range cow but one kept inside the family house in order to fatten it up.[20] From an anthropological perspective, human sacrifice would be the best type of sacrifice as it is the closest to the individual doing the sacrifice.

There is a hierarchy among human sacrifices as well, one that attests to the differentiated personhood of the individuals within societies. Humans with minimal power and legal rights make the best victims.[21] Making one's way up the chain of hierarchy, the most valuable victim is a biological child. As an offspring of the sacrificer's own body, a child has the closest association with the sacrificer, while at the same time its lesser personhood fulfills the prerequisites of low social status and minimal legal rights generally required of sacrifices.[22] Ethnographic studies show that some societies viewed children as pure, providing the best communicative link to the divine, thus furthering the possibility that they might be sacrificial victims.[23] In such societies children might be sacrificed in times of trouble, where war, famine, or other social stressors were at play.

The Anthropology of Gift-Giving: Sacrifice and Fertility

In many societies sacrifice is linked to the fertility of the land and of the people.[24] The idea that sacrifice functioned as a means to fertility can be viewed in tandem with the anthropology of gift-giving, which functions as a second lens for exploring the texts referencing child sacrifice.[25] Societies like ancient Israel operated under a system where gifts embodied a part of the gift-giver and reciprocation in kind was necessitated.[26] According to the biblical text, children (created in the image of God) were understood as a gift from God.[27] Such a grand gift demanded a counter-gift of equal measure. Reciprocity is at the very heart of the gift-giving process. At its core, reciprocity functioned to strengthen ties between two individuals or between people and their deity.[28] Refusing to give a counter-gift therefore brought shame and dishonor. Personhood, created and recreated through gift-giving and the relationships that were formed and re-formed, could be "occupied by animals and objects" as well as people, and the exchange of gifts "may force people to change perspectives in relation to one another: to now be in debt, or now be owed."[29] The biblical text further adds to this formula by bringing in power dynamics between humans and the divine.

Within the framework of gift-giving, the sacrifice of the firstborn (the return of the firstborn to God) was understood as a means of strengthening ties or showing devotion.[30] Hannah's vow that she would give her firstborn child back to God, and Abraham's sacrifice of Isaac, make sense in a world where giving up one child meant receiving more (1 Samuel 1; Genesis 22). In this framework, one can understand the requests from the deity to humankind to give up the firstborn and first fruits (Exodus 13:1–2, 22:28). Since children were created by their parents, they embody both the gift-giver and the recipient turned counter-giver.

Considered this way, the firstborn or *lmlk* sacrifice (often designated with the Hebrew verb נתן, "to give/take") recognizes the cyclical nature of the gift.

152 INTERPRETING THE BURIALS OF CHILDREN

The gift given and taken would again be re-given. Much ink has been spilled over the interpretation of the *lmlk* sacrifice. The current consensus is that these are a type of offering but not an offering to the god Molech.[31] Whether the text envisioned the children as sacrificed to a specific deity or as a type of sacrificial offering themselves, the fact remains that the texts suggest children were offered as a sacrifice. Phrases such as offering up *lmlk*, consigning sons and daughters to fire, burning sons and daughters in the Tophet, and crossing children through fire in the Hinnom imply the use of fire.[32] Yet no archaeological evidence exists for child sacrifice or tophets in ancient Israel. Because of this, some have suggested that the biblical text was speaking metaphorically.[33] However, if we compare the biblical texts to what *is* present in the archaeological record, a different picture develops.

Examining first the references to sacrifice in the Punic world and then revisiting children in the Phoenician, Philistine, and Israelite burial records, I argue that when the biblical writers lambaste child sacrifice, they have in mind non-Judahite burial practices being used for children. The specific practices in question are cremations and jar burials, both of which displace the child from the family tomb collective.

Child Sacrifice in the Punic World in Brief

The interpretation of infant tophets (ca. eighth to third c. BCE) that were discovered in the Phoenician colonies of North Africa, Sardinia, Sicily, and so forth is contentious, with some arguing that the cemeteries full of cremated infants were simply cemeteries and others arguing that they represent sacrificed infants.[34] The vast number of very young infants found cremated in the Phoenician diaspora have traditionally been used as the standard for understanding what remains of child sacrifice would look like in the Levant. The cremated infants were found placed in urns and in cemeteries designated for infants. While some animals were also found buried in the cemeteries, no adult cremations were found.[35] Most notably, the cremated infants were of very similar ages. This has suggested to some archaeologists that only infants of a certain age were cremated, leading to the assertion that these children were intentionally sacrificed before they grew up.

The stelae that accompanied many of the infant burials, along with the assertion of classical writers that the Punics sacrificed children during times of distress, further add to the matrix.[36] The stelae mention vows made to the deity.

Consider the following two examples: *RES* 339 (= Costa 93): "To the Lord, to Ba'l Hammon, a *mlk 'dm*, the vow which Ba'l-Pado' son of Magon vowed. He heard his voice; be blessed him."[37] Neopun. 30 (Lidzzbarski): "To the holy Lord Ba'l, in a fortunate day, for a *mlk*."[38] The question becomes, did erecting a stele fulfill the vow, or did the stele mean that the cremated child was sacrificed to fulfill the vow? The use of the word *mulk* on the stele has also raised the possibility that they are one and the same as the *mlk* sacrifices found in the biblical text.[39]

It is not my purpose here to reassess these data for the Punic world and make a firm declaration on the nature of infant sacrifice at those sites. Rather, I would assert that the practices happening in the Phoenician diaspora— infant cremation cemeteries, urns containing cremated infants, stelae referencing vows to deities—and the later interpretation of these cremations as child sacrifice by the classical writings were not the main concern of the biblical text and its understanding of child sacrifice / passing children through fire. Rather, I think that these practices became conflated with a practice much closer to home, that of cremation and jar burials.

Cremations, Urns, and Jars in the Phoenician Homeland and on the Israelite Coast

In Chapter 1, I presented the different ways in which infants were buried during the Bronze and Iron Ages. While they enjoyed burials in family caves and tombs, far and away the most common type of burials were infant jar burials, generally found within the domicile. This pattern suggested a certain Canaanite practice and belief about how deceased infants were incorporated into their cult of the dead kin. Chapters 4 and 5 showed how jar burials fell out of popularity within areas associated with the Kingdom of Judah. Jar burials, however, remained in use on the coast and in a few places within the north, places the Judahite writers of the biblical text chastised for their errant religious practices.[40] In examining the "why" of jar burials, Chapter 5 argued that the materiality of the jar presents the possibility of a return to the womb and a belief in infant rebirth. The use of jar burials in these areas seems to be intricately connected to a particular construction of fertility and intragenerational connections. These beliefs are fundamentally different from the way Judahites constructed intergenerational links in bench tombs.

Chapter 3 presented the archaeological data for sites on the Israelite coast that had connections to the Phoenician homeland. With the exception of

154   INTERPRETING THE BURIALS OF CHILDREN

'Atlit, these sites included a mix of burial styles including tombs, jars, urns, inhumations, and cremations. Again, these sites presented non-Judahite-looking burials. Looking further north, to the Phoenician homeland, sites such as Khaldé (ca. 9.6 km south of Beirut), Tyre, and Rachideyeh (ca. 4 km south of Tyre) also show a diverse burial record, including evidence for their increasingly common practice of cremation. Yet the age of those cremated at these sites is much different from those found in the Punic lands and on the coast of Israel. A brief look at three Phoenician homeland sites and their burials of children will help contextualize this point.

Khaldé is notable because it contains perhaps the largest Phoenician necropolis from the Iron Age (tenth to eighth c. BCE); unfortunately, it has not been fully published.[41] However, that which has been published offers a snapshot of the burial grounds. Like many Phoenician cemeteries, the cemetery was situated in sand and overlooked the water.[42] It included "single inhumations in unlined cist burials, multiple inhumations and cremations in a single built tomb, and so on."[43] The necropolis also had cremations and urns, and much like 'Arqa to the north, also had an area dedicated for cremation.[44] Overall, the picture that emerges from Khaldé is a cemetery that contained all ages; however, it appears that children were not cremated, but rather buried in tombs.

Closer to the ancient Israelite homeland are the sites of Tyre, originally an island, and Rachideyeh, its twin "land" sister city. They are located about fifty-six kilometers due west of Tel Dan and roughly eighty kilometers north of Haifa. Like Khaldé, the necropolis area of Rachideyeh contained a variety of burial styles (ninth to fifth c. BCE). The undisturbed shaft tombs found by Theodore Macridy contained a mix of primary and secondary burials dated to the late Iron Age.[45] Entrances for the tombs were dug into the side of a hill and closed with a stone slab. From the drawings, the tombs appear to have benches on which burials were laid along with ceramics.[46] Within the tombs Macridy references a large number of funerary urns with cremated remains.[47] In the years following his report, more tombs containing a variety of burial practices have been found, including more than one hundred urns containing burned bones and ashes dating to the Iron II period.[48] Unfortunately, a full analysis of the cremated remains was not undertaken, and the excavation is not fully published, leaving our understanding of whether children and infants were cremated there incomplete.

Tyre is also important to the current discussion. It had control of the southern Phoenician plain, including the region stretching up to Sidon and down to the Carmel.[49] The excavations at Tyre Al-Bass uncovered a cremation cemetery in 1990 (used ca. ninth to seventh c. BCE). Two things stand out with respect to the present study. First, unlike other Phoenician sites, this necropolis contains only cremations, placed in urns.[50] It included single urns, double urns buried in a single pit, and stacked double- urn burials with markers of wood or stone atop the burial. Common to all the burials was the presence of broken ceramic food vessels placed on top of the closed grave. The ceramics appeared to have been smashed at the time of burial.[51] The other reason the necropolis of Tyre Al- Bass stands out is for its almost total lack of infant and child remains.[52] Out of over eighty cremation urns whose remains were studied, only two contained nonadults.[53] One was a fetus buried along with an adult female, and the other was that of a juvenile between twelve and fourteen years of age.[54] The overall average age of the cremated individuals was thirty-two, which is much higher than that of other Phoenician necropolises.[55] Aubet reaches the following conclusion:

> It is therefore safe to assume that children did not have access to formal burial in this funerary space. As a result, we can conclude that, not only did they have no right to be buried with adults, but that they were not entitled to full membership in the funerary community.[56]

Where then are the children of ancient Tyre? Given what is known of the rest of the Phoenician world, it is possible that children were buried in a different section of the cemetery or in a separate cemetery. However, the almost complete lack of children in the burial record at Tyre does pose questions concerning their position within their society. Perhaps, as Aubet suggests, they did not have full membership in the funerary community. This would imply that membership in death occurred when an individual had reached an age of majority in society. The fetus buried with the adult female would then be understood not as a separate entity, but as related to the adult female (mother?). The juvenile between twelve and fourteen years of age would represent the youngest end of "adulthood."

What does this mean for the personhood of children in Tyrian society? If they were not a part of the community in death, were they understood as a part of the community in life? Was membership in the community understood in terms of contribution to the household economic system or something different?[57] Such questions still need to be explored. The dearth of burials also calls into question family ties. Unless family burials are subsequently uncovered, it certainly appears that burying a child near other members of their family was not a priority at Tyre. Most important, this means there were no overt intergenerational links.

A Summary of Non-Judahite Child Burials

Taken as a whole, the spectrum of Phoenician and Phoenician-influenced burials shows a mixed attitude toward the burials of infants and children. In the Phoenician homeland, the records suggest the presence of children in tombs, in individual cist burials, or alongside cremated adults. Along the Iron II Phoenician coast of Israel, infants and children continued to be included in tombs and cemeteries alongside other members of their society.[58] The ashlar family tombs, shaft family burials, pits, and jar burials at Achzib contained infants and children. So too, the shaft tombs at 'Atlit contained individuals of all ages. Excavations at Tell er-Reqeish and Tell el-Far'ah South found cemeteries with multiple burial types and ages interspersed with one another. These burial sites are much closer to the picture of infants and children in the Phoenician homeland burials than the Punic burials.

Regarding cremation, cremation in the Phoenician homeland was primarily for adults, while in Punic lands it was used for children. However, unlike the Phoenician homeland, sites on the coast of Israel, specifically 'Atlit, Tell er-Reqeish, and Tell el-Far'ah South, used cremation as a burial option for infants and children. To repeat for emphasis: while infant and child cremation is seen in Punic lands, it is not seen in the Phoenician homeland.[59] Yet cremation of infants and children occurred on the Phoenician coast of Israel, where it existed alongside other burial forms for infants and children. As an aggregate, the burials of infants and children at the Iron II Phoenician-influenced sites on the coast of Israel are very different from those found in neighboring Iron II Judah.

The Ideal Judahite Burial in Peril

The previous chapters argued that the Judahite burial record presents a people who placed a great deal of importance on maintaining the Judahite household of the living in the household of the dead. From the layout of the tombs, which parallel the four-room house, to the use of benches as beds, to the gathering of bones and grave goods in the repository, the ideology focuses on keeping the family or kin group together, marking them as Judahite in death. For Judahites, it was not only adults who were gathered to the ancestors, but according to the burial record, infants and children were routinely included in this ideal. As Matthew Suriano convincingly argues, the Judahite burial record in turn echoes burial ideals presented in the Hebrew Bible. Thus, we might understand the elite writers of the biblical text to be describing what they understand as the "correct" type of burial (family bench tomb) for an elite member of Judahite society.[60]

As the biblical texts present this ideology, they do so alongside reference to the heterodox nature of the praxis the writers were witnessing.[61] The critique of these nonorthodox practices is seen mostly with respect to religion. There is condemnation of foreign gods, foreign religions, cults of the dead, necromancy, and so forth.[62] Sometimes these critiques are done as a polemic, while other times the critique is forthright. I would assert that the charge of child sacrifice, specifically in the passages discussing passing one's children through fire or passages related to these texts, may have operated as a polemic against not only foreign religious practices, but against cremation burials and the individual burials (non-family burials, but burials in pits or cists) often found on the Phoenician coast of Israel in the vicinity of cremations and cremation urns.

Understanding the texts about child sacrifice, specifically those mentioning passing a son or a daughter (through fire) as a reference to a foreign burial practice, sheds new light on the biblical texts. For example, while there is no evidence of child sacrifice or infant tophets in Jerusalem or Judah, we do have evidence of children "passed through/over fire" and buried in cremation grounds to the north and west of Judah. Consider too that the fall of the Northern Kingdom to the Assyrians in 721 BCE is attributed to the sins of the north, of which child sacrifice was one. 'Atlit and Achzib, both places that had crematoriums, border the Kingdom of Israel. Furthermore, there is the possibility that infants were cremated at Iron II Megiddo. If the biblical texts used child sacrifice as a polemic or roundabout code for engaging in a cultural practice that was non-Judean, namely excluding infants and children in family burials and disrupting the household of death, then we might extrapolate that such texts also chastised the continued use of jar burials placed outside of family burials, such as are found in the Iron II at Achzib, Tel Zeror, Dothan, and Tel Dan North.

158   INTERPRETING THE BURIALS OF CHILDREN

Case Study Isaiah 57: The Changing Ideologies of
Children and Death

The place of children in the cult of the dead kin and the use of child sacrifice is seen most clearly in Isaiah 57:3–13. Written sometime after the fall of the First Temple, the text echoes the sentiment of those that came before, addressing the ongoing concern in the post-exilic period (Iron III).[63] It describes child sacrifice taking place in Jerusalem, the place where Abraham sacrificed Isaac, where tophets were said to exist, and where child sacrifice in the wadis seemingly still took place. The poem utilizes imagery of fertility, child sacrifice, and death cults.[64] The Hebrew employs multiple puns and double entendres to subtly weave together these different themes. According to Ackerman, the themes are related.[65] Her analysis points out that the *ilim* of verse 5 are simultaneously terebinth trees and gods. In verses 5–6 the wordplay with *n-ḥ-l* "inheritance / possession / ancestral estate" echoes in the mind alongside the meaning "wadi." In verses 7 and 8 the word *mishkav* can mean bed or grave, while the *zikron* and *yad* can mean both a burial memorial and also phallus.[66] To these puns, I would add some additional resonances. Verses 3 and 4 use the term *zera* for offspring. This word links back to covenantal language, where God promises Abraham *zera* (Genesis 17:7–10). I will return to the issue of *zera* below. Verse 4 also obliquely hints perhaps at an Egyptian practice related to the cult of the dead and the revivification of the deceased, called "the opening of the mouth."[67] All these things that the Israelites are doing to try to ensure life will bring about death. Furthermore, the multivalent resonances of the terms mean that one can hear the poem with multiple meanings.

Ackerman divides the poem into two groups of three. In the first group the *fertility cult* is seen in the sex under trees (v. 5a), *child sacrifice* with the slaughter of children in wadis (v. 5b), and *cult of the dead* where offerings are given to the perished (vv. 6a and b). The second group begins again with a *fertility cult* when the harlot sets up her bed (vv. 7–8), followed by *child sacrifice* as offerings are anointed (v. 9a), and then *cult of the dead* as necromancy is condemned (v. 9b). She argues the cult of the dead is linked to fertility inasmuch as the dead needed continuous offerings to remain happy in the afterlife. They needed continuous generations to rise up (fertility) and to care for them. The fertility of the land was also necessary in that offerings are fruits of the land.[68] Sacred sex was one way to provide fertility. "Some ancient Israelites, like their neighbors, believed that the way to stimulate this

DEATH OF CHILDREN IN THE HEBREW BIBLE   159

fertility was through fertility rituals involving sacred sexual intercourse. That is, fertility rituals that encourage agricultural fecundity are necessary if there is to be fitting observance of the cult of the dead."[69] By this rationale there is a link between cults of fertility and cults of the dead. She then links child sacrifice to fertility, noting just as agricultural items must be sacrificed in order to obtain a fertile land, so too must "bounty reaped from human fertility." Yet a direct link between child sacrifice and cults of the dead is only implied, not specified. Difficulties like this one have led some scholars to argue that the poem is not about fertility or a cult of the dead. Rather, it should be taken at face value as a direct condemnation of the literal sacrifice of children.[70]

A turn to Judahite burial practices and their cult of the dead kin moves the conversation forward, providing the missing link between child sacrifice and cults of the dead. Verse 5b states that the Israelites slaughter children in the wadis / in the clefts of rocks. This verse is important. Situating the poem as discussing acts that are happening in Jerusalem, in the wadis, perhaps near the *mishkan* itself, hearkens back to the frustrations expressed in Jeremiah 7:31: "And they have built the shrines [high places] of Tophet, which is in the Valley of Ben-hinnom, to burn their sons and their daughters in the fire, which I never commanded, which never came to My mind" (NJPS). The translation of verse 6 is difficult because the object of "to spill out libations" is unclear. Ackerman shifts the object of verse 6 to adults in the cult of the dead, who are presumably the ancestors that are being offered libations and offerings. Francesca Stavrakopoulou reads the recipients as "divine."[71] I read this verse as referring back to the dead children, the antecedent found earlier in verse 5.[72] Verse 6 then reads: "With the perished of the wadi [i.e., *the children that you sacrificed*] is your portion [i.e., *your inheritance*], they, they are your lot; to them [i.e., *the sacrificed children*] you have spilt a libation (and) offered up an offering."

Moreover, as Francesca Stavrakopoulou points out, the subject of child sacrifice picks up again in verse 9.[73] While the MT reads, "You have anointed the king (*melek*) with oil," most commentators read *mulk*-sacrifice in place of king (*melek*).[74] Thus, "You have anointed the *mulk*-sacrifice with oil." As noted above, in Leviticus 18:21, 20:2–5; 2 Kings 23:10; and Jeremiah 32:35, child sacrifice is linked with *mulk*-sacrifices. Whether *melek* or *mulk*, the sound is so close that, as in verses 5–6, in verse 9 one again hears echoes of children who were sacrificed receiving offerings, libations, and oils.

The poem is troubling. Using the rhetoric of child sacrifice raises red flags as the practice does not accord with the Judahite religion as described by

160 INTERPRETING THE BURIALS OF CHILDREN

laws and prophets. However, as a piece of poetry, the poem need not have a single static meaning. This is not to dismiss the possibility that child sacrifice was occurring, but to encourage a reading that considers something else may also be going on. Indeed, scholars have no problem reading other parts of the poem metaphorically.[75] References mixing harlotry and death cults, sexual deviance and cultic fertility rituals, fertility rituals and child sacrifice abound.[76] But as suggested above, a reference to child sacrifice can also be read as a more subtle critique. The adults, presumably Judahites, are not behaving according to proper Judahite burial practices. If we take the poem at face value, describing a link between fertility, cults of the dead, and child sacrifice, then some Judahites are elevating the children to an inappropriate place. They are separating out children from the collective family.[77]

Reading Isaiah 57:6 again with fresh eyes, ones that are attentive to burial practices for children, reveals such a meaning. "Among the departed (*ḥăliqē*) of the wadi is your portion (*ḥelek*), they are your lot. Ever to them have you poured libation and brought offerings."[78] The verse now becomes ironic, another "two-faced" metaphor. On the surface it refers to the child sacrifice of verse 5 and a judgment of the adults who practice it (they are as good as dead).[79] My reading sees it as *also* functioning as a reminder as to where and how children *should* be buried. They should not be separated out in individual burials. Rather, as described in Chapters 4 and 6, the Judahite ideal is burial in a family bench tomb, gathered to the ancestors. The continuance of the family line, the collective personhood distributed within the repository pits, and the distributed personhood of grave goods was of utmost importance. Here the charge, among other things, is that what was once being done is now not being done; the ideal is not being upheld.

To sum up: the exact audience of Isaiah 57:3– 13 is unknown. They could be inhabitants of Judah who were not exiled but stayed in the land, or returnees. Whoever they were, the polemic in the poem is a multivalent critique of a practice that links child sacrifice, fertility, death, and burial together. Accordingly, in Isaiah 57 children are not a part of the collective family; their place within the household of death has become different. Their place is highlighted through the repeated use of the word *zera*. The *zera* are no longer covenantal links; they are not a promised seed or a link to life. The *zera* here represent the exact opposite. In verse 3 the *zera* are linked to adultery and harlotry, words used to indicate foreign religious practices, while in verse 4 the *zera* are offspring of lies. Isaiah 57 then describes a cult of the dead that is no longer a cult of dead kin collectively, where the *zera* are linked to the *'avot*, but a cult wherein children have their own separate place, which remains linked to fertility and foreign practices.

Conclusions

In the archaeological record, the link between children, death, and fertility is most clearly seen with children in jar burials and cremations.[80] Jar burials and cremations played into an understanding wherein anything other than Judahite family burials were seen as "other" and therefore "bad." Cremated burials, represented in the text by children who were "sacrificed," that is, "passed over the fire," were synonymous with "non-Judahite" in a way that no other burials were. They were the quintessential "foreign" burial. Without writings to explain how Phoenicians understood cremation and personhood to intersect, it is difficult to say whether they believed cremation burned up, renewed, or reorganized the personhood of their dead, or whether all cremated individuals were understood to be sacrificed in some capacity upon death. What does seem clear, however, is that the biblical texts did not agree with what cremation stood for.

In the same way that the texts in the Hebrew Bible argue for Yahweh-centric worship, pushing against other heterodox practices, the texts on child sacrifice can be understood to push for their agenda regarding the cult of the dead kin. In a world where exile was either about to happen or had happened, where the writers saw foreign influences trickling into every aspect of life, the ethnic identity bound up in Judahite burial became especially important. Upholding a cult in which infants and children retained their place in the household via their differentiated personhood thus constructed a way to keep the Judean family unit together in death.

Notes

1. T. M. Lemos, *Violence and Personhood in Ancient Israel and Comparative Contexts* (Oxford: Oxford University Press, 2017), 133.
2. While the final form of Genesis 22 has Isaac surviving his trip up Mt. Moriah, there appears to be an older stratum of the texts wherein he does not come down with Abraham and return home (Genesis 22:19). See also Y. Amit, *Hidden Polemics in Biblical Narrative* (Leiden: Brill, 1998), 66–72. On the death of the children in 2 Kings 6 as sacrifice, see K. H. Garroway, "2 Kings 6:24–30: A Case of Unintentional Elimination Killing," *JBL* 137 (2018): 53–70.
3. The laws in Exodus are later emended so that firstborn sons must be redeemed rather than sacrificed (Exodus 13:12–13, 34:19–20; Numbers 3:11–12, 8:15–17).

162 INTERPRETING THE BURIALS OF CHILDREN

4. Among others, see M. Bauks, "The Theological Implications of Child Sacrifice in and beyond the Biblical Context in Relation to Genesis 22 and Judges 11," in *Human Sacrifice in Jewish and Christian Tradition*, SHR 112, ed. K. Finsterbusch, A. Lange, and D. Römheld (Leiden: Brill, 2007), 65–86; H. Dewrell, *Child Sacrifice in Ancient Israel*, EANEC 5 (Winona Lake, IN: Eisenbrauns, 2017), 108–15; S. W. Flynn, *Children in Ancient Israel: The Hebrew Bible and Mesopotamia in Comparative Perspective* (Oxford: Oxford University Press, 2018), 163–69; S. M. Olyan, *Asherah and the Cult of Yahweh in Ancient Israel*, SBLMS 34 (Atlanta: Scholars Press, 1988), 13–14, 38–61, 74.

5. J. D. Levenson, *Death and Resurrection of the Beloved Son: The Transformation of Child Sacrifice in Judaism* (New Haven: Yale University Press, 1993), 5, 111–24; S. Niditch, *War in the Hebrew Bible: A Study in the Ethics of Violence* (Oxford: Oxford University Press, 1995), 47; M. S. Smith, *The Early History of God: Yahweh and the Other Deities in Ancient Israel*, Biblical Resource Series (Grand Rapids: Eerdmans, 2002), 172–78. See also S. Ackerman, *Under Every Green Tree: Popular Religion in Sixth-Century Judah*, HSM 46 (Atlanta: Scholars Press, 1992), 137.

6. F. Stavrakopoulou points out that these passages have been interpreted by some as ritual practices of a nonlethal nature. F. Stavrakopoulou, *King Manasseh and Child Sacrifice: Biblical Distortions of Historical Realities*, BZAW 338 (Berlin: de Gruyter, 2012), 142–43.

7. Garroway, "2 Kings 6:24–30," 64.

8. Lemos, *Violence and Personhood*, 133.

9. The Aztec thought that their rain god Tlāoc needed the tears of children. T. Benjamin, *The Atlantic World: Europeans, Africans, Indians, and Their Shared History (1400–1900)* (Cambridge: Cambridge University Press, 2009), 13. Aztec towers of human skulls, called *tzompantli*, have been found throughout the Aztec empire. The one recently discovered in Mexico City attested to the sacrifice not just of young men but of women and children as well. BBC News, "Aztec Tower of Human Skulls Uncovered in Mexico City," 2 July 2017, www.bbc.com/news/world-latin-america-40473547.

10. The archaeological record demonstrates that sacrificed individuals were not simply discarded. The Punic record, discussed later in the chapter, shows care for (potentially) sacrificed children. In the Americas, recent investigations into the Maya and Inca civilizations have found sacrificed subadults as well as adults buried in a ceremonial manner. C. Verdugo, K. Zhu, M. Prout, N. Broomandkhosbacht, A. Galloway, L. Fehren-Schmitz, and J. E. Bradey, "Implications of Age and Sex Determinations of Ancient Maya Sacrificial Victims at Midnight Terror Cave," *International Journal of Osteoarchaeology* 30.4 (2020): 458–68; V. Tiesler and A. Cucina, eds., *New Perspectives on Human Sacrifice and Ritual Body Treatments in Ancient Maya Society* (New York; Springer, 2007); D. Socha, M. Sykutera, J. Reinhard, and R. Chávez Perea, "Ritual Drug Use during Inca Human Sacrifices on Ampato Mountain (Peru): Results of a Toxicological Analysis," *Journal of Archaeological Science: Reports* 43 (2022): 103415, https://doi.org/10.1016/j.jasrep.2022.103415.

11. T. Arden, "Empowered Children in Classic Maya Sacrificial Rites," *Childhood in the Past* 4 (2011), https://doi.org/10.1179/cip.2011.4.1.133.

12. See H. Seiwert, "Opfer," *Handbuch religionswissenschaftlicher Grundbegriffe* 4:268–84; B. Pongratz-Leisten, "Ritual Killing and Sacrifice in the Ancient Near East," in Finsterbusch, Lange, and Römheld, *Human Sacrifice*, 10–11.

13. B. Pongratz-Leisten, "Sacrifice in the Ancient Near East: Offering and Ritual Killing," in *Sacred Killing: The Archaeology of Sacrifice in the Ancient Near East*, ed. A. M. Porter and G. M. Schwartz (Winona Lake, IN: Eisenbrauns, 2012), 295–96. Such offerings often work on a gift-giving system; they are given out of gratitude and serve an economic function.

14. Pongratz-Leisten, "Sacrifice," 291.

15. Pongratz-Leisten, "Sacrifice," 292–94.

16. E. Morris, "Sacrifice for the State: First Dynasty Royal Funerals and the Rites at Macramallah's Rectangle," in *Performing Death: Social Analyses of Funerary Traditions in the Ancient Near East and Mediterranean*, OIS 3, ed. Nicola Laneri (Chicago: Oriental Institute of the University of Chicago, 2007), 15–38; F. H. Gorman, *The Ideology of Ritual: Space, Time and Status in the Priestly Theology*, JSOT Supp. 91 (Sheffield: JSOT Press, 1990), 19.

17. M. Suriano, *A History of Death in the Hebrew Bible* (Oxford: Oxford University Press, 2018), 20; C. Bell, *Ritual Theory, Ritual Practice* (New York: Oxford University Press, 1992), 74, and C. Bell, *Ritual: Perspectives and Dimensions* (New York: Oxford University Press, 1997), 136–37.

18. For a bibliography on appropriate sacrificial victims, see G. Schwartz, "Archaeology and Sacrifice," in Porter and Schwartz, *Sacred Killing*, 5. See also J. Beattie, "On Understanding

DEATH OF CHILDREN IN THE HEBREW BIBLE 163

Sacrifice," in *Sacrifice*, ed. M. F. C. Bourdillon and M. Fortes (New York: Academic Press, 1980), 41–44; R. Girard, *Violence and the Sacred*, trans. P. Gregory, new ed. (London: Continuum, 2005); H. Hubert and M. Mauss, *Sacrifice: Its Nature and Function*, trans. W. D. Halls (Chicago: University of Chicago Press, 1964), 52.

19. Descartes held that animals had no souls or mind and therefore had no personhood. B. Morris, *Western Conceptions of the Individual* (Oxford: Berg, 1991), 11. However, this position does not hold in ethnographic studies. See the overview and sources in C. Fowler, *The Archaeology of Personhood: An Anthropological Approach* (London: Routledge, 2004), 11, 16–17, 30.

20. Amos 6:4 chastises those who eat these animals rather than sacrifice them. So too, the prophetic corpus makes reference to stall-fed calves as luxury items (1 Samuel 28:24; Jeremiah 46:21; Malachai 4:2). See P. King and L. Stager, *Life in Biblical Israel* (Louisville, KY: Westminster John Knox, 2001), 34.

21. Schwartz, "Archaeology and Sacrifice," 8.

22. Garroway, "2 Kings 6:24–30," 61. Consider the biblical narratives describing Mesha's *firstborn* son (2 Kings 3:27), Abraham's *beloved* son (Genesis 22:2), and Jephthah's *only* daughter (Judges 11:34) that emphasize the value of these children to their parents.

23. Archaeologists have found evidence of child sacrifice for communicative purposes in high-altitude Incan tombs, where the children were interred as ice mummies (Schwartz, "Archaeology and Sacrifice," 7; M. Constanza Ceruti, "Frozen Mummies from Andean Mountaintop Shrines: Bioarchaeology and Ethnohistory of Inca Human Sacrifice," *BioMed Research International* 2015, https://doi.org/10.1155/2015/439428). Mayans sacrificed children for a similar reason. See Arden, "Empowered Children."

24. This belief is found in the Maya, Aztec, and Inca myths, as well as the Norse, Japanese, and Hawaiian myths. ANE myths about the dying (and rising) gods also attest to this connection: the Ba'al Cycle, the deaths of Tiamat and Kingu in the Enuma Elish, as well as with Ishtar, Persephone, and Osiris.

25. On the anthropology of gift-giving, see inter alia B. Malinowski, *Argonauts of the Western Pacific* (New York: Dutton, 1961); M. Mauss, *The Gift: Forms and Functions of Exchange in Archaic Societies* (New York: Norton, 1967); C. Lévi-Strauss, *The Elementary Structures of Kinship*, trans. J. Bell, J. von Strumer, and R. Needham (Boston: Beacon, 1969), C. Lévi-Strauss, *Introduction to the Work of Marcel Mauss*, trans. F. Baker (London: Routledge & Kegan Paul, 1987); P. Bourdieu, *The Logic of Practice*, trans. R. Nice (Stanford: Stanford University Press, 1990).

26. G. Stansell, "The Gift in Ancient Israel," *Semeia* 87 (1999): 65–90; V. H. Matthews, "The Unwanted Gift: Implication of Obligatory Gift Giving in Ancient Israel," *Semeia* 87 (1999): 91–104; T. M. Lemos, *Marriage Gifts and Social Change in Ancient Palestine, 1200 BCE to 200 CE* (Cambridge: Cambridge University Press, 2010), 1–19; K. H. Garroway, "The Case of Joseph's Coat: Giving Gifts to Children in the Hebrew Bible," *AVAR* 1.2 (2022): 189–90.

27. Genesis 16:2, 17:15–16, 21:1–2, 30:2; Judges 13:5; Ruth 4:12–14; 1 Samuel 1:11; Job 1:21.

28. Matthews, "The Unwanted Gift," 91–104.

29. Fowler, *The Archaeology of Personhood*, 11; M. Strathern, *Property, Substance and Effect; Anthropological Essays on Persons and Things* (London: Athlone, 1999), 239.

30. K. H. Garroway, *Children in the Ancient Near Eastern Household*, EANEC 3 (Winona Lake, IN: Eisenbrauns, 2014), 191.

31. See inter alia O. Eissfeldt, *Molk als Opferbegriff im Punischen und Hebräischen und das Ende des Gottes Moloch*, Beiträge zur Religionsgechichte des Altertums 3 (Halle: Niemeyer, 1935); G. C. Heider, *The Cult of Molek: A Reassessment*, JSOT Supp 43 (Sheffield: JSOT Press, 1985); P. G. Mosca, "Child Sacrifice in Canaanite and Israelite Religion: A Study in *Mulk* and מלך," (PhD dissertation, Harvard University, 1975); J. Day, *Molech: A God of Human Sacrifice in the Old Testament*, University of Cambridge Oriental Publications 41 (Cambridge: Cambridge University Press, 1989); B. H. Reynolds, "Molek: Dead or Alive? The Meaning and Derivation of *mlk* and למלך," in Finsterbusch, Lange, and Römheld, *Human Sacrifice*, 133–50; M. Bauks, "Kinderopfer als Weihe- oder Gabeopfer: Anmerkungen zum *mlk*-Opfer," in *Israeliten und Phönizier: Ihre Beziehungen im Spiegel der Archäologie und der Literatur des Alten Testaments und seiner Umwelt*, OBO 235, ed. M. Witte and J. F. Diehl (Fribourg: Academic Press, 2008), 233–51; Dewrell, *Child Sacrifice*.

32. Leviticus 18:21, 20:3; Jeremiah 32:35 (*lmlk*); Deuteronomy 12:30–31, 18:10; Isaiah 30:27–33; Jeremiah 7:31, 19:5; 2 Kings 21:6 // 2 Chronicles 33:6 (fire and tophets).

33. Stavrakopoulou, *King Manasseh*, 141–48 and bibliography within.

34. J. H. Schwartz, F. Houghton, L. Bondioli, and R. Macchiarelli, "Skeletal Remains from Punic Carthage Do Not Support Systematic Sacrifice of Infants," *PLoS ONE* 5 (2010): e9177; J. H. Schwartz, F. Houghton, R. Macchiarelli, and L. Bondioli, "Bones, Teeth, and Estimating Age of Perinates: Carthaginian Infant Sacrifice Revisited," *Antiquity* 86 (2012): 738–45. See also the sources cited in Chapter 3, note 3.

35. The lack of adult cremations in a cemetery stands in stark contrast to the adult-only cremation sites in the Phoenician homeland. On faunal remains at Carthage see D. Fulton and P. Hesse, "Considering Carcasses: Sheep and Goat Sacrifice at Carthage, Tunisia and Al Qisha, Yemen," in *The Wide Lens in Archaeology: Honoring Brian Hesse's Contribution to Anthropological Archaeology*, ed. J. Lev-Tov, A. Gilbert, and P. Hesse (London: Lockwood Press, 2017), 245–56.

36. A. Alquier and J. Alquier, "Stèles votives à Saturne découvertes près de N'Gaous (Algérie)," *CRAI* 75.1 (1931): 21–26; Dewrell, *Child Sacrifice*, 11–13; Mosca, "Child Sacrifice," 55–97. See the comprehensive treatment of the inscriptions in H. Dixon, "Phoenician Mortuary Practice in the Iron Age I–III (ca. 1200–ca. 300 BCE) Levantine 'Homeland'" (PhD dissertation, University of Michigan, 2013), 25–162. On the classical writers, see Diodorus Siculus or Philo of Byblos, who suggest the Phoenicians/Punics would eagerly sacrifice children to their god Kronos. See also Mosca, "Child Sacrifice," 2–23; Day, *Molech*, 86–91.

37. Dewrell, *Child Sacrifice*, 14.

38. Dewrell, *Child Sacrifice*, 16 and 16 n. 29.

39. P. Eissfeldt was the first to link the Punic *mlk* sacrifices with the biblical *lmlk* sacrifices and see them both as referring to the sacrifice of children. For an overview of Eissfeldt and the defense of his position by Mosca, see Eissfeldt, *Molk als Opferbegriff*; Mosca, "Child Sacrifice"; and the discussion and bibliography in Dewrell, *Child Sacrifice*, 15–19.

40. Inter alia, 1 Kings 12:25–33, 16:31; 2 Kings 16:1–4; Amos 2:6–8; Jeremiah 3:3–9.

41. The site reports from Roger Saidah include "Fouilles de Khaldé: Rapport préliminarire sure la première et deuxième campagnes (1961–1962)," *Bulletin du Musée Beyrouth* 19 (1966): 51–90; "Chronique: Fouilles de Khaldé," *Bulletin du Musée Beyrouth* 20 (1967): 165–68; "Archaeology in the Lebanon 1968–69," *Berytus* 18 (1969): 119–42. For a detailed analysis of the site and its excavation history year by year, see Dixon, "Phoenician Mortuary Practice," 495–519.

42. Tyre's necropolis was also at the edge of an ancient creek, which was turned into a lake in the ninth to eighth c. BCE, again showing the Phoenician preference to bury near water. M. Aubet, "The Phoenician Cemetery of Tyre," *NEA* 73 (2010): 144–55.

43. Dixon, "Phoenician Mortuary Practice," 75.

44. Saidah, "Chronique," 166. Of the 422 Iron II burials discovered, 178 were given a general age. Dixon, "Phoenician Mortuary Practice," 517; H. Sader, "Necropoles et tombes phénicinnes du Liban," *Cuadernos de Arquelogía Mediterránea* 1 (1995): 17. Helen Dixon's compilation records 119 adults, 37 "adolescents," and 22 "*enfants en bas âge*" (i.e., infants or toddlers or simply young children)—the French terminology again highlighting the difficulty in interpreting excavation reports with regard to age. Of these 178 burials, the physical anthropology report offers comments only on around thirty individuals, whose remains have since gone missing. W. Shanklin and M. Ghantus, "A Preliminary Report on the Anthropology of the Phoenicians," *Bulletin du Musée de Beyrouth* 19 (1966): 91–96. Of these thirty, only two were children. Shaklin and Ghantus say little about these children other than they were included in the sampling ("A Preliminary Report," 91). Dixon's overview of the Khaldé level III tombs in which two adolescents were discovered, along with an infant of undetermined age and adults, suggests that the adolescents might be between eleven and thirteen years old (Dixon, "Phoenician Mortuary Practice," 505–10; Saidah, "Fouilles de Khaldé").

45. Specifically, the last quarter of the eighth through the first quarter of the sixth century BCE. E. Bloch-Smith, *Judahite Burial Practices and Beliefs about the Dead*, JSOT Sup. 123 (Sheffield: JSOT, 1992), 242–43. Another Iron Age II tomb was discovered by Chéhab and dated by its pottery to the eighth c. The tomb conditions were not ideal for preservation: "L'eau suintant sans cesse et l'humidité qui en résultait avaient rendu le matériel très friable." C. Doumet, "Les Tombes IV et V de Rachidieh," *Annels d'Histoire et d'Archaélogie de la FLSH de l'Université Saint-Joseph* 1 (1982): 92. The conditions likely account for why no skeletal remains were located.

46. T. Macridy, "A travers les nécropoles sidoniennes," *RB* 1.4 (1904): 567, Figure 13.

47. Plate VI: 14 and 15 are images of uncovered urns with bones sticking out of the top. They appear to be long bones and part of a cranium (Macridy, "A travers les nécropoles sidoniennes," plate VI). Ironically, Macridy found the practice of cremation very "un-Phoenician-like": it

DEATH OF CHILDREN IN THE HEBREW BIBLE 165

"n'appartenaient pas à des Phéniciens, pour qui l'incinération du cadavre eût été un crime abominable." Macridy, "A travers les nécropoles sidoniennes," 569.

48. M. Chéhab, "Chronique," *Bulletin du Musée de Beyrouth* 4 (1942–43): 123–24; Doumet-Serhal, "Les Tombes IV et V."

49. Aubet, "Phoenician Cemetery of Tyre," 144–55; M. Edrey, E. Arie, H. May, and A. Yasur-Landau, "The Iron Age II Tombs of Area E, Tel Achziv," *IEJ* 68.2 (2018): 173–74.

50. M. Aubet, F. J. Núñez, and L. Trelliśo, "La necropolis fenicia de Tiro-Al Bass: En el contexto funerano fenicio oriental," in *Huelra Arquelógica* 20 (Barcelona: Universitat Pompeu Fabra, 2003), 60.

51. Aubet, "Phoenician Cemetery of Tyre," 148.

52. Aubet et al., "La necropolis fenicia," 41–62; Aubet, "Phoenician Cemetery of Tyre," 144–45.

53. Helen Sader notes that there were hundreds of ninth to seventh c. cremation urns, most of which were dug up by looters. Sader, "Necropoles et tombes phénicinnes," 21.

54. Aubet et al., "La necropolis fenicia," 56.

55. Aubet et al., "La necropolis fenicia," 56.

56. Aubet, "Phoenician Cemetery of Tyre," 146.

57. On membership in the household as a criterion for personhood and burial status, see Garroway, *Children*, 239–44. Ultimately, lacking data, the answer to these questions is speculative at best.

58. See Chapter 3.

59. Stavrakopoulou draws parallels between the Phoenician sacrificial *mlk* practice and the burials found at Achzib, 'Atlit, Tell el- 'Ajjul, and Tell el- Far'ah South. She is careful to note that one cannot say for sure whether these southern Levantine sites are sacrificial sites. Notably absent in her discussion is the importance of the ages of the cremated remains. Stavrakopoulou, *King Manasseh*, 224–25.

60. That the masses were not privy to bench tombs, or the texts of the Bible, seems a given based on the burial record itself and understandings of the transmission of biblical texts and literacy in the Iron Age. For the latter two, see, for example, the discussion of Torah transmission in M. Satlow, *How the Bible Became Holy* (New Haven: Yale University Press, 2015). On scribalism as a trained profession and the notion that not everyone would have been able to read and write, see W. Schniedewind, *The Finger of the Scribe: How Scribes Learned to Write the Bible* (New York: Oxford University Press, 2019); C. Rollston, *Writing and Literacy in the World of Ancient Israel: Epigraphic Evidence from the Iron Age* (Atlanta: SBL, 2010).

61. On the heterodox nature of Israelite religions, see the overview by C. B. Hays, *A Covenant with Death: Death in the Iron Age II and Its Rhetorical Uses in Proto-Isaiah* (Grand Rapids, MI: Eerdmans, 2011), 133–34.

62. Deuteronomy 18:10–11; 2 Kings 21:6 // 2 Chronicles 33:6; Isaiah 44, 46.

63. As Lewis notes, there is no consensus in modern critical scholarship regarding the compositional history of Isaiah 56:9– 57:13, nor is there agreement on the target audience. T. Lewis, *Cults of the Dead in Israel and Ugarit*, HSM 39 (Atlanta: Scholars Press, 1989), 143–44. Those arguing for a pre-exilic date of Isaiah 17 include O. Eissfeldt, *The Old Testament: An Introduction* (New York: Harper and Row, 1965), 345, and C. Westermann, *Isaiah 40– 66*, trans. D. M. G. Stalker; OTL (London: SCM Press, 1969), 325. I follow Ackerman (and others), who make a convincing linguistic case for placing the text in the sixth c. Ackerman goes so far as to say that the poem's emphasis on child sacrifice sits nicely in the years 535–520 BCE. Ackerman, *Under Every Green Tree*, 114.

64. T. J. Lewis, "Death Cult Imagery in Isaiah 57," *HAR* 11 (1987): 267–84; Lewis, *Cults of the Dead*, 143–58; Ackerman, *Under Every Green Tree*, 143–52; S. Ackerman, "Sacred Sex, Sacrifice, and Death," *BR* 6 (1990): 40, https://www.baslibrary.org/bible-review/6/1/9. Ackerman translates the poem with slight differences in *Under Every Green Tree*, 102– 11. J. Blenkinsopp, *Isaiah 56– 66: A New Translation and Commentary*, AB 19B (New York: Doubleday, 2003), 152– 66; Stavrakopoulou, *King Manasseh*, 170–79.

65. Ackerman treats the poem in a more detailed manner in *Under Every Green Tree*, 115–63. There she focuses on whether child sacrifice or a cult of the dead occurred. The strength of her *BR* article for the current study rests in how she describes the relationship between fertility, child sacrifice, and a cult of the dead. On the other hand, Lewis (*Cults of the Dead*, 143–58) reads this poem as solely concerned with the cult of the dead, while Stavrakopoulou understands it as only concerned with child sacrifice (*King Manasseh*, 170–76, 254–61).

66. Non- sanctioned cults are typically described as taking place on high places or under leafy trees: 1 Kings 14:13; 2 Kings 17:10; Hosea 4:14; Jeremiah 2:20; Ezekiel 6:13.

166 INTERPRETING THE BURIALS OF CHILDREN

67. On the Egyptian opening of the mouth or *wpt r* ritual, see M. Roth, "The *pss-kf* and the 'Opening of the Mouth' Ceremony: A Ritual of Birth and Rebirth," *Journal of Egyptian Archaeology* 78 (1992): 113–47; S. Bjerke, "Remarks on the Egyptian Ritual of 'Opening the Mouth' and Its Interpretation," *Numen* 12.1 (1965): 201–16. Lewis comments that the mouth imagery may also be related to Mot, the god of death who swallowed up Baal. He posits it is Mot who is "licking his lips with anticipated delight as he is about to satisfy once again his voracious appetite" (Lewis, *Cults of the Dead*, 512–53; cf. *CTA* 5.2.2–4).
68. Exodus 23:19; Leviticus 23:9–14; Numbers 15:17–21; Deuteronomy 26:1–11.
69. Ackerman, "Sacred Sex, Sacrifice, and Death." Stavrakopoulou argues for a connection between the *mlk* sacrifice and fertility. She also discusses the relationship of the *mlk* sacrifices to the royal cult of the dead. Stavrakopoulou, *King Manasseh*, 292–95.
70. "The poem as a whole clearly condemns child sacrifice as a practice at odds with the correct worship of YHWH" (Stavrakopoulou, *King Manasseh*, 171).
71. "The heavy emphasis upon the practitioners of child sacrifice in Isa 57:3–13 contrasts with the surprising lack of any clear focus upon the deity to whom the children are offered" (Stavrakopoulou, *King Manasseh*, 172).
72. See also H. W. Irwin, "'The Smooth Stones of the Wady'? Isaiah 57, 6," *CBQ* 29 (1967): 37–39; and Blenkinsopp, *Isaiah 56–66*, 158–59.
73. Stavrakopoulou, *King Manasseh*, 171.
74. See references to this reading ad loc in BHS.
75. Lewis praises the "author's artistry in mixing metaphors" (*Cults of the Dead*, 149).
76. Westermann, *Isaiah 40–66*, 324; S. McKenzie, *Second Isaiah: Introduction, Translation and Notes*, AB 20 (Garden City, NJ: Doubleday, 1968), 156; Ackerman, *Under Every Green Tree*, 101–63.
77. The monumental tombs of the Iron II period in the Silwan are evidence of the movement toward the more individualized nature of burials. The tombs of the Royal Steward, Pharaoh's Daughter, and Shebna are the most well known of this corpus. These stand in contrast to the family tombs found at Ketef Hinnom and St. Étienne. The rebuke given to Shebna in Isaiah 22:15–19 "is thus directed at Shebna's decision to build his own tomb rather than choosing interment in a family tomb. This is consistent with the tombs in Silwan, which were individual funerary monuments rather than communal burial sites." Suriano, *History of Death*, 110. See also Hays, *A Covenant with Death*, 232–49.
78. Translation by Lewis, *Cults of the Dead*, 149.
79. As Irwin, "Smooth Stones," notes, the wadis surrounding Jerusalem are a common place of burial. They are also related to child sacrifice. In this reading verse 6 is a polemic against child sacrifice.
80. See Chapters 5 and 6.

8

The Personhood of Children Revealed in Death

Given that burial involves a form of commemoration and public ritual, and that burials can provide the dying body a form of protection, these categories are helpful for investigating conceptions of personhood. While the preceding chapters touched upon personhood with respect to these categories, this chapter wraps up the study, asking what we might discern regarding personhood from different rituals and commemorative practices for children. It then moves beyond these categories to think more broadly about the personhood of children displayed in death throughout the different regions of ancient Israel, ending with a focus on Judahite children. The study concludes that across the burials examined, infants and children appear to have had some degree of personhood that was measurable in relationship to that of the adults in their communities.

Commemoration and Public Ritual

Commemoration can take many forms. Chapter 5 explored the ways in which writing played a role in remembering the deceased. From writing found on tomb entrances, to the tomb itself, to jewelry found within the tomb, writing served as a means of protecting the dying individuals, thus attesting to the fact that they needed protection. This idea is not new or novel but has been expressed in prior scholarship on death. However, where earlier scholarship focused on the individuals as adults, the work here brought the focus onto the children in the burials. Children too needed protection; ergo, children associated with writing had something worth protecting. I would argue that the "something" that needed protection was their personhood as the living child transitioned through the dying process.

Commemoration can also take the form of a burial that is marked in some manner. With intramural burials, the marking could be a newly laid floor, as

The Dying Child. Kristine Henriksen Garroway, Oxford University Press. © Oxford University Press 2025.
DOI: 10.1093/9780197566718.003.0009

168   INTERPRETING THE BURIALS OF CHILDREN

seen in the sites associated with Philistia. They might also be associated with a particular space in a room, like a threshold or corner. Space may have also been marked with a movable object set on top of the burial.[1] More permanent commemorative markers could take the form of pillars, walls, or roads. Finally, the "container" for the burial, whether a jar, a tomb, or a cave, could also serve as a locus for protection and commemoration. Having a marked location for commemoration would be a way in which a child's personhood might be protected and, in some cases, remembered for generations to come.

The relationship between public ritual and personhood might be best understood with respect to burials in cemeteries. These burials are often argued to have been attended by individuals of the wider community, whereas intramural burials, especially within the house, are seen as "less public," attended by a limited number of family members. We might ask, then, whether external burials argue for a more socially recognized understanding of personhood by age. One could argue yes for societies that buried children in cemeteries and infants in houses, such as found throughout Bronze Age Canaan. In these societies we see a ceramic burial kit both given to all ages and yet differentiated by age. Infants, buried intramurally, routinely received an abbreviated ceramic burial kit: a juglet (bottle?) and at times a bowl. If ceramic grave goods were meant to feed the deceased while they went through the dying process or even in the afterlife, this kit was appropriate for infants as it served their needs; infants consume only liquid, so they would not need elaborate ceramic kits of bowls, plates, jars, and jugs for solid foods.

Attitudes toward the Death and Burial of Children in the Iron Age

The examination of infants in Philistine and Phoenician sites within the land of Iron Age Israel provides a set of comparative data, a foil if you will, for investigating attitudes toward the dying child in Israel and Judah. Inhabitants of Iron I Philistia had a distinct attitude toward infants and the way in which they were to be incorporated into the household cult, for the intramural burials were quite literally a part of the household. The peoples of Ashkelon were exemplary in their propensity to bury things under their house floors.[2] The frequency of intramural infant burials perhaps, as has been suggested, is related to the idea of rebirth. However, rebirth has been argued more for intramural jar burials, not intramural pit burials such as were common in

Ashkelon. While the difference might seem minor, it could attest to a variance in the way infants were viewed. Jar burials, like those seen in Bronze Age Canaan (and at Bronze Age Ashkelon), may well be evidence of an idea of rebirth, as discussed in Chapter 6. Conversely, pit burials within a house could point more toward an idea of the infant anchoring the family to the house. Given that infant burials often occurred in liminal spaces within the domicile, they could even have been providing protection to the house. Intramural burials have been interpreted in this way for other cultures, as the dead are associated with the cult of the ancestors. However, the so-called protective burials are generally adults.[3] The difficulty of interpreting intramural burials as ancestors who become household gods is that burials are not found in every house, and houses are bought and sold. As Daniel Flemming observes:

> The very genealogical bonds maintained by remembrance of ancestors reach across individual households to a wider circle of kin. So far as "the dead" may be addressed at a burial site, this grave does not appear to be located inside the house. House sales at Emar are common, and the families of sellers seem to be in no danger of losing contact with their dearly departed.[4]

In pushing us to think about the locale of the ancestor cult, Flemming suggests that the locus of the rites was not always a burial within the house. On the other hand, within Ugarit the ancestral dead were often buried under houses. So, while each society had its differences, the consensus appears to suggest that many societies understood the dead to have an influence on the living—what that influence was and where the dead were buried, however, varies. Those exploring the relationship between the ancestral dead and household religion note the importance of family matters in household religion.[5] No one to my knowledge has considered the role of children and intramural burials within the context of household religion and a cult of the dead.

Returning to Ashkelon, given the number of infants found within the domestic region of Ashkelon's Grid 38, I suggest these burials may represent a certain household religious practice or belief. It could be that the protection provided by the burial was not meant as literal protection offered by the dead child working from beyond the grave, but was more of a symbolic protection. The burial of a child within a house may have acted as sympathetic magic. Given the high rate of infant mortality, perhaps

170 INTERPRETING THE BURIALS OF CHILDREN

burying a deceased infant within the domicile acted as a means of warding off the exact thing that was feared—infant death. The placement of burials in corners of buildings, as well as under thresholds and other such liminal spaces, lends support to the argument that the burials were protective. Other positives for such an understanding also exist. It has been suggested that burials can "anchor" a family to a plot of land or a house. Because residency may turn over more frequently in a city, I would argue that we should not think about infant and child burials as anchoring family to a plot of land or a house. Rather, we should envision these burials as having relevance not for a greater kinship group but for a specific natal family.[6] As this brief discussion demonstrates, more work on Philistine rituals and household religion needs to be done, and that work needs to include children in the discussion.

Regarding extramural burials, Dan Master and Adam Aja suggest that the Ashkelon cemetery finds similarities with Phoenician burial practices. They point to cremation, subterranean header blocks, ceramic assemblage, and covering children with sherd "blankets,"[7] to which I might also add a burial near water. They contrast this similarity with the distinctly non-Phoenician aspects in the Ashkelon cemetery, such as lack of food offerings and cooking vessels. This, combined with the fact that burials were often burials of single individuals, buried apart from family members, and without grave markers, suggested to them that the cemetery was not Phoenician and, moreover, that there was not an ongoing relationship with the dead.[8]

Yet earlier in the report there are hints that their conclusion might not be entirely accurate. There is reference to the possibility that store jars associated with pit burials were left partially exposed above ground and that the built chamber tombs may well have had a superstructure above ground.[9] They also note that the placement of the pit graves seem to be between the built tombs, not on top of them. Some indication of where individuals were laid out must have been present; otherwise in such a densely populated cemetery multiple graves would have cut into one another.[10]

All of this to say that it is quite possible the living inhabitants of Ashkelon remained in relationship with the dead and cared for them. If store jars did indeed protrude above ground, then so too would the bowls and dipper juglets placed on top of them. Perhaps these were related to a post-burial libation ceremony. If this is the case, then there are implications for the care given to children. Since the store jar, bowl, and juglet kit is not associated with children, it would seem that children did not receive the same kind

PERSONHOOD OF CHILDREN REVEALED IN DEATH 171

of care post-burial as their adult counterparts. Yet care given at the time of burial, the high frequency of personal adornment items afforded to the Ashkelon children, and their careful inhumation demonstrate that there was a conscious effort to afford them the same kind of pre-burial care as adults. It would appear, then, that children needed the same kind of pre-burial care but not post-burial care. If care is related to personhood, then the care given to children suggests that the bodies of the dying children chosen for burial in the Ashkelon cemetery were understood to have a measurable amount of personhood. Again, that personhood need not be on par with the adults in the cemetery, but their personhood certainly appears to be something, not nothing.

For their part, the Phoenicians are frequently described in the literature as not favoring a single type of burial. Cremation, inhumation, jars, tombs, and pits are all employed. At times, Phoenician burials even resemble earlier Canaanite family cave burials and contemporaneous Judahite bench tombs. However, it is cremation burials that, for many, are the hallmark of Phoenician burials. The fact that infants and children are not always buried like adults suggests that Phoenicians held a differentiated conception of an infant's or child's needs in death, as related to an understanding of their differentiated personhood. While cremation was not something used for infants within the Phoenician homeland, it was used in the Phoenician diaspora, in Punic lands. Not surprisingly, in the land between these areas, ancient Israel, we see differing attitudes toward the use of cremation for infants in cities under Phoenician influence or hosting Phoenician trade colonies. In ʿAtlit children were cremated, while at Tell el-Farʿah and Tell er-Reqeish children and infants alike were cremated and placed in cemeteries along with adults. Given this data, comments such as the following deserve rethinking.

> The bias against inclusion of infants and children in cremations therefore holds good for all the Levantine Iron Age cemeteries described above. It appears to represent a commonly held attitude in the past whereby the majority of infants and young children did not receive full funerary rites.[11]

The comments go on to explain how the lack of infant and child burials represents a society's view that these individuals were "not considered members of the community, or even fully human, until they had reached a specific stage of biological development." They also reference the pragmatic

172 INTERPRETING THE BURIALS OF CHILDREN

concerns wherein society did not want to put time, energy, and expenses into the burial of infants and children.

I too have argued that infants and children were treated differently, according to their age, and that their burials, especially within the Bronze Age, represent the degree to which they were considered full members of their society. Indeed, by such logic, one might argue, as I have, the same things regarding expense and energy expenditure for infants and child burials of every kind. However, I would push back against the statement regarding "full funerary rites." The data provided in the current study present a more complex picture. To say infants and children did not receive full funerary rites has merit only to a limited extent. It approaches the subject from the perspective of the adult and assumes a standardized practice of funerary rites for all individuals. With the data provided here, we can move the discussion further. Just as we have come to understand Philistine, Phoenician, Canaanite, and Judahite societies to be complex entities, so too are their burials.[12] Yes, burials differed by age and by culture, but for good reason. In fact, what I have shown is that infants and children could receive "full" funerary rites, but that what was considered "full" funerary rites differed by age and also differed across sites and within cultural groups.

Looking to other areas in the land of ancient Israel, older Canaanite practices continued to persist into the Iron Age, most notably in areas outside of Judah. Cave burials, some rock-cut tombs, and even jar burials remain viable options for burying infants and children. Such burials again stand in contrast to the uniformity of the burial record found in Iron II Judah. The burials in the north continued to utilize unique burials, namely jar burials, for infants and young children. Intramural burials are not found in Judah, yet sites such as Tel Kinnerot / Tell el-'Orēme, Megiddo, and possibly Dothan attest to the continued use of these burials for infants and children, including intramural jar burials. Other sites in the north took care to include infants and children in cemeteries or family cave burials. Taken as a whole, the areas outside of Judah present a fractured approach to caring for the youngest members of society in death. While it seems likely in some cases that these young ones were afforded a measure of personhood, it is also apparent that infants and children were not routinely buried in proximity to other family members and adults in their community, or commemorated with any form of ritual, private or public. The picture for Judahite children, however, is much different.

A Child's Story: The Social Memory of the Child in Judah

Social memory, membership in the household, and elevated status of individuals are all important issues for constructing a social history of death. Who is kept close to the house and who is buried with the family are indications of a family's attachment to an individual and the person's ascribed status within the community: "Only certain individuals were selected for burial in reused spaces where the living would periodically interact with their remains for years or even decades after [their] biological death."[13] Studies of Middle Bronze Age Megiddo have related this locus of spatial reuse to intramural residential burials and place-making, and group membership in death.[14] I would argue that similar elements can be seen in the Judahite bench tombs, which also functioned as a locus of social memory.

The Judahite bench tomb stood as the locus of mortuary rites for extended kin groups. Interment within the family tomb meant the living interacted with those individuals who had previously passed on. It also meant that dying individuals were brought to a place where they would be gathered with their ancestors. The uniformity of bench tombs—in the construction, layout, and deposition of bodies and grave goods—suggests a measure of standardized mortuary practices and beliefs. As laid out at the start of the chapter, burials are a form of commemoration and public ritual, as well as a means of protecting the dying body. Moving the bodies to the tombs, preparing them for burial, opening the tomb, depositing them, and then closing up the tomb would require more than just one or two individuals. Burial in a rock-cut bench tomb would lean to the side of public ritual and commemoration. Whereas infants and children in surrounding regions experienced differentiated burials, Judahite infants and children did not.[15] When it comes to the issue of personhood, I also argued that the personhood and place an individual held in the household of the living was understood to continue into the household of the dead. To this end, infants remained infants and children remained children, so that their degree of personhood remained fixed in the household of death as they were brought into the collective household of the afterlife.

Unpacking this conclusion has implications for previous understandings of Judahite religion and the afterlife. Early on Yehizkiel Kaufmann maintained that the Israelite religion was distinct. He came down definitively on the issue that where other societies practiced a cult of the ancestors, there was no cult of the ancestors in ancient Israel.[16] His conclusion was based on

174 INTERPRETING THE BURIALS OF CHILDREN

his desire to keep the Israelites and biblical text separate from those cultures around it. While coming from a different starting point, Brian B. Schmidt also argued against a cult of ancestors. His stance was that any references to a cult of the dead in the biblical texts were late adoptions of Mesopotamian religion related to necromancy and the beneficent dead.[17] Views rejecting the existence of a cult of the dead have not found favor in the scholarly community. The pendulum swings to the side of scholarship that sees death cult vocabulary in texts of the Hebrew Bible and ancient Near East, as well as in the mortuary remains of the Levant, as indicative of such a cult.

The general arguments both for and against a cult of ancestors have approached the question as one related specifically to adults. And this approach comes as no surprise, for the arguments were based on data that privileged adults. The Hebrew Bible and ancient Near Eastern texts were written by adults, specifically educated, elite, adult men. The concerns within the texts thus reflected those of the writers. As heads of a household, men in a patriarchal society would need others to care for them in death, remember their name, carry on their lineage, and inherit their goods. In reading the biblical texts in light of the archaeological record and the various burials that were discovered in Judah, scholars naturally paid attention to the individuals in the texts, and for whom the texts were concerned: men. And hence, we arrive at a cult of the ancestors that revolved around the patriarch.

Like others, I find the propensity of textual and now archaeological evidence to speak in favor of some sort of a cult of the dead. However, what I have argued here is for a more nuanced understanding. For example, it may well be that the broader conclusions of those, like Kaufmann and Schmidt, have some merit in that the Judahite cult may have been distinct from its neighbors, and it may not have been, strictly speaking, a cult of the ancestors. In focusing on the place of Judahite children in the afterlife, we see a picture unfold in the archaeological record that upholds and preserves not a single male ancestor but the entire family. Within the tomb, the deposition of infants and children is found alongside women and men. They are not treated differently on the basis of age or status within the family. In this way death appears as something of an equalizer. I would argue that one of the most important factors in reaching this conclusion has to do with the intermingling of the bones and grave goods within the repository pits. As Chapter 6 explained, through a theory of partible personhood, a mixing of skeletal remains can be understood as the intermingling of each individual's personhood into the collective. Therefore, what appears in the archaeological record of ancient

Judah might more accurately be described as a cult of the dead kin, not a cult of the ancestors.

This Judahite cult of the dead kin differs from that of surrounding cultures.[18] The concerns represented in the tomb are not solely those commonly cited as pertaining to the concerns of a cult of the ancestor as seen in, inter alia, Mesopotamia, Emar, Nuzi, and Ugarit, namely, the upkeep of a man's grave, mortuary offerings given by a son to a father, written curses or blessings to protect a king or patriarch, or prayers or offerings given post-burial. The concerns of the Judahite cult likely included these but also appear to reach beyond, extending to the household as a whole. Most importantly, Judahite bench tombs show intergenerational links by presenting a unified approach to the way in which children and infants were incorporated into death-way rituals. As demonstrated in Chapters 2–4, this sets Judah apart as different from the more immediate surrounding regions. The archaeological remains in the Judahite bench tombs show care for all members deposited there, stressing the importance of the continuity of the Judahite family unit and personhoods, including infants and children, in life as well as in death.

Notes

1. While a logical idea, it is only a hypothesis since the objects would likely not remain in situ for the archaeologist to discover.
2. The relationship between the intramural animal deposits and intramural infant burials at Ashkelon needs further investigation.
3. K. van der Toorn, "Second Millennium West Asian Family Religion," in *Household and Family Religion in Antiquity*, ed. J. Bodel and S. Olyan (Malden, MA: Wiley-Blackwell, 2012), 26; M. Stol, "Wirtschaft und Gesellschaft in altbablyonischer Zeit," in *Mesopotamien: Die altbabylonische Zeit*, Orbis Biblicus et Orientalis 160/4, ed. D. Charpin, D. O. Edzard, and M. Stol (Fribourg: Academic Press, 2004), 643–975; F. R. Kraus, ed., *Altbabylonische Brief im Umschrift und Übersetzung*, vol. 1 (Leiden: Brill, 1964), no. 140: 17–25.
4. D. Flemming, "Household and Community Religion in Syria," in *Household and Family Religion in Antiquity*, ed. J. Bodel and S. Olyan (Malden, MA: Wiley-Blackwell, 2012), 42.
5. R. Albertz and R. Schmitt, eds., *Family and Household Religion in Ancient Israel and the Levant* (Winona Lake, IN: Eisenbrauns, 2012); J. Bodel and S. Olyan, eds., *Household and Family Religion in Antiquity* (Malden, MA: Wiley-Blackwell, 2012); C. Meyers, *Rediscovering Eve: Ancient Israelite Women in Context* (Oxford: Oxford University Press, 2013); S. Ackerman, *Women and the Religion of Ancient Israel* (New Haven: Yale University Press, 2022).
6. The idea of foundation burials, which have also been suggested for intramural infant burials broadly, also does not hold water for Iron I Ashkelon Grid 38. If these were indeed foundation burials, then we would expect to see such burials in more buildings and in more public buildings.
7. See Chapter 3 and D. Master and A. Aja, "The Philistine Cemetery of Ashkelon," *BASOR* 377 (2017): 156.
8. Master and Aja, "Philistine Cemetery of Ashkelon," 156–57.
9. Master and Aja, "Philistine Cemetery of Ashkelon," 139, 141.
10. Interestingly, the description by Aja is like the description given by Tufnell of the graves at Tell el-Far'ah. She notes that no previous burials were cut into, meaning the living had a way of

176 INTERPRETING THE BURIALS OF CHILDREN

marking or remembering where the burials were located. O. Tufnell, "Burials in Cemeteries 100 and 200," in *Beth-Pelet I (Tell Fara)*, ed. W. F. Petrie (London: British School of Archaeology in Egypt, 1930), 12.

11. P. Smith and G. Kahila Bar- Gal, "Age Biases in Phoenician Funerary Practices," *Eretz-Israel: Archaeological, Historical and Geographical Studies* 33 (2018): 170.

12. Various expressions of cultic practices (to which burials are related) surely occurred within different societies, as the different studies of Philistine and Phoenician sites discussed in this book have pointed out. Note too, the scholarly consensus that Israelite religion was not singular, and it does not appear likely that it was widely practiced according to how it is set out in the biblical text until the Hasmonean period. Y. Adler, *The Origins of Judaism: An Archaeological-Historical Reappraisal* (New Haven: Yale University Press, 2022).

13. M. Cradic, "Residential Burial and Social Memory in the Middle Bronze Age Levant," *NEA* 81.3 (2018): 199.

14. Cradic, "Residential Burial," 199; A. Brody, "Late Bronze Age Intramural Tombs," in *Ashkelon I: Introduction and Overview, 1985– 2006*, Final Reports of the Leon Levy Expedition of Ashkelon 1, ed. L. Stager, J. Schloen, and D. Master (Winona Lake, IN: Eisenbrauns, 2008), 516, 529; A. Brody, "New Perspectives on Levantine Mortuary Ritual: A Cognitive Interpretive Approach to the Archaeology of Death," in *Historical Biblical Archaeology and the Future: The New Pragmatism*, ed. T. Levy (London: Equinox, 2010), 126.

15. This statement is accurate to the extent that one is discussing only rock-cut bench tombs. As a caveat, these were likely the burials of the wealthy class, so conclusions drawn here apply to the socioeconomic stratum under discussion. Without other burial types for comparison, it seems logical that the "missing" pit burials or field burials of the Iron I continued to be the preferred burial in Iron II Judah as well. Yet here too children and infants are hypothetically treated the same as adults. We see, perhaps, a standardized attitude toward death in the community based on social strata.

16. Y. Kaufmann, *The Religion of Ancient Israel: From Its Beginnings to the Babylonian Exile*, trans. M. Greenberg (Chicago: University of Chicago Press, 1972).

17. B. B. Schmidt, *Israel's Beneficent Dead: Ancestor Cult and Necromancy in Ancient Israelite Religion and Tradition* (Winona Lake, IN: Eisenbrauns, 1996). P. Johnston also argues against a cult of the ancestors in *Shades of Death and Afterlife in the Old Testament* (Downers Grove, IL: InterVarsity, 2002).

18. Kerry Sonia has argued persuasively for the unique nature of the cult of dead kin within Judah using the texts of the Hebrew Bible. The arguments made here support her conclusions from an archaeological perspective. K. Sonia, *Caring for the Dead in Ancient Israel*, ABS 27 (Atlanta: SBL Press, 2020). On a non-royal cult of the dead kin more broadly in Mesopotamia, see M. Bayliss, "The Cult of the Dead Kin in Assyria and Babylonia," *Iraq* 35.2 (1973): 115– 25, as well as the various essays covering household religion in West Asia, Ugarit, Emar, the Levant, Egypt, and Greece in J. Bodel and S. Olyan, eds., *Household and Family Religion in Antiquity* (Malden, MA: Wiley-Blackwell, 2012).

Bibliography

Abercrombie, J. R. "Palestinian Burial Practices from 1200 to 60 BCE." PhD dissertation, University of Pennsylvania, 1979.

Ackerman, S. "Sacred Sex, Sacrifice, and Death." *BR* 6 (1990): 40. https://www.baslibrary.org/bible-review/6/1/9.

Ackerman, S. *Under Every Green Tree: Popular Religion in Sixth-Century Judah.* HSM 46. Atlanta: Scholars Press, 1992.

Ackerman, S. *Women and the Religion of Ancient Israel.* New Haven: Yale University Press, 2022.

Adler, Y. *The Origins of Judaism: An Archaeological-Historical Reappraisal.* New Haven: Yale University Press, 2022.

Adler, Y. "Watertight and Rock Solid: Stepped Pools and Chalk Vessels as Expressions of Jewish Ritual Purity." *BAR* 47 (2021): 44–51.

Aḥituv, S. "A Rejoinder to Nadav Naʾaman's 'A New Appraisal of the Silver Amulet from Ketef Himmom.'" *IEJ* 62 (2012): 223–32.

Aizik, N. and Y. Peleg. "An Iron Age IIb Burial Cave to the East of Khirbet Shemsin." Pages 201–4 in *Excavations and Discoveries in Samaria.* Judea and Samaria Publications 9. Edited by I. Yezerski. Jerusalem: IAA, 2009. In Hebrew.

Aja, A. "Grid 38." Pages 20–126 in *Ashkelon 7: The Iron Age I.* Edited by L. Stager, D. Master, and A. Aja. Winona Lake, IN: Eisenbrauns, 2020.

Aja, A. "Philistine Domestic Architecture in the Iron Age I." PhD dissertation, Harvard University, 2009.

Aja, A. and D. Master. "Conclusions: Uncovering Philistines." Pages 854–62 in *Ashkelon 7: The Iron Age I.* Edited by L. Stager, D. Master, and A. Aja. Winona Lake, IN: Eisenbrauns, 2020.

Albertz, R., B. Alpert Nakhai, S. Olyan, and R. Schmitt, eds. *Family and Household Religion: Toward a Synthesis of Old Testament Studies, Archaeology, Epigraphy, and Cultural Studies.* Winona Lake, IN: Eisenbrauns, 2014.

Albertz, R. and R. Schmitt. *Family and Household Religion in Ancient Israel and the Levant.* Winona Lake, IN: Eisenbrauns, 2012.

Albright, W. F. *Yahweh and the Gods of Canaan.* Winona Lake, IN: Eisenbrauns, 1968.

Alexandre, Y. "An Iron Age IB/IIA Burial Cave at Har Yona, Upper Nazareth." *ʿAtiqot* 44 (2003): 183–89.

Alexandre, Y. "Burial Caves from the Intermediate Bronze, Middle Bronze and Iron Ages at Nazareth." *ʿAtiqot* 93 (2018): 1–44.

Alexandre, Y. and E. Stern. "Phoenician Cremation Burials at Tel Bira." *ʿAtiqot* 42 (2001): 183–95.

Alpert Nakhai, B. "When Considering Infants and Jar Burials in the Middle Bronze Age Southern Levant." Pages 100–128 in *Tell It in Gath: Studies in the History and Archaeology of Israel. Essays in Honor of A. M. Maier on the Occasion of His Sixtieth Birthday.* Ägypten und Altes Testament 90. Edited by I. Shai, J. R. Chadwick, L. Hitchcock, A. Dagan, C. McKinney, and J. Uziel. Münster: Zaphon, 2018.

Alpert Nakhai, B., J. P. Dressel, and B. Wisthoff. "Tell el-Wawiyat." *IEJ* 37 (1987): 181–85.

Alpert Nakhai, B., J. P. Dressel, and B. Wisthoff. "Tell el-Wawiyat." *IEJ* 40 (1990): 72.

Alquier, A. and J. Alquier. "Stèles votives à Saturne découvertes près de N'Gaous (Algérie)." *CRAI* 75.1 (1931): 21–26.

Amit, Y. *Hidden Polemics in Biblical Narrative.* Leiden: Brill, 1998.

178   BIBLIOGRAPHY

Amster, M. "Gender Complementarity and Death among the Kelabit." Pages 251–308 in *Journeys of the Soul: Anthropological Studies of Death, Burial, and Rebirth Practice in Borneo*. Borneo Research Council Monograph 7. Edited by W. Wilder. Philips, ME: Borneo Research Council, 2003.

Appell, G. and L. Appell. "Death among the Rungus Momogun of Sabah, Malaysia: The Dissolution of Personhood and Dispersion of the Multiple Souls and Spiritual Counterparts." Pages 41–121 in *Journeys of the Soul: Anthropological Studies of Death, Burial, and Rebirth Practice in Borneo*. Borneo Research Council Monograph 7. Edited by W. Wilder. Philips, ME: Borneo Research Council, 2003.

Arden, T. "Empowered Children in Classic Maya Sacrificial Rites." *Childhood in the Past* 4 (2011): 133–45. https://doi.org/10.1179/cip.2011.4.1.133.

Arensburg, B. "Human Skeletal Remains from Tel Batash." Page 313 in *Timnah (Tel Batash) III*. Qedem 45. Edited by A. Mazar and N. Panitz-Cohen. Jerusalem: Hebrew University, 2006.

Arensburg, B. and Y. Rak. "Jewish Skeletal Remains from the Period of the Kings of Judah." *PEQ* 117 (1985): 30–34.

Arnett, J. "Broad and Narrow Socialization: Family in the Context of a Cultural Theory." *Journal of Marriage and Family* 57 (1995): 617–28.

Assmann, J. "Death and Initiation in the Funerary Religion of Ancient Egypt." Pages 135–59 in *Religion and Philosophy in Ancient Egypt*. Yale Egyptiological Studies 3. Edited by J. P. Allen et al. New Haven: Yale University Press, 1989.

Assmann, J. *Death and Salvation in Ancient Egypt*. Translated by D. Lorton. Ithaca, NY: Cornell University Press, 2005.

Aubet, M. "Cremation and Social Memory in Iron Age Phoenicia." Pages 77–87 in *Ritual, Religion and Reason: Studies in the Ancient World in Honour of Paolo Xella*. Alter Orient und Altes Testament 404. Edited by O. Loretz et al. Münster: Ugarit-Verlag, 2013.

Aubet, M. "The Phoenician Cemetery of Tyre." *NEA* 73 (2010): 144–55.

Aubet, M., F. J. Núñez, and L. Trellisó. "La necropolis fenicia de Tiro-Al Bass: En el contexto funerano fenicio oriental." Pages 41–62 in *Huelra Arquelógica* 20. Edited by J. Fernández Jurado, C. García Sanz, and P. Rufete Tomico. Barcelona: Universitat Pompeu Fabra, 2003.

Avissar Lewis, R. *Children of Antiquity: A View of Archaeology and Childhood in the Land of Israel during the Biblical Period*. Haifa: Haifa University Press, 2020. Hebrew.

Bacvarov, K., ed. *Babies Reborn: Infant/ Child Burials in Pre- and Protohistory*. BAR International Series 1832. Oxford: Archaeopress, 2008.

Baker, B., T. Dupras, and M. Tocheri. *Osteology of Infants and Children*. College Station: Texas A&M University Press, 2005.

Baker, J. "The Funeral Kit: A Newly Defined Canaanite Mortuary Practice Based on the MB and LBA Tomb Complex at Ashkelon." *Levant* 38 (2006): 1–31.

Baker, J. *The Funeral Kit: Mortuary Practices in the Archaeological Record*. Walnut Creek, CA: Left Coast Press, 2012.

Barkay, G. "Burial Headrests as a Return to the Womb—a Reevaluation." *BAR* 14 (1988): 48–50.

Barkay, G. "Excavations at Ketef Hinnom in Jerusalem." Pages 95–105 in *Ancient Jerusalem Revealed*. Edited by H. Geva. Jerusalem: Israel Exploration Society, 1994.

Barkay, G. "The Priestly Benediction on Silver Plaques from Ketef Hinnom in Jerusalem." *TA* 19 (1992): 139–92.

Bauks, M. "Kinderopfer als Weihe- oder Gabeopfer: Anmerkungen zum *mlk*-Opfer." Pages 233–51 in *Israeliten und Phönizier: Ihre Beziehungen im Spiegel der Archäologie und der Literatur des Alten Testaments und seiner Umwelt*. OBO 235. Edited by M. Witte and J. F. Diehl. Fribourg: Academic Press, 2008.

Bauks, M. "Soul-Concepts in Ancient Near Eastern Mythical Texts and Their Implications for the Primeval History." *VT* 66 (2016): 181–93.

Bauks, M. "The Theological Implications of Child Sacrifice in and beyond the Biblical Context in Relation to Genesis 22 and Judges 11." Pages 65–86 in *Human Sacrifice in Jewish and Christian Tradition*. Edited by K. Finsterbusch, A. Lange, and D. Römheld. Leiden: Brill, 2007.

BIBLIOGRAPHY 179

Baxter, J. *Archaeology of Childhood: Children, Gender and Material Culture.* Walnut Creek, CA: AltaMira Press, 2005.

Bayliss, M. "The Cult of Dead Kin in Assyria and Babylonia." *Iraq* 35 (1973): 115–25.

BBC News. "Aztec Tower of Human Skulls Uncovered in Mexico City." 2 July 2017. www.bbc.com/news/world-latin-america-40473547.

Beattie, J. "On Understanding Sacrifice." Pages 41–44 in *Sacrifice*. Edited by M. F. C. Bourdillon and M. Fortes. New York: Academic Press, 1980.

Beauchesne, P. and S. Agarwal. *Children and Childhood in Bioarchaeology.* Gainesville: University of Florida Press, 2018.

Beit-Arieh, I. and A. G. Baron. "The Cemetery." Pages 129–69 in *Tel 'Ira: A Stronghold in the Biblical Negev.* Sonia and Marco Nadler Institute of Archaeology Monograph Series 15. Edited by I. Beit-Arieh. Tel Aviv: Emery and Claire Yass Publications in Archaeology, Institute of Archaeology, Tel Aviv University, 1999.

Bell, C. *Ritual: Perspectives and Dimensions.* New York: Oxford University Press, 1997.

Bell, C. *Ritual Theory, Ritual Practice.* New York: Oxford University Press, 1992.

Bender, S. *The Social Structure of Ancient Israel: The Institution of the Family* (beit 'ab) *from Settlement to the End of the Monarchy.* Jerusalem: Simor, 1996.

Benjamin, T. *The Atlantic World: Europeans, Africans, Indians, and Their Shared History (1400–1900).* Cambridge: Cambridge University Press, 2009.

Ben-Shlomo, D., ed. *Ashdod VI: The Excavations of Areas H and K (1968–1969).* IAA Reports 24. Jerusalem: Israel Antiquities Authority, 2005.

Ben-Shlomo, D. "The Cemetery of Azor and Early Iron Age Burial Practices." *Levant* 40.1 (2008): 29–54.

Binford, L. "Mortuary Practices: Their Study and Their Potential." Pages 6–29 in *Approaches to the Social Dimension of Mortuary Practices.* Memoirs for the Society for American Archaeology 25. Edited by J. A. Brown. New York: Society for American Archaeology, 1971.

Biran, A. "Tell er-Ruqeish to Tell er-Ridan." *IEJ* 24.2 (1974): 141–42.

Birney, K. and B. R. Doak. "Funerary Iconography on an Infant Jar Burial from Ashkelon." *IEJ* 61 (2011): 32–53.

Bjerke, S. "Remarks on the Egyptian Ritual of 'Opening the Mouth' and Its Interpretation." *Numen* 12.1 (1965): 201–16.

Blenkinsopp, J. "Deuteronomy and the Politics of Post-mortem Existence." *VT* 45 (1995): 1–16.

Blenkinsopp, J. *Isaiah 56–66: A New Translation and Commentary.* AB 19B. New York: Doubleday, 2003.

Bloch-Smith, E. *Judahite Burial Practices and Beliefs about the Dead.* JSOT Supp. 123, JSOT/ASOR Monograph Series 7. Sheffield: JSOT Press, 1992.

Bloch-Smith, E. "Resurrecting the Iron I Dead." *IEJ* 54 (2004): 77–91.

Bodel, J. and S. Olyan, eds. *Household and Family Religion in Antiquity.* Malden, MA: Wiley-Blackwell, 2012.

Bohstrom, P. "Whole Nuclear Family Found in Ancient Phoenician Tomb in Israel." *Haaretz*, 24 December 2019. https://www.haaretz.com/archaeology/2019-12-24/ty-article-magazine/.premium/tomb-of-phoenician-father-mother-and-child-found-in-israel/0000017f-da7c-dea8-a77f-de7ebabd0000

Bonatz, D. *Das syro-hethitische Grabdenkmal: Untersuchungen zur Entstehung einer neuen Bildgattung in der Eisenzeit im nordsyrisch-südostanatolischen Raum.* Mainz: van Zabern, 2000.

Bonatz, D. "Katumuwa's Banquet Scene." Pages 39–44 in *Remembrance of Me: Feasting with the Dead in the Ancient Middle East.* Edited by V. Rimmer Herrmann and J. D. Scholeon. Chicago: Oriental Institute of the University of Chicago, 2014.

Boretto, E. "Radiocarbon Dates from Cave T1." Pages 235–36 in *Tell es-Safi/Gath II: Excavations and Studies.* Ägypten und Altes Testament 105. Edited by A. Maeir and J. Uziel. Münster: Zaphon, 2020.

Bourdieu, P. *The Logic of Practice.* Translated by R. Nice. Stanford: Stanford University Press, 1990.

180 BIBLIOGRAPHY

Bourdieu, P. *Outline of a Theory of Practice*. Translated by R. Nice. Cambridge: Cambridge University Press, 1977.

Boutin, A. "Crafting a Bioarchaeology of Personhood: Osteobiographical Narratives from Alalakh." Pages 109–34 in *Breathing New Life into the Evidence of Death: Contemporary Approaches to Bioarchaeology*. Edited by A. Baadsgaard, A. T. Boutin, and J. E. Buikstra. Santa Fe, NM: School for Advanced Research Press, 2011.

Boyd, M. "Destruction and Other Material Acts of Transformation in Mycenaean Funerary Practice." Pages 155–65 in *THRAVSMA: Contextualizing the Intentional Destruction of Objects in the Bronze Age Aegean and Cyprus*. Edited by K. Harrell and J. Driessen. Louvain; Presses Universitaires de Louvain, 2015.

Brichto, H. "Kin, Cult, Land and Afterlife—a Biblical Complex." *HUCA* 44 (1973): 1–54.

Brody, A. "Late Bronze Age Canaanite Mortuary Practices." Pages 515–32 in *Ashkelon: Introduction and Overview 1985–2000*, vol. 3: *Studies in the Archaeology and History of the Levant*. Edited by L. Stager, D. Schloen, and D. Master. Winona Lake, IN: Eisenbrauns, 2008.

Brody, A. "New Perspectives on Levantine Mortuary Ritual: A Cognitive Interpretive Approach to the Archaeology of Death." Pages 123–41 in *Historical Biblical Archaeology and the Future: The New Pragmatism*. Edited by T. Levy. London: Equinox, 2010.

Brown, B. "Kingship and Ancestral Cult in the Northwest Palace at Nimrud." *JANER* 10 (2010): 1–53.

Brown, J. "On Mortuary Analysis—With Special Reference to the Saxe-Binford Research Program." Pages 3–26 in *Regional Approaches to Mortuary Analysis*. Interdisciplinary Contributions to Archaeology. Edited by L. A. Beck. Boston: Springer, 1995.

Buchennino, A. and E. Yannai. "Iron Age I Tombs in the Azor Cemetery." *Atiqot* 63 (2010): 17–40. In Hebrew, English summary 231–32.

Buckberry, J. "Where Have All the Children Gone? The Preservation of Infant's and Children's Remains in the Archaeological Record." Paper presented at the "Archaeology of Infancy and Childhood" conference, 6–8 May 2005.

Buckley, J. "Techniques for Identifying Age and Sex of Children at Death." Pages 55–70 in *The Oxford Handbook of the Archaeology of Childhood*. Edited by S. Crawford, D. Hadley, and G. Shepherd. Oxford: Oxford University Press, 2018.

Burke, S. *God, Self, and Death: The Shape of Religious Transformation in the Second Temple Period*. Leiden: Brill, 2003.

Canevaro, L. G. "Review Article, Materiality and Classica: (Re)turning to the Material." *Journal of Hellenic Studies* 139 (2019): 222–32.

Casella, E. and K. Croucher. "The Materiality of Personhood." *Feminist Theory* 12.2 (2011): 209–17.

Cerezo-Roman, J. I. "Unpacking Personhood and Funerary Customs in the Hohokam Area of Southern Arizona." *American Antiquity* 80 (2015): 353–75.

Constanza Ceruti, M. "Frozen Mummies from Andean Mountaintop Shrines: Bioarchaeology and Ethnohistory of Inca Human Sacrifice." *BioMed Research International* 2015.1. http://dx.doi.org/10.1155/2015/439428.

Chapman, C. *The House of the Mother: The Social Roles of Maternal Kin in Biblical Hebrew Narrative and Poetry*. New Haven: Yale University Press, 2016.

Chéhab, M. "Chronique." *Bulletin du Musée de Beyrouth* 4 (1942–43): 123–24.

Chesson, M. "Libraries of the Dead: Early Bronze Age Charnel Houses and Social Identity at Urban Bab edh-Dhra', Jordan." *JAA* 18 (1999): 137–64.

Cline, E. *1177 B.C.: The Year Civilization Collapsed*. Princeton: Princeton University Press, 2014.

Conklin, B. and L. Morgan. "Babies, Bodies, and Production of Personhood in North America and Native Amazonian Society." *Ethos* 24 (1996): 657–94.

Cooley, R. and G. Pratico. "The Western Cemetery, with Comments on Joseph Free's Excavations, 1953–1964." Pages 147–90 in *Preliminary Excavation Report: Sardis, Bir Umm*

BIBLIOGRAPHY 181

Fawakhir, Tell el-'Umeiri, the Combined Caeserea Expeditions, and Tell Dothan. Edited by W. Dever. Winona Lake, IN: Eisenbrauns, 1995.

Cradic, M. "Residential Burial and Social Memory in the Middle Bronze Age Levant." *NEA* 81.3 (2018): 191–201.

Cradic, M. "Transformations in Death: The Archaeology of Funerary Practices and Personhood in the Bronze Age Levant." PhD dissertation, University of California, Berkeley, 2017.

Crass, B. "Gender and Mortuary Analysis: What Can Grave Goods Really Tell Us?" Pages 10–18 in *Gender and the Archaeology of Death.* Edited by B. Arnold and N. L. Wicker. Walnut Creek, CA: AltaMira, 2001.

Crawford, S., D. Hadley, and G. Shepherd, eds. *The Oxford Handbook of the Archaeology of Childhood.* Oxford: Oxford University Press, 2018.

Crossland, Z. "Materiality and Embodiment." Pages 386–405 in *The Oxford Handbook of Material Culture Studies.* Edited by D. Hicks and M. C. Beaudry. Oxford: Oxford University Press, 2010.

Culican, W. "The Graves at Tell er-Requeish." *Australian Journal of Biblical Archaeology* 2 (1973): 66–105.

Darby, E. *Interpreting Judean Pillar Figurines: Gender and Empire in Apotropaic Ritual.* FAT 2. Reihe 69. Tübingen: Mohr Siebeck, 2014.

Darby, E. "Judean Pillar Figurines (JPFs)." Pages 401–14 in *Archaeology and History of Eighth-Century Judah.* ANEM 23. Edited by Z. Farber and J. Wright. Atlanta: SBL Press, 2018.

Day, J. *Molech: A God of Human Sacrifice in the Old Testament.* University of Cambridge Oriental Publications 41. Cambridge: Cambridge University Press, 1989.

Dayagi-Mendels, M. *The Akhziv Cemeteries: The Ben-Dor Excavations, 1941–1944.* Jerusalem: Israel Antiquities Authority, 2002.

Dever, W. *Gezer II: Report of the 1967–70 Seasons in Fields I and II.* Jerusalem: Keter, 1974.

Dever, W. *Gezer IV: The 1969–71 Seasons in Field VI, the "Acropolis".* Jerusalem: Keter, 1986.

Dever, W. *The Lives of Ordinary People in Ancient Israel: Where Archaeology and the Bible Intersect.* Grand Rapids, MI: Eerdmans, 2012.

Dever, W., H. D. Lance, and G. E. Wright. *Gezer I: Preliminary Report of the 1964–66 Seasons.* Jerusalem: Keter, 1970.

Deverenski, J. S. "Engendering Children, Engendering Archaeology." Pages 192–202 in *Invisible People and Processes: Writing Gender and Childhood into European Archaeology.* Edited by J. Moore and E. Scott. London: Leicester University Press, 1997.

Dewrell, H. *Child Sacrifice in Ancient Israel.* EANAC 5. Winona Lake, IN: Eisenbrauns, 2017.

Dixon, H. "Phoenician Mortuary Practice in the Iron Age I–III (ca. 1200–ca. 300 BCE) Levantine 'Homeland.'" PhD dissertation, University of Michigan, 2013.

Dothan, M. "The Excavations at 'Afula." *'Atiqot* 1 (1955): 19–70.

Dothan, M. "Excavations at Azor, 1960." *IEJ* 11.4 (1961): 171–75.

Dothan, M. *Ashdod II–III: The Second and Third Seasons Excavations 1963.* 'Atiqot [ES] 9–10. Jerusalem: Department of Antiquities, 1965.

Dothan, M. *Ashdod II–III: The Second and Third Seasons of Excavations 1963, 1965: Soundings in 1967.* Jerusalem: Department of Antiquities, 1971.

Dothan, M. "A Cremation Burial at Azor—a Danite City." *EI* 20 (1989): 164–74. In Hebrew.

Dothan M. and Y. Porath. *Ashdod IV: Excavation of Area M.* 'Atiqot [ES] 15. Jerusalem: Department of Antiquities, 1982.

Dothan M. and Y. Porath. *Ashdod V: Excavation of Area G.* 'Atiqot 23 [ES]. Jerusalem: Department of Antiquities, 1993.

Dothan, M. and D. Ben-Shlomo, eds. *Ashdod VI: Excavations of Areas H and K (1968–1969).* IAA Reports No. 24. Jerusalem: Israel Antiquities Authority, 2005.

Dothan, M. and D. Ben-Shlomo. "Stratigraphy and Building Remains." Pages 11–62 in *Ashdod VI: The Excavations of Areas H and K (1968–1969).* IAA Reports No. 24. Edited by M. Dothan and D. Ben-Shlomo. Jerusalem: Israel Antiquities Authority, 2005.

182 BIBLIOGRAPHY

Dothan, T. and S. Gitin. *Tel Miqne (Ekron) Excavation Project: Spring, 1982; Field Report, Field I NE-Areas 2, 3, 4, 5, 6, 7*. Jerusalem: Tel Miqne (Ekron) Excavation Project Publications Office, 1982.

Dothan, T. and S. Gitin. *Tel Miqne-Ekron: Eighth Excavation Season and Field School. June 10–July 27, 1990. Program*. Jerusalem: W.F. Albright Institute of Archaeological Research, 1990.

Douglas, M. *Purity and Danger: An Analysis of Concepts of Pollution and Taboo*. Harmondsworth: Penguin, 1970.

Doumet, C. "Les Tombes IV et V de Rachidieh." *Annels d'Histoire et d'Archaélogie* 1 (1982): 89–136.

Drower, E. "Women and Taboo in Iraq." *Iraq* 5 (1938): 105–17.

DuQuesne, T. *The Salakhana Trove: Votive Steale and Other Objects from Asyut*. London: Darengo, 2009.

Durkheim, É. *The Elementary Forms of Religious Life*. Translated by C. Cosman. Oxford: Oxford University Press, 2001.

Edrey, M., E. Arie, H. May, and A. Yasur-Landau. "The Iron Age II Tombs of Area E, Tel Achziv." *IEJ* 68.2 (2018): 150–81.

Eissfeldt, O. *Molk als Opferbegriff im Punischen und Hebräischen und das Ende des Gottes Moloch*. Beiträge zur Religionsgechichte des Altertums 3. Halle: Niemeyer, 1935.

Eissfeldt, O. *The Old Testament: An Introduction*. New York: Harper and Rowe, 1965.

Ekengren, F. "Contextualizing Grave Goods: Theoretical Perspectives and Methodological Implications." Pages 173–92 in *The Oxford Handbook of the Archaeology of Death and Burial*. Edited by S. Tarlow and L. N. Stutz. New York: Oxford University Press, 2013.

Eshed, V., S. Wish-Baratz, and I. Hershkovitz. "Human Skeletal Remains." Pages 495–510 in *Tel 'Ira: A Stronghold in the Biblical Negev*. Sonia and Marco Nadler Institute of Archaeology Monograph Series 15. Edited by I. Beit-Arieh. Tel Aviv: Emery and Claire Yass Publications in Archaeology, Institute of Archaeology, Tel Aviv University, 1999.

Eshel, H. "The Late Iron Age Cemetery at Gibeon." *IEJ* 37.1 (1987): 1–17.

Ewbank, D. C. and J. N. Gribble. *Effects of Health Programs on Child Mortality in Sub-Saharan Africa*. Washington, DC: National Academy Press, 1993.

Faerman, M. "Human Skeletal Remains of the Intermural Pit and Jar Burials from Area K." Pages 418–42 in *Megiddo VI: The 2010–2014 Seasons*. Vol 1. Edited by I. Finkelstein and M. Martin. University Park, PA: Eisenbrauns and Tel Aviv: Emery and Claire Yass Publications in Archaeology, 2022.

Faerman, M., N. Lev-Tov, and P. Smith. "Infants." Pages 701–4 in *Ashkelon 7: The Iron Age*. Edited by L. Stager, D. Master, and A. Aja. University Park, PA: Eisenbrauns, 2020.

Faerman, M., and P. Smith. "The Human Remains from Cave T1." Pages 221–34 in *Tell es-Safi / Gath II: Excavations and Studies*. Edited by A. Maeir and J. Uziel. Münster: Zaphon, 2020.

Faerman M. and P. Smith. "Human Skeletal Remains from Chamber—Tomb 100." Pages 402–17 in *Megiddo VI: The 2010–2014 Seasons*. Vol 1. Edited by I. Finkelstein and M. Martin. University Park, PA: Eisenbrauns and Tel Aviv: Emery and Claire Yass Publications in Archaeology, 2022.

Faerman, M., P. Smith, E. Boaretto, J. Uziel and A.M. Maeir. ". . . in Their Lives, and in Their Death . . .": A Preliminary Study of an Iron Age Burial Cave at Tell eṣ-Ṣāfī, Israel." *ZDPV* 127 (2011): 29–48.

Faust, A. "The Bible, Archaeology, and the Practice of Circumcision in Israelites and Philistine Societies." *JBL* 134 (2015): 273–90.

Faust, A. "'Mortuary Practices, Society, and Ideology': The Lack of Iron Age I Burials in the Highlands in Context." *IEJ* 54.2 (2004): 174–90.

Faust, A. and S. Bunimovitz. "The Four Room House: Embodying Iron Age Israelite Society." *NEA* 66.1–2 (2003): 22–31.

Faust, A. and S. Bunimovitz. "The Judahite Rock-Cut Tomb: Family Response at a Time of Change." *IEJ* 58.2 (2008): 150–70.

Feder, Y. "Contagion and Cognition: Bodily Experience and the Conceptualization of Pollution (*ṭum'ah*) in the Hebrew Bible." *JNES* 72 (2013): 151–67.

BIBLIOGRAPHY 183

Feldman, M. et al. "Ancient DNA Sheds Light on the Genetic Origins of Early Iron Age Philistines." *Science Advances* 5.7 (2019): 1–10, eaax0061. https://doi.org/10.1126/sciadv.aax0061.

Finlay, N. "Kid Knapping: The Missing Children in Lithic Analysis." Pages 203–12 in *Invisible People and Processes: Writing Gender and Childhood into European Archaeology*. Edited by J. Moore and E. Scott. London: Leicester University, 1997.

Fleishman, J. "Legal Innovation in Deuteronomy XXI 18–20." *VT* 53 (2003): 311–27.

Flemming, D. "Household and Community Religion in Syria." Pages 37–59 in *Household and Family Religion in Antiquity*. Edited by J. Bodel and S. Olyan. Malden, MA: Wiley-Blackwell, 2012.

Flynn, S. *Children in Ancient Israel: The Hebrew Bible and Mesopotamia in Comparative Perspective*. Oxford: Oxford University Press, 2018.

Foster, C. and B. Parker. "Introduction: Household Archaeology in the Near East and Beyond." Pages 1–14 in *New Perspectives in Household Archaeology*. Edited by C. Foster and B. Parker. Winona Lake, IN: Eisenbrauns, 2012.

Fowler, C. *The Archaeology of Personhood: Anthropological Approach*. London: Routledge, 2004.

Fowler, C. "From Identity and Material Culture to Personhood and Materiality." Pages 352–85 in *The Oxford Handbook of Material Culture Studies*. Edited by D. Hicks and M. D. Beaudry. Oxford: Oxford University Press, 2010.

Frank, T. *Household Food Storage in Ancient Israel and Judah*. Oxford: Archaeopress, 2018.

Franklin, N. "The Tombs of the Kings of Israel—Two Recently Identified 9th-Century Tombs from Omride Samaria." *ZDPV* 119 (2003): 1–11.

Free, J. P. "The Second Season at Dothan." *BASOR* 135 (1954): 14–20.

Free, J. P. "The Third Season at Dothan." *BASOR* 139 (1955): 3–9.

Free, J. P. "The Sixth Season at Dothan." *BASOR* 156 (1959): 22–29.

Free, J. P. "The Seventh Season at Dothan." *BASOR* 160 (1960): 6–15.

Freud, L. "Iron Age." Pages 189–289 in *Tel 'Ira: A Stronghold in the Biblical Negev*. Sonia and Marco Nadler Institute of Archaeology Monograph Series 15. Edited by I. Beit-Arieh. Tel Aviv: Emery and Claire Yass Publications in Archaeology, Institute of Archaeology, Tel Aviv University, 1999.

Fulton, D. N. and P. Hesse. "Considering Carcasses: Sheep and Goat Sacrifice at Carthage, Tunisia and Al Qisha, Yemen." Pages 245–56 in *The Wide Lens in Archaeology: Honoring Brian Hesse's Contribution to Anthropological Archaeology*. Edited by J. Lev-Tov, A. Gilbert, and P. Hesse. London: Lockwood Press, 2017.

Gadotti, A. *"Gilgamesh, Enkidu, and the Netherworld" and the Sumerian Gilgamesh Cycle*. UAVA 10. Boston: de Gruyter, 2014.

Garroway, K. H. "The Anthropology of Death in Ancient Israel." Pages 455–68 in *The T & T Clark Handbook of Anthropology and the Hebrew Bible*. Edited by E. Pfoh. London: Bloomsbury, 2023.

Garroway, K. H. "The Case of Joseph's Coat: Giving Gifts to Children in the Hebrew Bible." *AVAR* 1.2 (2022): 185–211.

Garroway, K. H. "Children and Religion in the Archaeological Record of Ancient Israel." *JNEAR* 17 (2017): 116–39.

Garroway, K. H. *Children in the Ancient Near Eastern Household*. EANEC 3. Winona Lake, IN: Eisenbrauns, 2014.

Garroway, K. H. "Children in the Ancient World: A Methodology." Pages 67–90 in *A Handbook to Children and Childhood in the Biblical World*. Edited by J. F. Parker and S. Betsworth. London: T & T Clark, 2019.

Garroway, K. H. *Growing Up in Ancient Israel: Children in Material Culture and Biblical Texts*. ABS 23 Atlanta: SBL, 2018.

Garroway, K. H. "Judean Pillar Figurines (JPFs)." Pages 301–14 in *Archaeology and History of Eighth-Century Judah*. ANEM 23. Edited by Z. Farber and J. Wright. Atlanta: SBL Press, 2018.

184 BIBLIOGRAPHY

Garroway, K. H. "Rattle and Hum: A Reassessment of Closed-Form Rattles in the Southern Levant." *JAOS* 143.1 (2023): 173–94.

Garroway, K. H. "2 Kings 6:24–30: A Case of Unintentional Elimination Killing." *JBL* 137 (2018): 53–70.

Gelb, I. "The Ancient Mesopotamian Ration System." *JNES* 24 (1965): 238–41.

Gennep, A. van. *The Rites of Passage*. Chicago: University of Chicago Press, 1960.

Gillespie, S. "Personhood, Agency, and Mortuary Ritual: A Case Study from the Ancient Maya." *Journal of Anthropological Archaeology* 20 (2001): 73–112.

Girard, R. *Violence and the Sacred*. Translated by P. Gregory. New ed. London: Continuum, 2005.

Goldstein, L. G. "One-Dimensional Archaeology and Multi-dimensional People: Spatial Organization and Mortuary Analysis." Pages 53–69 in *The Archaeology of Death*. Edited by R. Chapman, G. Kinnes, and K. Randsborg. Cambridge: Cambridge University Press, 1981.

Gonen, R. *Burial Patterns and Cultural Diversity in Late Bronze Age Canaan*. ASOR Dissertation Series 7. Winona Lake, IN: Eisenbrauns, 1992.

Goodman, A. H. and G. J. Armelagos. "Infant and Childhood Morbidity and Mortality Risks in Archaeological Populations." *WA* 21 (1989): 225–43.

Gorman, F. H. *The Ideology of Ritual: Space, Time and Status in the Priestly Theology*. JSOT Supp. 91. Sheffield: JSOT Press, 1990.

Graham, E.-J. "Becoming Persons, Becoming Ancestors: Personhood, Memory and the Corpse in Roman Rituals of Social Remembrance." *Archaeological Dialogues* 16 (2009): 51–74.

Green, J. "Anklets and the Social Construction of Gender and Age in the Late Bronze and Early Iron Age Southern Levant." Pages 283–311 in *Archaeology and Women: Ancient and Modern Issues*. Edited by S. Hamilton, R. D. Whitehouse, and K. I. Wrights. Walnut Creek, CA: Left Coast Press, 2007.

Grimm, L. "Apprentice Flintknapping: Relating Material Culture and Social Practice in the Upper Paleolithic." Pages 53–71 in *Children and Material Culture*. Edited by J. S. Derevenski. New York: Routledge, 2000.

Guy, H., C. Masset, and C. Baud. "Infant Taphonomy." *International Journal of Osteoarchaeology* 7 (1997): 221–29.

Guy, P. L. O. *Megiddo Tombs*. Chicago: University of Chicago Press, 1938.

Haas, N. "Anthropological Observation on the Skeletal Remains Found in Area D (1962–1963)." Pages 212–14 in *Ashdod II–III: The Second and Third Seasons of Excavation 1963, 1965, Soundings in 1967*. Edited by M. Dothan. Jerusalem: Department of Antiquities and Museums in the Ministry of Education and Culture, Hebrew University, 1971.

Hallam, E. and J. Hockney. *Death, Memory and Material Culture*. Oxford: Berg, 2001.

Hallote, R. *Death, Burial and Afterlife in the Biblical World: How the Israelites and Their Neighbors Treated the Dead*. Chicago: Ivan R. Dee, 2001.

Hallote, R. "Mortuary Archaeology and the Middle Bronze Age Southern Levant." *Journal of Mediterranean Archaeology* 8.1 (1995): 93–122.

Hallote, R. "Real and Ideal Identities in Middle Bronze Age Tombs." *NEA* 65 (2002): 105–11.

Hardin, J. *Lahav II: Households and the Use of Domestic Space at Iron II Tell Halif: An Archaeology of Destruction*. Reports of the Lahav Research Project at Tell Halif, Israel. Ed. J. Seger. Winona Lake, IN: Eisenbrauns, 2012.

Hardin, J. "Understanding Houses, Household, and the Levantine Archaeological Record." Pages 9–26 in *Household Archaeology in Ancient Israel and Beyond*. Edited by A. Yasur-Landau, J. Ebling, and L. Mazow. Leiden: Brill, 2011.

Härke, H. "Data Types in Burial Analysis." Pages 31–39 in *Prehistoric Graves as a Source of Information: Symposium at Kastlösa, Öland, May 21–23, 1992*. Edited by B. Stjernquist. Stockholm: Kungl. Vitterhets Historie och Antikvites Akademien, 1994.

Harris, R. *Gender and Aging in Mesopotamia: The Gilgamesh Epic and Other Ancient Literature*. Norman: University of Oklahoma Press, 2000.

Harrison, T. P. *Megiddo 3: Final Report on the Stratum VI Excavations*. OI Publications 127. Chicago: Oriental Institute, 2004.

BIBLIOGRAPHY   185

Hartal, M. "Tel Dan (North)." *Hadashot Arkheologiyot* 118 (2006). https://www.hadashot-esi.org.il/report_detail_eng.aspx?id = 342.

Hays, C. B. *A Covenant with Death: Death in the Iron Age II and Its Rhetorical Uses in Proto-Isaiah.* Grand Rapids, MI: Eerdmans, 2011.

Hays, C. B. "The Covenant with Mut: A New Interpretation of Isaiah 28:1– 22." *VT* 60 (2010): 212–40.

Hays, C. B. "The Egyptian Goddess Mut in Iron Age Palestine: Further Data from Amulet and Onomastics." *JNES* 71 (2012): 299–313.

Hays, C. B. "'My Beloved Son, Come and Rest in Me': Job's Return to His Mother's Womb (Job 1:21a) in Light of Egyptian Mythology." *VT* 62 (2012): 607–21.

Hazard, S. "The Material Turn in the Study of Religion." *Religion and Society* 4.1 (2013): 58–78.

Healey, J. F. "Death in West Semitic Texts: Ugaritic and Nabatea." Pages 188– 91 in *The Archaeology of Death in the Ancient Near East.* Oxbow Monographs 51. Edited by S. Campbell and A. Green. Oxford: Oxbow Press, 1995.

Heider, G. C. *The Cult of Molek: A Reassessment.* JSOT Supp. 43. Sheffield: JSOT Press, 1985.

Hershkovitz, I. "The Effect of Mating Type on Growth and Development of Children in South Sinai Bedouin Isolates." PhD dissertation, Tel Aviv University, 1984.

Hertz, R. *Death and the Right Hand.* Translated by R. Needham and C. Needham. Glencoe, IL: Free Press, 1960.

Hesse, P. and D. N. Fulton. "Faunal Remains." Pages 705– 26 in *Ashkelon 7: The Iron Age I.* Edited by L. Stager, D. Master, and A. Aja. University Park, PA: Eisenbrauns, 2020.

Hodder, I. *The Present Past: An Introduction to Anthropology for Archaeologists.* London: Batsford, 1982.

Hodder, I. "Post- processual Archaeology." *Advances in Archaeology Method and Theory* 8 (1985): 1–26.

Hodder, I. "Social Structure and Cemeteries: A Critical Appraisal." Pages 161– 69 in *Anglo-Saxon Cemeteries 1979: The Fourth Anglo-Saxon Symposium at Oxford.* BAR 82. Edited by P. A. Rahtz, T. M. Dickinson, and L. Watts. Oxford: BAR Publishing, 1980.

Hodder, I. *Symbols in Action: Ethnoarchaeological Studies of Material Culture.* Cambridge: Cambridge University Press, 1982.

Hodder, I. and C. Cressford. "Daily Practice and Social Memory at Çatalhöyük." *American Antiquity* 69.1 (2004): 17–40.

Holz, B. A. "A Recent Application of the Saxe- Binford Hypothesis in Establishing Social Persona." MA thesis, University of Nevada at Las Vegas, 1996.

Hubert, H. and M. Mauss. *Sacrifice: Its Nature and Function.* Translated by W. D. Halls. Chicago: University of Chicago Press, 1964.

Humphrey, C. and J. Laidlaw. *The Archetypal Actions of Ritual: A Theory of Ritual Illustrated by the Jain Rite of Worship.* Oxford: Clarendon Press, 1994.

Ilan, D. "Iron Age Mortuary Practices and Beliefs in the Southern Levant." Pages 51– 66 in *Engaging with the Dead: Exploring Changing Human Beliefs about Death, Mortality and the Human Body.* Studies in Funerary Archaeology 13. Edited by J. Bradbury and C. Scarre. Oxford: Oxbow Press, 2017.

Ilan, D. "Mortuary Practices at Tel Dan in the Middle Bronze Age: A Reflection of Canaanite Society and Ideology." Pages 117– 37 in Oxbow Monographs 51. *The Archaeology of Death in the Ancient Near East.* Edited by S. Campbell and A. Green. Oxford: Oxbow Press, 1995.

Irwin, H. W. "'The Smooth Stones of the Wady'? Isaiah 57, 6." *CBQ* 29 (1967): 31–40.

Johns, C. N. "Discoveries in Palestine since 1939." *PEQ* 80.2 (1948–49): 81–101.

Johns, C. N. "Excavation of Pilgrims' Castle, 'Atlit (1933): Cremated Burials of Phoenician Origin." *QDAP* 6 (1937–38): 135.

Johns, C. N. "Excavations at 'Atlit (1930–1)." *QDAP* 2 (1933): 41–104.

Johnston, P. *Shades of Death and Afterlife in the Old Testament.* Downers Grove, IL: InterVarsity, 2002.

186 BIBLIOGRAPHY

Joyce, R. "Life with Things: Archaeology and Materiality." Pages 119–32 in *Archaeology and Anthropology: Past, Present and Future.* Edited by D. Shankland. London: Routledge, 2012.

Kan, S. *Symbolic Immortality: The Tlingit Potlatch of the Nineteenth Century.* Washington, DC: Smithsonian Institution Press, 1989.

Kaufmann, Y. *The Religion of Ancient Israel: From Its Beginnings to the Babylonian Exile.* Translated by M. Greenberg. Chicago: University of Chicago Press, 1972.

Keel, O. "The Peculiar Headrests for the Dead in First Temple Times." *BAR* 13.4 (1987): 50, 52–53.

Kenyon, K. *Digging Up Jericho.* London: Ernst Benn, 1957.

Killebrew, A. "Canaanite Roots, Proto-Phoenicia, and the Early Phoenician Period 1300–1000 BCE." Pages 38–55 in *The Oxford Handbook of the Phoenician and Punic Mediterranean.* Edited by C. Lópex-Ruiz and B. Doak. Oxford: Oxford University Press, 2019.

King, J. E. "Infant Burials." *Classical Review* 17.1 (1903): 83.

King, P. and L. Stager. *Life in Biblical Israel.* Louisville, KY: Westminster John Knox, 2001.

Klass, D. and T. Walter. "Processes of Grieving: How Bonds Are Continued." Pages 431–48 in *Handbook of Bereavement Research: Consequences, Coping and Care.* Edited by M. Stroebe, R. Hansson, W. Stroebe and H. Schut. Washington, DC: American Psychological Association, 2001.

Kletter, R. *Judean Pillar Figurines and the Archaeology of Ashera.* BAR International Series 636. Oxford: Tempus Reparatum, 1996.

Kletter, R. "People without Burials? The Lack of Iron I Burials in the Central Highlands of Palestine." *IEJ* 52 (2002): 28–48.

Kletter, R. and Y. Nagar. "An Iron Age Cemetery and Other Remains at Yavne." *Atiqot* 81 (2015): 1–33.

Kloner, A. "Iron Age Burial Caves in Jerusalem and Its Vicinity." *BAIAS* 19–20 (2001): 95–118.

Kloner, A. and D. Davis. "A Burial Cave of the Later First Temple Period on the Slope of Mount Zion." Pages 107–10 in *Ancient Jerusalem Revealed.* Edited by H. Geva. Jerusalem: Israel Exploration Society, 1994.

Knight, D. A. *Law Power and Justice in Ancient Israel.* Louisville, KY: Westminster John Knox, 2011.

Knüsel, C. and J. Robb. "Funerary Taphonomy: An Overview of Goals and Methods." *Journal of Archaeological Reports* 10 (2016): 655–73.

Koch, I. "Judahite Stamped and Incised Jar Handles: A Tool for Studying the History of Late Monarchic Judah." *TA* 38 (2011): 5–41.

Koepf-Taylor, L. *Give Me Children or I Shall Die.* Minneapolis: Fortress, 2013.

Kogan-Zehavi, E. "Tombs and Installations from the Iron Age II to the Byzantine Period from S. Ḥorbat Tittora." *Atiqot* 72 (2012): 13–92. In Hebrew.

Králik, M., P. Urbanová, and M. Hložek. "Finger, Hand and Foot Imprints: The Evidence of Children on Archaeological Artefacts." Pages 1–15 in *Children, Identity and the Past.* Edited by L. H. Dommasnes and M. Wrigglesworth. Newcastle: Cambridge Scholars, 2008.

Kraus, F. R., ed. *Altbabylonische Brief im Umschrift und Übersetzung.* Vol. 1. Leiden: Brill, 1964.

Lally, M. and A. Moore, eds. *(Re)thinking the Little Ancestor: New Perspectives on the Archaeology of Infancy and Childhood.* BAR International Series 2271. Oxford: Archaeopress, 2011.

Laneri, N. "A Family Affair: The Use of Intramural Funerary Chambers in Mesopotamia during the Late Third and Early Second Millennia B.C.E." Pages 121–35 in *Residential Burial: A Multiregional Exploration.* Archaeological Papers of the American Anthropological Association 20. Edited by R. L. Adams and S. M. King. Walden, MA: Wiley Periodicals, 2011.

Lehmann, G. "The Levant." Pages 464–79 in *The Oxford Handbook of the Phoenician and Punic Mediterranean.* Edited by C. López-Ruiz and B. Doak. Oxford: Oxford University Press, 2019.

Lemaire, A. "Prières en temps de crise: Les inscriptions de Khirbet Beit Lei." *RB* 83 (1976): 558–68.

BIBLIOGRAPHY 187

Lemos, T. M. *Marriage Gifts and Social Change in Ancient Palestine. 1200 BCE to 200 CE.* Cambridge: Cambridge University Press, 2010.

Lemos, T. M. *Violence and Personhood in Ancient Israel and Comparative Contexts.* Oxford: Oxford University Press, 2017.

Levenson, J. D. *Death and Resurrection of the Beloved Son: The Transformation of Child Sacrifice in Judaism.* New Haven: Yale University Press, 1993.

Lévi-Strauss, C. *The Elementary Structures of Kinship.* Translated by J. Bell, J. von Strumer, and R. Needham. Boston: Beacon, 1969.

Lévi-Strauss, C. *Introduction to the Work of Marcel Mauss.* Translated by F. Baker. London: Routledge & Kegan Paul, 1987.

Lévi-Strauss, C. *The Way of the Masks.* London: Jonathan Cape, 1983.

Lewis, M. *The Bioarchaeology of Children: Perspectives from Biological and Forensic Anthropology.* Cambridge: Cambridge University Press, 2007.

Lewis, M. "The Osteology of Infancy and Childhood: Misconceptions and Potential." Pages 1–13 in *(Re)thinking the Little Ancestor: New Perspectives on the Archaeology of Infancy and Childhood.* BAR International Series 2271. Edited by M. Lally and A. Moore. Oxford: BAR Publishing, 2011.

Lewis, M. *Paleopathology of Children.* London: Academic Press, 2018.

Lewis, T. *Cults of the Dead in Ancient Israel and Ugarit.* HSM 39. Atlanta: Scholars Press, 1989.

Lewis, T. "Death Cult Imagery in Isaiah 57." *HAR* 11 (1987): 267–84.

Lewis, T. "Review: *Israel's Beneficent Dead.*" *JAOS* 119 (1999): 512–14.

Lillehammer, G. "A Child Is Born: The Child's World in an Archaeological Perspective." *NAR* 22 (1989): 89–105.

Lipschits, O., O. Sergi, and I. Koch. "Royal Judahite Jar Handles: Reconsidering the Chronology of the lmlk Stamp Impressions." *TA* 37 (2010): 3–32.

Livingston, D. "A MBA II and IA I Tomb (no. 65) at Khirbet Nisya." *'Atiqot* 43 (2002): 17–35.

López-Bertran, M. "Funerary Ritual." Pages 293–309 in *The Oxford Handbook of the Phoenician and Punic Mediterranean.* Edited by C. López-Ruiz and B. Doak. Oxford: Oxford University Press, 2019.

López-Ruiz, C. C. *Phoenicians and the Making of the Mediterranean.* Cambridge, MA: Harvard University Press, 2021.

Lucy, S. "Children in Early Medieval Cemeteries." *Archaeological Review from Cambridge* 13 (1994): 21–34.

MacAlister, R. A. S. *The Excavation of Gezer 1902– 1905 and 1907– 1909.* 3 vols. London: Palestine Exploration Fund, 1912.

Macridy, T. "A travers les nécropoles sidoniennes." *RB* 1.4 (1904): 547–72.

Maeir, A. *Tell es-Safi/ Gath I: The 1996–2005 Seasons Part 1. Text.* Ägypten und Altes Testament 69. Wiesbaden: Harrassowitz Verlag, 2012.

Maeir, A. and J. Uziel. *Tell es- Safi / Gath II: Excavations and Studies.* Ägypten und Altes Testament 105. Münster: Zaphon, 2020.

Malinowski, B. *Argonauts of the Western Pacific.* New York: Dutton, 1961.

Mandell, A. and J. Smoak. "The Material Turn in the Study of Israelite Religion: Spaces, Things, and the Body." *Journal of Hebrew Scriptures* 19 (2019): 1–42. https:// doi.org/ 10.5508/ jhs29397.

Mandell, A. and J. Smoak. "Reconsidering the Function of Tomb Inscriptions in Iron Age Judah: Khirbet Beit Lei as a Test Case." *JANER* 16 (2016) 192–245.

Martin, M. A. S., M. S. Cradic, and R. Kalisher. "Area K: Intramural Pit and Jar Burials (Level K-10)." Pages 239–41 in *Megiddo VI: The 2010-2014 Seasons.* Vol 1. Emery and Claire Yass Publications in Archaeology. Edited by Israel Finkelstein and M. S. S. Martin. Winona Lake, IN: Eisenbrauns, 2022.

Master, D. and A. Aja. "The Philistine Cemetery of Ashkelon." *BASOR* 337 (2017): 135–59.

Master, D., J. Monson, E. Lass, and G. Pierce, eds. *Dothan I: Remains from the Tell (1952-1964).* Winona Lake, IN: Eisenbrauns, 2005.

188 BIBLIOGRAPHY

Matthews, V. H. "The Unwanted Gift: Implication of Obligatory Gift Giving in Ancient Israel." *Semeia* 87 (1999): 91–104.

Maurice, C. "Chronique." *Bulletin du Musée de Beyrouth* 4 (1942–43): 123–24.

Mauss, M. *The Gift: Forms and Functions of Exchange in Archaic Societies.* Translated by Ian Cunnison. New York: Norton, 1967.

Mazar, A., ed. *Timnah (Tel Batash) I: Stratigraphy and Architecture.* Qedem 37. Edited by A. Mazar. Jerusalem: Hebrew University, 1997.

Mazar, E. "The Achziv Burials: A Test-Case for Phoenician-Punic Burial Customs." PhD dissertation, Hebrew University, 1996.

Mazar, E. *The Northern Cemetery of Achziv (10th–6th c. BCE): The Tophet Site. Sam Turner Excavations. Final Report of the Excavations (1992-2004).* Cuadernos de Arqueología Mediterránea 19–20. Barcelona: Edicions Bellaterra, 2013.

Mazar, E. *The Phoenician Family Tomb N. 1 at the Northern Cemetery of Achziv (10th–6th Centuries BCE): Sam Turner Expedition, Final Report of the Excavations.* Cuadernos de Arquelogía Mediterránea. Barcelona: Edicions Bellaterra, 2004.

Mazar, E. *The Phoenicians in Achzib: The Southern Cemetery. Jerome L. Joss Expedition, Final Report of the Excavations, 1988-1990.* Cuadernos de Arquelogía Mediterránea 7. Barcelona: Laboratorio de Arqueología, Universidad Pompeu Fabra de Barcelona, Carrera edició, 2001.

Mazow, L. "The 'Bathtub Coffin' from Tel Qitaf: A Re-examination of Its Context and Function." *PEQ* 146.1 (2014): 31–39.

Mazow, L. "Competing Material Culture: Philistine Settlement at Tel Miqne-Ekron in the Early Iron Age." Pages 131–64 in *Material Culture Matters: Essays on the Archaeology of the Southern Levant in Honor of Seymour Gitin.* Edited by J. Spencer, R. Mullins, and A. Brody. Winona Lake, IN: Eisenbrauns, 2014.

Mazow, L. "Throwing the Baby Out with the Bathwater: Innovations in Mediterranean Textile Production at the End of the 2nd / Beginning of the 1st Millennium BCE." Pages 213–21 in *Textile Production and Consumption in the Ancient Near East Archaeology, Epigraphy, Iconography.* Ancient Textile Series. Edited by M. L. Nosch, H. Kofoed, and E. Anderson Strand. Oxford: Oxbow Press, 2013.

McGeough, K. "Birth Bricks, Potter's Wheels, and Exodus 1:16." *Biblica* 87 (2006): 305–18.

McKenzie, S. *Second Isaiah: Introduction, Translation and Notes.* AB 20. Garden City, NJ: Doubleday, 1968.

Meehl, M. W., T. Dothan, and S. Gitin. *Tel Miqne-Ekron Excavations, 1995-1996: Field INE East Slope. Iron Age I (Early Philistine Period).* Jerusalem: W.F. Albright Institute of Archaeological Research and the Hebrew University, 2007.

Meskell, L. *Private Life in New Kingdom Egypt.* Princeton: Princeton University Press, 2002.

Metcalf, P. and R. Huntington, eds. *Celebrations of Death.* Cambridge: Cambridge University Press, 1991.

Meyers, C. "Engendering Syro-Palestinian Archaeology: Reasons and Resources." *NEA* 66 (2003): 185–97.

Meyers, C. *Households and Holiness: The Religious Culture of Israelite Women.* Minneapolis: Augsburg Fortress, 2005.

Meyers, C. *Rediscovering Eve: Ancient Israelite Women in Context.* Oxford: Oxford University Press, 2013.

Milgrom, J. "The Rationale for Biblical Impurity." *JANES* 22 (1993): 107–11.

Miller, P. "Psalms and Inscriptions." Pages 210–32 in *Israelite Religion and Biblical Theology: Collected Essays.* JSOT Supp. 267. Sheffield: Sheffield Academic Press, 2000.

Miller, S. *At the Intersection of Texts and Material Finds: Stepped Pools, Stone Vessels, and Ritual Purity among the Jews of Roman Galilee.* Göttingen: Vandenhoeck and Ruprecht, 2019.

Mills, A. and R. Slobodin. *Amerindian Rebirth: Reincarnation Belief among North American Indians and Inuit.* Toronto: University of Toronto Press, 1994.

BIBLIOGRAPHY   189

Morris, B. *Western Conceptions of the Individual*. Oxford: Berg, 1991.

Morris, E. "Sacrifice for the State: First Dynasty Royal Funerals and the Rites at Macramallah's Rectangle." Pages 15– 38 in *Performing Death: Social Analyses of Funerary Traditions in the Ancient Near East and Mediterranean*. OIS 3. Edited by N. Laneri. Chicago: Oriental Institute of the University of Chicago, 2007.

Mosca, P. G. "Child Sacrifice in Canaanite and Israelite Religion: A Study in *Mulk* and מלך." PhD dissertation, Harvard University, 1975.

Mosca, P. G. "The Tofet: A Place of Infant Sacrifice?" *SEL* 29–30 (2012–13): 119–36.

Murphy, E. and M. LeRoy, eds., *Children, Death and Burial: Archaeological Discourses*. Oxford: Oxbow Press, 2017.

Na'aman, N. "The lmlk Seal Impressions Reconsidered." *TA* 43 (2016): 111–25.

Na'aman, N. "Population Changes in Palestine following the Assyrian Deportation." *TA* 20 (1993): 104–24.

Nagar, Y. "Skeletal Remains from the Excavation at Ketef Hinnom, Jerusalem." *'Atiqot* 80 (2015): 55–58. In Hebrew.

Naveh, J. "Old Hebrew Inscriptions in a Burial Cave." *IEJ* 13 (1963): 74–92.

Niditch, S. *War in the Hebrew Bible: A Study in the Ethics of Violence*. Oxford: Oxford University Press, 1995.

O'Shea, J. M. *Mortuary Variability: An Archaeological Investigation*. Studies in Archaeology Series. Orlando, FL: Academic Press, 1984.

Ohata, K. *Tel Zeror II: Preliminary Report of the Excavation Second Season, 1965*. Tokyo: Society for Near Eastern Studies in Japan, 1967.

Ohata, K. *Tel Zeror III: Report of the Excavation Third Season, 1966*. Tokyo: Society for Near Eastern Studies in Japan, 1970.

Olyan, S. *Asherah and the Cult of Yahweh in Ancient Israel*. SBLMS 34. Atlanta: Scholars Press, 1988.

Olyan, S. *Biblical Mourning: Ritual and Social Dimensions*. Oxford: Oxford University Press, 2004.

Olyan, S. "Some Neglected Aspects of Israelite Interment Ideology." *JBL* 124 (2005): 601–16.

Ory, J. "Other Discoveries: 1 July 1938 to 30 June 1940." *QDAP* 10 (1944): 205.

Osbourne, J. "Secondary Mortuary Practice and the Bench Tomb: Structure and Practice in Iron Age Judah." *JNES* 70.1 (2011): 35–53.

Pardee, D. "A New Aramaic Inscription from Zincirli." *BASOR* 365 (2009): 51–71.

Parker, J. F. *Valuable and Vulnerable: Children in the Hebrew Bible, Especially the Elisha Cycle*. BJS 355. Providence, RI: Brown University Press, 2013.

Pearson, M. P. *The Archaeology of Death and Burial*. College Station: Texas A&M University Press, 2000.

Pearson, M. P. "Mortuary Practices, Society and Ideology: An Ethnoarchaeological Study." Pages 99– 113 in *Symbolic and Structural Archaeology*. Edited by I. Hodder. Cambridge: Cambridge University Press, 1982.

Petrie, W. F. *Ancient Gaza II*. London: British School of Archaeology in Egypt, 1933.

Petrie, W. F. *Beth-Pelet I (Tell Fara)*. London: British School of Archaeology in Egypt, 1930.

Pickworth, D. "Excavations at Nineveh: The Halzi Gate." *Iraq* 67.1 (2005): 295–316.

Pitard, W. T. "The 'Libation Installations' of the Tombs at Ugarit." *BA* 51 (1994): 20–37.

Pitard, W. T. "Tombs and Offerings: Archaeological Data and Comparative Methodology in the Study of Death in Israel." Pages 149– 50 in *Sacred Time, Sacred Place: Archaeology and the Religion of Israel*. Edited by B. M. Gittlen. Winona Lake, IN: Eisenbrauns, 2002.

Polychronakou-Sgouritsa, N. "Children Burials in Mycenean Greece." Αρχαιολογικόν Δελτίον, Μελέτες 42 (1987): 8–29.

Pongratz- Leisten, B. "Ritual Killing and Sacrifice in the Ancient Near East." Pages 3– 34 in *Human Sacrifice in Jewish and Christian Tradition*. Edited by K. Finsterbusch, A. Lange, and D. Römheld. Leiden: Brill, 2007.

190 BIBLIOGRAPHY

Pongratz-Leisten, B. "Sacrifice in the Ancient Near East: Offering and Ritual Killing." Pages 289–302 in *Sacred Killing: The Archaeology of Sacrifice in the Ancient Near East.* Edited by A. M. Porter and G. M. Schwartz. Winona Lake, IN: Eisenbrauns, 2012.

Pope, M. "The Cult of the Dead at Ugarit." Pages 159–79 in *Ugarit in Retrospect: Fifty Years of Ugarit and Ugaritic.* Edited by G. D. Young. Winona Lake, IN: Eisenbrauns, 1981.

Pope, M. "Cult of the Dead in Ugarit." Pages 225–50 in *Probative Pontification in Ugaritic and Biblical Literature: Collected Essays.* Edited by M. S. Smith. Münster: Ugarit-Verlag, 1994.

Pope, M. "Notes on the Rephaim Texts from Ugarit." Pages 163–82 in *Essays on the Ancient Near East in Memory of Jacob Joel Finkelstein.* Memoirs of the Connecticut Academy of Arts and Sciences 19. Edited by M. de Jong Ellis. Hamden, CT: Archon Books, 1977.

Popham, M. R. and J. H. Musgrave. "The Late Helladic UIC Intramural Burials at Lefkandi, Euboea." *Annual of the British School at Athens* 86 (1991): 273–96.

Power, R. and Y. Tristant. "From Refuse to Rebirth: Repositioning the Pot Burial in the Egyptian Archaeological Record." *Antiquity* 90. (2016): 1474–88.

Prausnitz, M. "Achvib." Page 34 in *New Encyclopedia of Archaeological Excavations in the Holy Land.* Vol. 1. Edited by E. Stern. Jerusalem: Israel Exploration Society & Carta; New York: Simon & Schuster, 1993.

Quick, L. *Dress, Adornment, and the Body in the Hebrew Bible.* Oxford: Oxford University Press, 2021.

Rad, G. von. *Old Testament Theology.* Vol. 1: *The Theology of Israel's Historical Traditions.* Louisville, KY: Westminster John Knox, 2001. German orig., 1957.

Radcliffe-Brown, A. A. *The Andaman Islanders: A Study in Social Anthropology.* Cambridge: Cambridge University Press, 1922.

Rahtz, P. A., T. Dickinson, and L. Watts, eds. Anglo-Saxon Cemeteries, 1979: The Fourth Anglo-Saxon Symposium at Oxford. BAR British Series 82. Oxford: British Archaeological Reports, 1980.

Rathinasabapathi, M. K. and H. K. Perumallapalli. "Bifid Rib: A Rare Anomaly." *Medical Journal DY of Patil University* 8.5 (2015): 607–71. https://doi.org/10.4103/0975-2870.16495.

Renfrew, C. *Approaches to Social Archaeology.* Cambridge, MA: Harvard University Press, 1984.

Renfrew, C. "Towards a Theory of Material Engagement." Pages 23–31 in *Rethinking Materiality: The Engagement of Mind with the Material World.* Edited by E. DeMarrais, C. Gosden and C. Renfrew. Cambridge: McDonald Institute for Archaeological Research, 2004.

Reynolds, B. H. "Molek: Dead or Alive? The Meaning and Derivation of *mlk* and למלך." Pages 133–50 in *Human Sacrifice in the Jewish and Christian Tradition.* SHR 112. Edited by K. Finsterbusch, A. Lange, and K. F. D. Römheld. Leiden: Brill, 2007.

Richardson, S. "Thy Neighbor's Ghost: Ideal Types, Stereotypes, All Types." *Metatron* 2.1 (2022). scholasticahq.com.

Ridson, D. "A Study of the Cranial and Other Human Remains from Palestine Excavated at Tell Duwier (Lachish) by the Wellcome-Marsont Archaeological Research Expedition." *Biometrika* 31 (1939): 99–166.

Robb, J. "Creating Death: An Archaeology of Dying." Pages 440–57 in *The Oxford Handbook of the Archaeology of Death and Burial.* Edited by L. N. Stutz and S. Tarlow. Oxford: Oxford University Press, 2013.

Rollston, C. *Writing and Literacy in the World of Ancient Israel: Epigraphic Evidence from the Iron Age.* Atlanta: SBL, 2010.

Roth, M. A. *Egyptian Phyles in the Old Kingdom: The Evolution of a System of Social Organization.* Studies in Ancient Oriental Civilization 48. Chicago: University of Chicago Press, 1991.

Roth, M. A. "The *pss-kf* and the 'Opening of the Mouth' Ceremony: A Ritual of Birth and Rebirth." *Journal of Egyptian Archaeology* 78 (1992): 113–47.

Roveland, B. "Footprints in the Clay: Upper Palaeolithic Children in Ritual and Secular Context." Pages 26–38 in *Children and Material Culture.* Edited by J. S. Derevenski. New York: Routledge, 2000.

BIBLIOGRAPHY 191

Sader, H. "Necropoles et tombes phénicinnes du Liban." *Cuadernos de Arquelogía Mediterránea* 1 (1995): 15–30.

Saidah, R. "Archaeology in the Lebanon 1968–69." *Berytus* 18 (1969): 119–42.

Saidah, R. "Chronique: Fouilles de Khaldé." *Bulletin du Musée Beyrouth* 20 (1967): 165–68.

Saidah, R. "Fouilles de Khaldé: Rapport préliminarire sure la première et deuxième campagnes (1961–1962)." *Bulletin du Musée Beyrouth* 19 (1966): 51–90.

Sanders, S. L. "Appetites of the Dead: The Language of the New Zincirli Stela and the History of a West Semitic Funerary Tradition." *BASOR* 369 (2013): 85–105.

Satlow, M. *How the Bible Became Holy.* New Haven: Yale University Press, 2015.

Saxe, A. A. Social Dimensions of Mortuary Practice. PhD dissertation, University of Michigan, 1970.

Scheuer, L. and S. Black, eds. *Developmental Juvenile Osteology.* San Diego, CA: Academic Press, 2000.

Schloen, J. D. *The House of the Father as Fact and Symbol: Patrimonialism in Ugarit and the Ancient Near East.* SAHL 2. Winona Lake, IN: Eisenbrauns, 2001.

Scholen, J. D. and A. Fink. ""New Excavations at Zincirli Höyük in Turkey (Ancient Sam'al) and the Discovery of an Inscribed Mortuary Stele." *BASOR* 365 (2009): 1–13.

Schmidt, B. B. *Israel's Beneficent Dead: Ancestor Cult and Necromancy in Ancient Israelite Religion and Tradition.* Winona Lake, IN: Eisenbrauns, 1996.

Schmitt, R. "Care for the Dead in the Context of the Household and Family." Pages 429–73 in *Family and Household Religion in Ancient Israel and the Levant.* Edited by R. Albertz and R. Schmitt. Winona Lake, IN: Eisenbrauns, 2012.

Schniedewind, W. *The Finger of the Scribe: How Scribes Learned to Write the Bible.* New York: Oxford University Press, 2019.

Schumacher, G. *Tell et Mutesellim: Bericht über die 1903 bis 1905 mit Unterstützung SR. Majestät des deutschen Kaisers und der Deutschen orient Gesellschaft vom Deutschen Verein zur Erforschung Palästinas veranstalteten Ausgrabung.* Leipzig: Ruldof Haupt, 1908.

Schwartz, G. "Archaeology and Sacrifice." Pages 1–32 in *Sacred Killing: The Archaeology of Sacrifice in the Ancient Near East.* Edited by A. Porter and G. Schwartz. Winona Lake, IN: Eisenbrauns, 2012.

Schwartz J. H., F. Houghton, R. Macchiarelli, and L. Bondioli. "Bones, Teeth, and Estimating Age of Perinates: Carthaginian Infant Sacrifice Revisited." *Antiquity* 86 (2012): 738–45.

Schwartz, J. H., F. Houghton, R. Macchiarelli, and L. Bondioli. "Skeletal Remains from Punic Carthage Do Not Support Systematic Sacrifice of Infants." *PLoS ONE* 5 (2010) e9177. https://doi.org/10.1371/journal.pone.0009177

Scott, E. *The Archaeology of Infancy and Infant Death.* BAR International Series 819. Oxford: Archaeopress, 1999.

Scurlock, J. "Ghosts in the Ancient Near East: Weak or Powerful?" *HUCA* 68 (1977): 77–96.

Scurlock, J. *Magico-Medical Means of Treating Ghost-Induced Illnesses in Ancient Mesopotamia.* Ancient Magic and Divination 3. Leiden: Brill, 2002.

Seiwert, H. "Opfer." *Handbuch religionswissenschaftlicher Grundbegriffe* 4 (1988): 268–84.

Shafer-Elliott, C. *The 5 Minute Archaeologist in the Southern Levant.* Sheffield: Equinox Publishing, 2016.

Shanklin, W. and M. Ghantus. "A Preliminary Report on the Anthropology of the Phoenicians." *Bulletin du Musée de Beyrouth* 19 (1966): 91–96.

Shay, T. "Differentiated Treatment of Deviancy at Death as Revealed in Anthropological and Archaeological Populations." *JAA* 4.3 (1989): 225–43.

Sheridan, S. "Coming of Age at St. Stephen's: Bioarchaeology of Children at a Byzantine Jerusalem Monastery (Fifth to Seventh Centuries CE)." Pages 150–94 in *Children in the Bible and the Ancient World: Comparative and Historical Methods in Reading Ancient Children.* Edited by S. W. Flynn. London: Rutledge, 2019.

Sherratt, S. and A. Sherratt, "The Growth of the Mediterranean Economy in the Early First Millennium B.C." *WA* 24.3 (1993): 361–78.

192 BIBLIOGRAPHY

Singer-Avitz, L. "The Pottery of Megiddo Strata III-II and a Proposed Subdivision of the Iron II Ca Period in Northern Israel." *BASOR* 372 (2014): 1123–45.

Smith, J. Z. *Imagining Religion*. Chicago: University of Chicago Press, 1982.

Smith, M. *The Early History of God: Yahweh and the Other Deities in Ancient Israel*. 2nd ed. Grand Rapids, MI: Eerdmans, 2002.

Smith, M. and E. Bloch- Smith. "Death and Afterlife in Ugarit and Israel." *JAOS* 108 (1988): 277–84.

Smith, P. "Approach to the Paleodemographic Analysis of Human Skeletal Remains from Archaeological Sites." Pages 2- 13 in *Biblical Archaeology Today, 1990: Proceedings of the Second International Congress on Biblical Archaeology*. Edited by A. Biran and J. Aviram. Jerusalem: Israel Exploration Society; Israel Academy of Sciences and Humanities, 1993.

Smith, P. and G. Avishai. "The Use of Dental Criteria for Estimating Postnatal Survival in Skeletal Remains of Infants." *Journal of Archaeological Science* 32 (2005): 83–89.

Smith, P., G. Avishai, J. A. Greene, and L. E. Stager. "Age Estimations Attest to the Practice of Infant Sacrifice at the Carthage Tophet." *Antiquity* 87 (2013): 1191–99.

Smith, P., G. Avishai, J. A. Greene, and L. E. Stager. "Aging Cremated Infants: The Problem of Sacrifice at the Tophet at Carthage." *Antiquity* 85 (2011): 859–74.

Smith, P. and G. Kahila Bar- Gal. "Age Biases in Phoenician Funerary Practices." *Eretz-Israel: Archaeology, History, and Geographical Studies* 33 (2018): 163–74.

Smith, P. and M. Faerman. "Has Society Changed Its Attitude to Infants and Children? Evidence from Archaeological Sites in the Southern Levant." Pages 211- 29 in *Nasciturus, infans, puerulus vobis mater terra: La muerte en la infancia*. Edited by F. G. Jener, S. Muriel and C. Olària. Castelló, Spain: Disputació de Castelló, Servei D'investigacions Arquelògiques Prehistòriques, 2008.

Smith, P., L. Horowitz, and J. Zias. "Human Remains from the Iron Age Cemeteries at Achziv: Part 1. The Built Tomb from the Southern Cemetery." *Rivista di Studi Fenici* 18.2 (1990): 137–54.

Smoak, J. *The Priestly Blessing in Inscription and Scripture: The Early History of Numbers 6:24– 26.* New York: Oxford University Press, 2016.

Smoak, J. "You Have Refined Us Like Silver Is Refined (Ps 66:10): Yahweh's Metallurgic Powers in Iron Age Judah." *AABNER* 1.3 (2021): 83–115.

Socha, D., M. Sykutera, J. Reinhard, and R. Chávez Perea. "Ritual Drug Use during Inca Human Sacrifices on Ampato Mountain (Peru): Results of a Toxicological Analysis." *Journal of Archaeological Science: Reports* 43 (2022): 103415. https://doi.org/10.1016/j.jas rep.2022.103415.

Sofaer, J. "Towards a Social Bioarchaeology of Age." Pages 285–311 in *Social Bioarchaeology*. Edited by S. Agarwal and B. Blencross. New York: Wiley-Blackwell, 2011.

Song, W., S. Kim, D. Park, and K. Koh. "Bifid Rib: Anatomical Considerations in Three Cases." *Yonsei Medical Journal* 50.2 (2009): 300–303. https://doi.org/10.3349/ymj.2009.50.2.300.

Sonia, K. *Caring for the Dead in Ancient Israel*. ABS 27. Atlanta: SBL, 2020.

Sonia, K. "Thinking with Clay: Procreation and the Ceramic Paradigm in Israelite Religion." *JANER* 21 (2021): 185–207.

Sourvinou-Inwood, C. *Reading Greek Death: To the End of the Classical Period*. Oxford: Oxford University Press, 1983.

Spronk, K. *Beatific Afterlife in Ancient Israel and in the Ancient Near East*. Alter Orient und Altes Testament 219. Neukirchen-Vluyn: Neukirchener Verlag, 1986.

Stager, L. E. "The Archaeology of the Family in Ancient Israel." *BASOR* 260 (1985): 1–35.

Stager, L. E. "Carthage: A View from the Tophet." Pages 115- 66 in *Phönizier im Westen: Die Beiträge des Internationalen Symposiums über "Die phönizische Expansion im westlichen Mittelmeerraum" in Köln vom 24 bis 27 April, 1979*. Edited by H. G. Niemeyer. Mainz am Rhein: Zabern, 1982.

Stager, L. E. "Introduction." Pages 3- 14 in *Ashkelon 7: The Iron Age I*. Edited by L. Stager, D. Master, and A. Aja. Winona Lake, IN: Eisenbrauns, 2020.

Stager, L.E. "New Discoveries in the Excavations of Ashkelon in the Bronze and Iron Ages." *Qadmoniot* 131 (2006): 2–19. In Hebrew.

Stager, L. E., J. D. Schloen, and D. M. Master, eds. *Ashkelon I: Introduction and Overview (1985–2006)*. Final Reports of the Leon Levy Expedition to Ashkelon 1. Winona Lake, IN: Eisenbrauns, 2008.

Stansell, G. "The Gift in Ancient Israel." *Semeia* 87 (1999): 65–90.

Stavrakopoulou, F. *King Manasseh and Child Sacrifice: Biblical Distortions of Historical Realities*. BZAW 338. Berlin: de Gruyter, 2012.

Stavrakopoulou, F. *Land of Our Fathers: The Roles of Ancestor Veneration in Biblical Land Claims*. LHBOTS 473. London: T & T Clark, 2010.

Stavrakopoulou, F. "Religion at Home: The Materiality of Practice." Pages 346–65 in *The Wiley Blackwell Companion to Ancient Israel*. Edited by S. Niditch. Malden, MA: Wiley-Blackwell, 2016.

Steinberg, N. *Kinship and Marriage in Genesis: A Household Economics Perspective*. Minneapolis: Fortress, 1993.

Steinberg, N. *The World of the Child in the Hebrew Bible*. HBM 51. Sheffield: Sheffield Phoenix, 2013.

Stern, E. *Archaeology of the Land of the Bible*. Vol. 2: *The Assyrian, Babylonian, and Persian Periods, 732–332 BCE*. New York: Doubleday, 2001.

Stol, M. "Wirtschaft und Gesellschaft in altbablyonischer Zeit." Pages 643–975 in *Mesopotamien: Die altbabylonische Zeit*. Orbis Biblicus et Orientalis 160/4. Edited by D. Charpin, D. O. Edzard, and M. Stol. Fribourg: Academic Press, 2004.

Strathern, M. *The Gender of the Gift: Problems with Women and Problems with Society in Melanesia*. Berkeley: University of California Press, 1998.

Strathern, M. *Property, Substance and Effect: Anthropological Essays on Persons and Things*. London: Athlone, 1999.

Stutz, L. N. and S. Tarlow. "Beautiful Things and Bones of Desire: Emerging Issues in the Archaeology of Death and Burials." Pages 1–16 in *The Oxford Handbook of the Archaeology of Death and Burial*. Edited by S. Tarlow and L. N. Stutz. Oxford: Oxford University Press, 2013.

Suriano, M. "Breaking Bread with the Dead: Katumuwa's Stele, Hosea 9:4, and the Early History of the Soul." *JAOS* 134 (2014): 385–405.

Suriano, M. *A History of Death in the Hebrew Bible*. Oxford: Oxford University Press, 2018.

Suriano, M. *The Politics of Dead Kings: Dynastic Ancestors in the Book of Kings and Ancient Israel*. Tübingen: Mohr Siebeck, 2010.

Suriano, M. "What Did Feeding the Dead Mean? Two Case Studies from Iron Age Tombs at Beth-Shemesh." *AABNER* 1.3 (2021): 117–42.

Tarlow, S. *Bereavement and Commemoration: An Archaeology of Mortality*. Oxford: Blackwell, 1999.

Tarlow, S. and L. N. Stutz, eds. *The Oxford Handbook of the Archaeology of Death & Burial*. Oxford: Oxford University Press, 2019.

Teinz, K. "How to Become an Ancestor—Some Thoughts." Pages 235–43 in *(Re)-constructing Funerary Rituals in the Ancient Near East: Proceedings of the First International Symposium of the Tübingen Post-Graduate School "Symbols of the Dead" in May 2009*. Qaṭna Studien Supplementa 1. Edited by P. Pfälzner, H. Niehr, E. Pernicka, and A. Wissing. Wiesbaden: Harrassowitz Verlag, 2012.

Tenney, J. *Life at the Bottom of Babylonian Society: Servile Laborers at Nippur in the 14th and 13th Centuries B.C.* CHANE 51. Leiden: Brill, 2011.

Tiesler, V. and A. Cucina, eds., *New Perspectives on Human Sacrifice and Ritual Body Treatments in Ancient Maya Society*. New York: Springer, 2007.

TOI Staff. "Archaeologists Discover Phoenician Family Tomb in Ancient City of Achziv." *Times of Israel*, 25 December 2019. https://www.timesofisrael.com/archaeologists-discover-pho enician-family-tomb-in-ancient-city-of-achziv/

194 BIBLIOGRAPHY

Toorn, K. van der. *Family Religion in Babylonia, Syria, and Israel: Continuity and Change in the Forms of Religious Life*. Leiden: Brill, 1996.

Toorn, K. van der. "Funerary Rituals and Beatific Afterlife in Ugaritic Texts and the Bible." *BO* 48 (1991): 40–66.

Toorn, K. van der. "Second Millennium West Asian Family Religion." Pages 20–36 in *Household and Family Religion in Antiquity*. Edited by J. Bodel and S. Olyan. Oxford: Blackwell, 2008.

Tropper, J. *Nekromantie: Totenbefragung im Alten Orient und im Alten Testament*. AOAT 223. Neukirchen-Vluyn: Kevelaer, 1989.

Tufnell, O. "Burials in Cemeteries 100 and 200." Pages 11–13 in *Beth-Pelet I (Tell Fara)*. Edited by W. F. Petrie. London: British School of Archaeology in Egypt, 1930.

Tufnell, O. *Lachish III (Tell ed. Duwier): The Iron Age*. London: Oxford University Press, 1953.

Turner, V. *The Forest of Symbols: Aspects of Ndembu Ritual*. Ithaca, NY: Cornell University Press, 1967.

Turner, V. *The Ritual Process: Structure and Anti-structure*. Chicago: Aldine, 1969.

Uko, P. "Ethnography and Archaeological Interpretation of Funerary Remains." *WA* 1 (1969): 262–80.

Usshishkin, D. "On the History of the High Place at Gezer." Pages 411–16 in *Timelines: Studies in Honor of Manfred Bietak*. Vol. 2. Edited by E. Czerny. Peeters: Leuven, 2006.

Uziel, J. and R. Avissar Lewis. "The Tel Nagila Middle Bronze Age Homes— Studying Household Activities and Identifying Children in the Archaeological Record." *PEQ* 145 (2013): 284–92.

Uziel, J. and A. Maeir. "Philistine Burial Customs in Light of the Finds at Tell eṣ-Ṣâfi/ Gath." *NEA* 81.1 (2018): 19–21.

Verduci, J. "The Iron Age I/IIA Jewelry from Cave T1." Pages 251–70 in *Tell es-Safi / Gath II: Excavations and Studies*. Ägypten und Altes Testament 105. Edited by A. Maeir and J. Uziel. Münster: Zaphon, 2020.

Verdugo, C., K. Zhu, M. Prout, N. Broomandkhosbacht, A. Galloway, L. Fehren-Schmitz, and J. E. Bradey. "Implications of Age and Sex Determinations of Ancient Maya Sacrificial Victims at Midnight Terror Cave." *International Journal of Osteoarchaeology* 30.4 (2020): 458–68.

Vitto, F. "An Iron Age Burial Cave in Nazareth." *'Atiqot* 42 (2001): 159–69.

Waetzoldt, H. "Compensation of Craft Workers and Officials in the Ur III Period." Pages 117–41 in *Labor in the Ancient Near East*. Edited by M. A. Powell. New Haven: American Oriental Society, 1987.

Wardlaw, T. et al. "Low Birth Weight: Country, Regional, and Global Estimates." UNICEF. New York: UNICEF, 2004. http://apps.who.int/iris/bitstr eam/ 10665/43184/1/9280638 327.pdf accessed 5/6/23.

Wason, P. K. *The Archaeology of Rank*. New Studies in Archaeology. Cambridge: AltaMira Press, 2004.

Wassén, C. "Stepped Pools and Stone Vessels: Rethinking Jewish Purity Practices in Palestine." *BAR* 45 (2019): 52–58.

Westermann, C. *Isaiah 40–66*. Translated by D. M. G. Stalker. OTL. London: SCM Press, 1969.

Wicker, N. "Selective Female Infanticide as Partial Explanation for the Dearth of Women in Viking Age Scandinavia." Pages 205–21 in *Violence and Society in the Early Medieval West*. Edited by G. Halstall. Woodbridge: Boydell Press, 1998.

Wilk, R. and W. Rathje. "Household Archaeology." *American Behavioral Scientist* 25.6 (1982): 618.

Wolff, S. and G. Edelstein. "The 1964 Excavation at Tell el-'Orēme." Pages 513–28 in *Kinneret II: Results of the Excavation at Tel el 'Orēme in 1994– 2008*. Vol. 1. Ägypten und Altes Testament 120. Edited by W. Zwickel and J. Pakkala. Münster: Zaphon, 2024.

Wright, D. P. *The Disposal of Impurity: Elimination Rites in the Bible and in Hittite and Mesopotamian Literature*. Atlanta: Scholars Press, 1987.

Wyatt, N. "Circumcision and Circumstance: Male Genital Mutilation in Ancient Israel and Ugarit." *JSOT* 33 (2009): 405–31.

Xella, P. "'Tophet': An Overall Interpretation." *SEL* 29–30 (2012–13): 259–81.

Xella, P., J. Quinn, V. Melchiorri, and P. van Dommeln. "Phoenician Bones of Contention." *Antiquity* 87 (2013): 1–9.

Yannai, E. and Y. Nagar. "A Burial Cave from the Iron Age II and Early Roman Period North of Tel Hadid." *'Atiqot* 70 (2012): 1–20. In Hebrew.

Yasur-Landau, A., J. Ebling, and L. Mazow. "Introduction: The Past and Present of Household." Pages 1–8 in *Household Archaeology in Ancient Israel and Beyond*. Edited by A. Yasur-Landau, J. Ebling, and L. Mazow. Leiden: Brill, 2011.

Yezerski, I. "Burial-Cave Distribution and the Borders of the Kingdom of Judah toward the End of the Iron Age." *TA* 26 (1999): 253–70.

Yezerski, I. "Iron Age Burial Customs in the Samaria Highlands." *TA* 40.1 (2013): 72–98.

Zevit, Z. *The Religions of Ancient Israel: A Synthesis of Parallactic Approaches*. London: Continuum, 2001.

Index

For the benefit of digital users, indexed terms that span two pages (e.g., 52–53) may, on occasion, appear on only one of those pages.

Note: Tables are indicated by an italic *t* following the page number.

Achzib site, 66
activities within households, 2–3
afterlife
  ceramic goods and, 30–31
  child burial overview and, 28–31, 35
  child sacrifice and, 158–59
  grave goods and, 168
  introduction to, 1, 2, 3–4, 9–11, 12–13, 15–16
  Iron Age I, 97
  Judahite burials and, 127, 129, 130–33, 137, 141, 173–75
  memorials and, 107–8, 111–12
  Philistine Plain Iron Age, 55–56
  Phoenician-influenced burials, 69, 76–78
Agarwal, Sabrina, 5
Aja, Adam, 112
Albright, William F., 10–11
ancestors *in potentia*, 36, 37–38, 129, 141
ancient Near East (ANE)
  childbirth in, 114
  child sacrifices in, 150
  circumcision in in, 128
  Hebrew Bible and, 173–74
  Judahite family tombs and, 128
  personhood in, 4–5, 9, 11
animal bones, 33, 46–47, 112
Ashdod site, 45
Ashkelon site
  attitudes toward death and burial, 168
  memorials, 14–15, 112–13
  Philistine Plain Iron Age burials, 46, 48*t*, 55, 57–58
'Atlit site, 70, 76–77, 171
Aubert, María, 65–66
Azor site, 51–52, 55

Bab edh-Dhra' cemetery, 7
baby burial kit, 38–39
Baker, Jill, 29–30
Beauchesne, Patrick, 5

behaviors within households, 2–3
bench tombs
  child sacrifice and, 153, 156–57, 160
  in Iron Age II, 85–89
  Judahite, 15, 38–39, 132, 135–36, 141, 171, 173, 175
  materiality approach to, 14–15
  memorials and, 14–15, 108, 111–12, 115, 117–19
Ben-Dor site, 67
Ben-Shlomo, David, 55
bet 'av, 2, 11, 126
Binford, Lewis, 28
bioarchaeology, 5–6
biological age, 5–6
Birney, Kathleen, 106
Bloch-Smith, Elizabeth, 70–71
bone repository pit, 14, 85
Brichto, Chanan, 10–11
Bunimovitz, Shlomo, 111, 127
burial kits, 38–39, 55, 57–58, 168
burial rites, 1, 12, 58–59, 98

Canaanite burials
  attitudes toward death and burial, 172
  cave burials, 98, 171, 172
  cult of the dead, 9
  cults of the dead, 9
  funeral kits, 29–30, 138
  intermural burials, 58
  Iron Age II, 51
Carmel coast sites, 66–70
Carthage, 64
cave burials
  in Bronze and Iron Ages, 25, 28–29, 33–34, 38–39, 87–88
  Canaanite, 98, 171, 172
  Central Highlands in Iron Age I, 83, 84, 85, 86*t*
  child sacrifices and, 153

198 INDEX

cave burials (*cont.*)
    Megiddo site, 91–92
    memorials and, 117
    Nazareth sites, 90–91
    Samarian Highlands, 94, 94*t*
    South of Ḥorbat Tittora site, 87–89, 88*t*
    Tel es-Safi/Gath, 49, 56
Central Highlands
    Galilee sites, 89
    Intermediate Bronze Age, 90–91
    in Iron Age I, 83, 84, 85, 86*t*
    in Iron Age II, 85
    Jezreel Valley sites, 91
    Late Bronze Age, 83–84, 89, 93–94
    Middle Bronze Age, 93, 95
    northern region burials, 89
    overview of, 97
    rock-cut tombs, 83, 85, 86*t*, 87, 88–89, 90–91, 94
    Samarian Highlands burials, 94, 94*t*
    Sharon Plain site, 93
    South of Ḥorbat Tittora site, 87–88, 88*t*
    Tel Hadid site, 85, 88
    Tel 'Ira site, 85, 87–88
ceramic goods
    Central Highlands, 89, 90–91, 93–94, 96–97
    child sacrifice and, 154–55
    introduction to, 4, 29–32, 32*t*, 168, 170
    Judahite family tombs, 126–27, 131–32, 134–35, 137–38
    memorials and, 110, 116–17
    Philistine Plain Iron Age burials, 45, 55, 56
    Phoenician-influenced burials, 67, 73–74, 76–77
chamber tombs, 47, 67, 68*t*, 87, 89, 170
charnel houses, 7
Chesson, Meredith, 7
child burials in Bronze and Iron Ages
    differentiated burials, 25, 26*t*, 27*t*
    graves and grave goods, 28, 32*t*
    introduction to, 25
    Megiddo tombs (Str. XII–IX), 36
    missing burials, 32
    personhood and, 34, 37
    rituals, 27–28, 35, 36, 37–38
    skeletal remains, 32–33
child sacrifice in Hebrew Bible
    afterlife and, 158–59
    anthropological perspective on, 149
    archaeological record on, 161
    bench tombs and, 153, 156–57, 160
    eliminatory sacrifices, 150
    fertility and gift-giving in, 151

    introduction to, 15
    Isaiah 57:3 13 case study, 158
    personhood and, 9, 148–51, 155–56, 160, 161
    pit burials and, 149–50, 154–55, 156, 157, 160
    Punics and, 152
    ritual killings, 150
    rituals and, 149–50, 158–60
chronological age, 4–6
circumcision of infants, 128–29
cist burials, 25–26, 47, 54–55, 67, 89, 93–94, 98, 125, 140, 154, 156, 157
collective generational spaces, 14–15, 108, 119
commemoration and personhood, 167
Cradic, Melissa, 58
cremations, 47, 64–76, 71*t*, 74*t*
cults of the dead
    Canaanite burials, 9
    child sacrifice and, 157–60
    Egyptian cult of the dead, 9
    introduction to, 1, 9–11
    Judahite burials, 12
    Judahite family tombs and, 139
    memorials and, 1, 9–11, 105–6, 110
    Ugarit state, 9
    See also death cult

death cult, 10–11, 27–28, 158, 159–60, 173–74. *See also* cults of the dead
Deverenski, Joanna Sofaer, 4–5
Doak, Brian, 106
drinking shoots, 67
Durkheim, Émile, 27–28

Early Bronze Age, 12–13, 30*t*, 31*t*, 127
Edrey, Meir, 93–94
Egyptian cult of the dead, 9
Ekron burial, 112–13
eliminatory sacrifices, 150
Epic of Gilgamesh, 3–4, 130–32
essential grave goods, 29–30
Exile, 15, 128–29, 160–61
extramural burials, 27, 47, 54, 58–59, 91–92, 94, 98–99, 170

family tombs, 14, 85. *See also* Judahite family tombs
faunal remains, 45–46, 57
Faust, Avraham, 83–84, 111, 127
feeding/feasting with dead, 137
fertility cult, 158–60
figurines, 1–2, 129–30
Flynn, Shawn, 4–5
Foster, Catherine, 3

INDEX 199

Free, Joseph, 95–96
Fulton, Deirdre, 112
funeral kits, 29–31, 138
funerary rites/rituals, 28, 35, 66, 97, 98, 171–72

Galilee sites, 89
Gilgamesh. *See* Epic of Gilgamesh
Gonen, Rivka, 84
grave burials in Bronze and Iron Ages, 25, 26*t*, 27*t*
grave goods
    afterlife and, 168
    child burials in Bronze and Iron Ages, 28
    essential goods, 29–30
    Judahite family bench tombs, 132
    non-ceramic, 29–30
    personal goods, 29–30, 32, 56, 65, 76–77, 110, 132–35, 170–71
    status goods, 29–30, 77
    Tel 'Ira site, 133–35, 134*t*

Hallote, Rachel, 7–8
Hays, Christopher B., 9–10, 119–20
Hebrew Bible, 4–5, 174. *See also* child sacrifice in Hebrew Bible
Hesse, Paula, 112
household archaeology, 2
House Societies, 7
human sacrifice, 149–51. *See also* child sacrifice in Hebrew Bible

Ilan, David, 83–84, 89
Intermediate Bronze Age, 90–91
intermural burials, 12–13, 27, 36, 46, 50, 57, 90, 112, 118–19
intramural burials
    in Bronze Ages, 27–28, 27*t*, 29, 33–34, 36
    in Iron Ages, 27–28, 27*t*, 29, 33–34, 36, 113–14
    personhood and, 167–69, 172–73
    Philistine Plain Iron Age burials, 43–45, 44*t*, 46–49, 48*t*, 51, 52–53, 57
Iron Age I
    afterlife and, 97
    Ashkelon site, 46
    attitudes toward death and burial, 168–69
    Azor site, 51, 52
    burial methods, 13
    Central Highlands in, 83, 84, 85, 86*t*, 89–90, 98
    extramural burials, 54
    Galilee sites, 89
    introduction to, 2, 13

Jezreel Valley sites, 91
    memorials and, 111–12, 119
    pit burials, 84, 89, 91–92, 168–69
    Sharon Plain site, 93
    skeletal remains, 90–92
    Tel es-Safi/Gath site, 49
    Tel Miqne/Ekron site, 50
    Timnah site, 53
Iron Age II
    Achzib site, 66, 67
    Ashkelon site, 46–47
    Azor site, 51
    bench tombs, 85–89
    burial methods, 13
    Canaanite burials, 51
    in Central Highlands, 85
    circumcision of infants, 129
    cremation, 154
    extramural burials, 54
    Judahite house plan, 127
    pit burials, 85
    rituals, 96–97
    Samarian Highlands burials, 94, 94*t*
    Sharon Plain site, 93
    skeletal remains, 85–89, 88*t*, 97–98
    Tel 'Ira site grave goods, 133–35, 134*t*
    Tel Yavne site, 54
    Timnah site, 53
Iron Age III, 117
Iron Age overview, 2, 12–14, 64, 117, 168
Isaiah 57:313 case study, 158

jar burials
    in Bronze and Iron Ages, 25–28
    under floors, 8
    Galilee sites, 89
    lmlk jars, 53, 114
    memorials and, 106, 110–19
    in Phoenician homeland, 153
    Samarian Highlands burials, 94, 94*t*
    Tel Miqne/Ekron site, 50
    tomb-to-womb theory, 115
Jezreel Valley sites, 91
Johns, C. N., 70
Judahite burials
    afterlife and, 127, 129, 130–33, 137, 141, 173–75
    bench tombs, 15, 38–39, 132, 135–36, 141, 171, 173, 175
    child sacrifice in Hebrew Bible, 148, 153–54, 156, 159–61
    cult of the dead, 12
    family tombs, 85

200 INDEX

Judahite family tombs
  afterlife and, 127, 129, 130–33, 137, 141
  cave burials, 132, 140–41
  circumcision of infants, 128–29
  cults of the dead and, 139
  feeding/feasting with dead, 137
  grave goods in bench tombs, 132
  house comparisons, 125–27
  introduction to, 125
  liminal stage/state of dying child, 127,
    130, 138
  pit burials, 129–30, 132, 133–34, 136–37,
    139, 174–75
  rituals, 126–27, 128, 129–31, 132–33, 137–39
  skeletal remains and, 130, 132–33, 134, 136,
    139, 141
  Tel 'Ira site, 133–35, 134t
Judean pillar figurines (JPFs), 129–30
juvenile osteology, 5

Kaufmann, Yehizkiel, 173–74
Ketef Hinnom amulets, 108
Khaldé site, 153–54
Khirbet Beit Lei tombs, 14–15, 85, 107, 110–
  11, 138
Khirbet Shemsin site, 85, 88–89, 91–92
kin-based burials, 26
Kletter, Raz, 83–84

Late Bronze Age, 36, 83–84, 89, 93–94, 137
legacy of dead adults, 130–31
Lemos, T. M., 35
liminal stage/state, 15, 37–38, 114, 127, 130,
  138, 168–70
lmlk jars, 53, 114
lmlk sacrifice, 151–52

Macridy, Theodore, 154
Maeir, Aren, 43–45
Mandell, Alice, 107–8
marzēaḥ, 10–11
maṣṣebot, 35, 89–90, 92, 105, 113
Master, Dan, 95
Mazar, Eliat, 67
McGeough, Kevin, 116
Megiddo tombs (Str. XII– IX), 36, 91–93, 113, 140
memorials
  afterlife and, 107–8, 111–12
  Ashkelon site, 14–15, 112–13
  bench tombs and, 14–15, 108, 111–12,
    115, 117–19
  burial receptacles as, 115

cave burials and, 117
ceramic goods and, 110, 116–17
cults of the dead and, 1, 9–11, 105–6, 110
introduction to, 105
Iron Age I, 111–12, 119
jar burials and, 106, 110–19
Ketef Hinnom amulets, 108
Khirbet Beit Lei inscriptions, 107
overview of, 119
pit burials and, 106, 110, 111
as rituals, 105, 107, 109–10, 114, 117,`
  118–20
skeletal remains and, 112, 114
structural, 14–15, 105, 111
written, 14–15, 105–10
Mesopotamia, 4–5, 9, 10–11, 115, 137, 173–
  74, 175
Middle Bronze Age, 7–8, 12–13, 27, 28–29, 32,
  36–37, 45, 52–54, 66, 93, 95, 127, 173
miniature vessels, 1–2
missing burials, 32, 83
mlk sacrifice, 152–53
mortuary archaeology, 6
mortuary record, 2, 8, 12, 14, 33–34, 75, 85,
  97, 125
mortuary rites, 28, 135–36, 173

necromancy, 10–11, 139–40, 157, 158–
  59, 173–74
Neo-Hittite state, 9
nonadult, 5, 154–55
non-ceramic goods, 29–30
non-Judahite burials, 156

Ohata, Kiyoshi, 93–94

Parker, Bradley, 3
Parker, Julie Faith, 4–5
personal grave goods, 29–30, 32, 56, 65, 76–77,
  110, 132–35, 170–71
personhood
  in Ancient Near East/Hebrew Bible, 9
  child burials and, 34, 37
  child sacrifice in Hebrew Bible, 9, 148–51,
    155–56, 160, 161
  defined, 1–2
  household archaeology, 2
  household infants and children, 3
  household living and dead, 11
  identifying infants and children, 4
  intramural burials and, 167–69, 172–73
  introduction to, 1–2

liminal stage/state of dying child, 127,
130, 138
mortuary archaeology, 6
public ritual and, 1–2, 14–15, 98, 105,
167, 173
social recognition and, 1–2, 34
Tel 'Ira site grave goods and, 133–35, 134*t*
personhood revealed in death
attitudes toward death and burial, 168
commemoration and, 167
introduction to, 15–16, 167
public ritual and, 167
rituals and, 167, 169–70, 172, 173, 175
social memory and, 173
Petrie, William Flinders, 73
Philistine Plain Iron Age burials
afterlife and, 55–56
Ashdod site, 45
attitudes toward death and burial, 168
Azor site, 51–52, 55
extramural burials, 47, 54, 58–59
intermural burials, 46, 50, 57
intramural burials, 43–45, 44*t*, 46–49, 48*t*, 51,
52–53, 57
introduction to, 13–14, 43
overview of, 43, 44*t*
pit burials, 45–47, 48*t*, 50, 51–53, 54–
55, 57–58
rituals and, 46, 47, 52–53, 57
skeletal remains, 47, 50–52
Tel es-Safi/Gath site, 49, 56
Tel Miqne/Ekron site, 50
Tel Yavne site, 54
Timnah site, 53
Phoenician-influenced burials
Achzib site, 66
afterlife and, 69, 76–78
'Atlit site, 70, 76–77
attitudes toward death and burial, 168
Carmel coast sites, 66–70
child sacrifice, 15
cremations, 64–76, 71*t*
introduction to, 64–66
jar burials, 153
overview, 74
pit burials, 65–66, 67–72, 74–75,
77–78, 171
rituals, 66, 76–77
skeletal remains, 67–68, 68*t*, 70, 73,
74*t*, 76–77
Tell el-Far'ah South site, 73, 77
Tell er-Reqeish site, 72

pit burials
in Bronze and Iron Ages, 25, 28–29, 33–
34, 36–37
child sacrifice and, 149–50, 154–55, 156,
157, 160
introduction to, 14
Iron Age I, 84, 89, 91–92, 168–69
Judahite family tombs, 129–30, 132, 133–34,
136–37, 139, 174–75
memorials and, 106, 110, 111
Philistine Plain Iron Age burials, 45–47, 48*t*,
50, 51–53, 54–55, 57–58
Phoenician-influenced burials, 65–66, 67–
72, 74–75, 77–78, 171
placement of, 170
Sharon Plain, 93
place-making, 14–15, 58, 113, 119, 173
place-marking, 14–15
Prausnitz, Moshe, 67
public ritual, 1–2, 14–15, 35, 98, 105, 167, 173.
See also rituals
Punics and child sacrifice, 152

rattles, 1–2
Rephaim, 10–11
ritual killings, 150
rituals
in Bronze and Iron Ages, 27–28, 35,
36, 37–38
child sacrifice and, 149–50, 158–60
funerary rites/rituals, 28, 35, 66, 97,
98, 171–72
introduction to, 1–2, 7, 8, 9, 10–11, 12, 14–15
Judahite family tombs, 126–27, 128, 129–31,
132–33, 137–39
memorials as, 105, 107, 109–10, 114,
117, 118–20
personhood revealed in death, 167, 169–70,
172, 173, 175
Philistine Plain Iron Age burials, 46, 47,
52–53, 57
Phoenician-influenced burials, 66, 76–77
public, 1–2, 14–15, 35, 98, 105, 167, 173
rock-cut tombs, 83, 85, 86*t*, 87, 88–89, 90–91,
94, 115, 117, 125, 127, 129–30, 172–73

Samarian Highlands burials, 94, 94*t*
Schmitt, Rüdiger, 139–40
Schumacher, x, 92–93
Sea Peoples, 38–39, 46
Second Temple Period, 28–29, 117–18
shaft tombs, 7, 25, 67–69, 70, 74–75, 154, 156

202 INDEX

Sharon Plain site, 93
silver amulets, 108
skeletal age, 5–6
skeletal remains
   animal bones, 33, 46–47, 112
   in Bronze and Iron Ages, 32–33
   introduction to, 5–6, 14
   Iron Age I, 90–92
   Iron Age II, 85–89, 88t, 97–98
   Judahite family tombs, 130, 132–33, 134, 136,
      139, 141
   memorials and, 112, 114
   Philistine Plain Iron Age burials, 47, 50–52
   Phoenician-influenced burials, 67–68, 68t,
      70, 73, 74t, 76–77
   Samarian Highlands, 94, 94t
Smith, Mark, 10–11
Smoak, Jeremy, 107–8, 109
social age, 4–6
socialization, 2–4
social memory, 36–37, 77–78, 112, 127–28,
      136, 173
social recognition, 1–2, 34
Sonia, Kerry, 10–11, 116, 127–28
Southern Levant, 2, 3, 7–8, 12–13, 34, 38–39,
      43, 49, 64, 72, 111, 119–20, 126
South of Ḥorbat Tittora site, 87–89, 88t
status grave goods, 29–30, 77
status of infants and children, 7–8, 15, 35, 36,
      37–38, 52–53, 56, 75–76, 111, 131–32, 138,
      140, 150–51, 173, 174–75
Stavrakopoulou, Francesca, 10–11, 159
Stratum VII (ca. 1200 1170 BCE), 50–51

structural memorials, 14–15, 105, 111
subadult, 5, 69, 141
Suriano, Matthew, 10–11, 108–9, 126, 130–
      31, 138

Tel es-Safi/Gath site, 49, 56
Tel Hadid site, 85, 88
Tel ʿIra site, 85, 87–88, 133–35, 134t
Tell el-Farʾah South site, 73, 77, 140, 156, 171
Tell er-Reqeish site, 72, 156, 171
Tel Miqne/Ekron site, 50, 112–13, 140–41
Tel Yavne site, 54
Timnah site, 53
tombs
   chamber tombs, 47, 67, 68t, 87, 89, 170
   child burials in Bronze and Iron Ages, 28
   missing tombs, 83
   rock-cut, 83, 85, 86t, 87, 88–89, 90–91, 94,
      115, 117, 125, 127, 129–30, 172–73
   shaft tombs, 7, 25, 67–69, 70, 74–75, 154, 156
   structural memorials, 14–15, 105, 111
   See also family tombs; Judahite family tombs
tomb-to-womb theory, 115
Torah, 148–49
Tyre Al-Bass necropolis, 65–66, 71–72, 154–55

Ugaritic corpus, 128
Ugarit state, 9
Uziel, Joel, 43–45

written memorials, 14–15, 105–10

Yahweh, 10–11, 108–9, 119–20, 148–49, 161